Air Fryer Cookbook for Advanced Users [4 Books in 1]

An Abundance of Fried Recipes to Godly Eat, Save Money and Improve Your Mood

By

Chef Ludovico L'Italiano

Table of Contents

Keto Air Fryer Cookbook with Pictures

Introduction..**20**

Cooking using an Air Fryer...21

Why Use It:..22

Selecting a Custom Air Fryer:...23

Accessories..23

How to clean an Air Fryer...24

Keto Diet..25

Tips for Usage:...25

CHAPTER 1: Breakfast Recipes...**26**

1. Loaded Cauliflower Breakfast Bake 26

2. Scrambled Eggs 27

3. "Hard-Boiled" Eggs 28

4. Breakfast Stuffed Poblanos 28

5. Cheesy Cauliflower Hash Browns 29

6. Egg, Cheese, and Bacon Roll-Ups 30

7. Pancake...31

8. Lemon Poppy Seed Cake 32

9. "Banana" Nut Cake 33

10. Bacon Strips 34

11. Pumpkin Spice Muffins 35

12. Veggie Frittata 36

13. Buffalo Egg Cups 37

14. Crispy Southwestern Ham Egg Cups 37

15. Jalapeño Popper Egg Cups...38

16. Crunchy Granola..39

CHAPTER 2: Air Fryer Chicken Main Dishes **40**

1. Chicken Fajitas 40

2. Pepperoni and Chicken Pizza Bake 40

3. Almond-Crusted Chicken 41

4. Southern "Fried" Chicken 42

5. Spinach and Feta-Stuffed Chicken Breast 43

6. Blackened Cajun Chicken Tenders 44

7. Chicken Pizza Crust 45

8. Chicken Enchiladas 45

9. Jalapeño Popper Hassel back Chicken 46

10.   Chicken Cordon Bleu Casserole 48

11.   Chicken Parmesan 48

12.   Fajita-Stuffed Chicken Breast 50

13.   Lemon Pepper Drumsticks 50

14.   Cilantro Lime Chicken Thighs 51

15.   Lemon Thyme Roasted Chicken 52

16.   Teriyaki Wings 53

17.   Crispy Buffalo Chicken Tenders 54

CHAPTER 3: Air Fryer Side Dish Recipes **55**

1. Pita-Style Chips 55

2. Avocado Fries 56

3. Flatbread 56

4. Radish Chips 57

5. Coconut Flour Cheesy Garlic Biscuits 58

6. Dinner Rolls 59

7. Cilantro Lime Roasted Cauliflower 60

8. Green Bean Casserole 61

9. Buffalo Cauliflower 62

10.   Kale Chips 62

11.   Roasted Garlic 63

12.   Zucchini Parmesan Chips 64

13.   Crispy Brussels sprouts 65

14.   Cheesy Cauliflower Tots 66

15.   Sausage-Stuffed Mushroom Caps 67

16.   Garlic Herb Butter Roasted Radishes 68

17.   Loaded Roasted Broccoli 68

CHAPTER 4: Air Fryer Snack and Appetizer Recipes **70**

1.   Bacon-Wrapped Brie 70

2.   Crust less Meat Pizza 71

3.   Garlic Cheese Bread 71

4.   Mozzarella Pizza Crust 72

5.   Spicy Spinach Artichoke Dip 73

6.   Mini Sweet Pepper Poppers 74

7.   Bacon-Wrapped Onion Rings 75

8.   Mozzarella Sticks 75

9.   Pork Rind Tortillas 76

10.   Bacon Cheeseburger Dip 77

11.   Pizza Rolls 78

12.   Bacon Jalapeño Cheese Bread 79

13.   Spicy Buffalo Chicken Dip 80

14.   Garlic Parmesan Chicken Wings 81

15.   Bacon-Wrapped Jalapeño Poppers 82

16.   Prosciutto-Wrapped Parmesan Asparagus 83

CHAPTER 5: Desserts **85**

1.   Mini Cheesecake 85

2.   Pecan Brownies...85

3.   Cinnamon Sugar Pork Rinds 86

4.   Almond Butter Cookie Balls 87

Conclusion **88**

The Complete Air Fryer Cookbook with Pictures

INTRODUCTION: 93

Chapter # 1: 94

An Overview & Benefits of an Air Fryer 94

Introduction: 94

The Air Fryer Usability: 94

The Air Fryer Works as: 94

What necessary to Search for in an Air Fryer? 95

Most Common - Five Guidelines for an Air Fryer usage: 95

1. Shake the food. 95

2. Do not overload. 95

3. Slightly spray to food. 95

4. Retain an Air fry dry. 95

5. Other Most Dominant cooking techniques. 96

An Air Fryer Helps to reduce fat content 96

Air Fryer provides an Aid in Weight Loss 96

Air Fried food may reduce the potentially harmful chemicals 96

Chapter # 2: 98

70 Perfectly Portioned Air Fryer Recipes for Busy People in Minimum Budget 98

1. Air fried corn, zucchini and haloumi fritters 98

2. Air fryer fried rice 99

3. Air fried banana muffins 100

4. Air fried Nutella brownies 101

5. Air fried celebration bites 101

6. Air fried nuts and bolts 102

7. Air fried coconut shrimps 103

8. Air fried Roasted Sweet and Spicy Carrots 104

9. Air fried Chicken Thighs 105

10. Air fried French Fries 106

11. Air fried Mini Breakfast Burritos 107

12. Air fried Vegan Tator Tots 108

13. Air fried Roasted Cauliflower 109

14. Air fried Cinnamon-Sugar Doughnuts 110

15. Air Fried Broiled Grapefruit 111

16. Air Fried Brown Sugar and Pecan Roasted Apples 112

17. Air Fried Breaded Sea Scallops 113

18. Air Fried Crumbed Fish..114

19. Air Fried Cauliflower and Chickpea Tacos 115

20. Air Fried Roasted Salsa 116

21. Air Fried Flour Tortilla Bowls 117

22. Air Fried Cheese and Mini Bean Tacos 118

23. Air Fried Lemon Pepper Shrimp 119

24. Air Fried Shrimp a la Bang Bang..120

25. Air Fried Spicy Bay Scallops 121

26. Air Fried Breakfast Fritatta..122

27. Air Fried Roasted Okra...123

28. Air Fried Rib-Eye Steak 124

29. Air Fried Potato Chips 125

30. Air Fried Tofu 126

31. Air Fried Acorn Squash Slices 127

32. Air Fried Red Potatoes 128

33. Air Fried Butter Cake 129

34. Air Fried Jelly and Peanut Butter S'mores 130

35. Air Fried Sun-Dried Tomatoes 131

36. Air Fried Sweet Potatoes Tots...132

37. Air Fried Banana Bread 133

38. Air Fried Avocado Fries 134

39. "Strawberry Pop Tarts" in an Air Fryer 135

40. Lighten up Empanadas in an Air Fryer 136

41. Air Fried Calzones...138

42. Air Fried Mexican Style Corns 139

43. Air Fryer Crunchy & Crispy Chocolate Bites 140

44. Doritos-Crumbled Chicken tenders in an Air fryer 141

46. Air Fryer Lemonade Scones 143

47. Air Fryer Baked Potatoes 144

48. Air Fryer Mozzarella Chips 145

49. Air Fryer Fetta Nuggets 146

50. Air Fryer Japanese Chicken Tender 147

51. Whole-Wheat Pizzas in an Air Fryer 148

52. Air Fryer Crispy Veggie Quesadillas 149

53. Air Fried Curry Chickpeas 150

54. Air Fried Beet Chips 151

55. Double-Glazed Air Fried Cinnamon Biscuits 152

56. Lemon Drizzle Cake in an Air Fryer 153

57. Air Fryer dukkah-Crumbed chicken 154

58. Air Fryer Vietnamese-style spring roll salad 155

59. Air Fryer Pizza Pockets 157

60. Air Fryer Popcorn Fetta with Maple Hot Sauce 158

61. Air fryer Steak Fajitas 159

62. Air-Fryer Fajita-Stuffed Chicken 160

63. Nashvilla Hot Chicken in an Air Fryer 161

64. Southern-style Chicken 163

65. Chicken Parmesan in an Air Fryer 163

66. Lemon Chicken Thigh in an Air Fryer 164

67. Salmon with Maple-Dijon Glaze in air fryer 165

68. Air Fryer Roasted Beans 166

69. Air Fried Radishes 167

70. Air Fried Catfish Nuggets 168

CONCLUSION: 170

Breville Smart Air Fryer Oven Cookbook

Introduction 176

Chapter 1: Health Benefits of Air and Deeply Fried Meals 180

1.1 Statistics of Deeply Fried Foods 180

1.2 Comparison of Deeply Fried and Air Fried Meals 181

Chapter 2: Breakfast & Main Dishes..**182**

1. Ninja Foodi Low-Carb Breakfast Casserole 182

2. Air Fryer Breakfast Sausage 183

3. Air Fryer Avocado Boats 184

4. Air Fryer Breakfast Stuffed Peppers 184

5. Air Fryer Breakfast Pockets 185

6. Air Fryer Bacon and Egg Breakfast Biscuit Bombs...............................186

7. Air Fryer Breakfast Potatoes 187

8. Breakfast Egg Rolls..187

9. Air Fryer Sausage Breakfast Casserole 188

10. Air Fryer Egg in Hole...190

11. Air Fryer Baked Egg Cups with Spinach & Cheese 191

12. Air Fryer French Toast Sticks 191

13. Air Fryer Apple Fritters 192

14. Air Fryer French Toast Sticks 193

15. Air Fryer Breakfast Toad-in-the-Hole Tarts..194

16. Air Fryer Churros...196

17. Air Fryer Hard Boiled Eggs 197

18. Air Fryer Omelette 197

19. Air Fryer McDonald's Copycat Egg McMuffin....................................198

20. Air Fryer Breakfast Pizza 198

21. Air Fryer Cherry and Cream Cheese Danish 199

22. Air-Fryer Southern Bacon, Egg, and Cheese Breakfast Sandwich 200

23. Air-Fried Breakfast Bombs 201

24. Air Fryer Breakfast Biscuit Bombs 201

25. Air Fryer Stuffed Breakfast Bombs with Eggs & Bacon 202

26. Air Fryer Breakfast Burritos 203

27. Air Fryer Breakfast Frittata...203

28. Air Fryer Crispy Bacon 204

29. Air Fryer Raspberry Muffins...204

30. Air Fryer Tofu..205

31. Air Fryer Brussel Sprouts 205

Air Fryer Main Dishes...**207**

1. Parmesan Breaded Air Fryer Chicken Tenders 207

2. Air Fryer Garlic Mushrooms Steaks 207

3. Air Fryer Falafels..209

4. Air Fryer Pita Bread Pizza 210

5. Air Fryer Chicken Quesadilla 210

6. Crispy Golden Air Fryer Fish..212

7. Air Fryer Chicken Fried Rice 213

8. Air Fryer Steak Bites and Mushrooms 213

9. Juicy Air Fryer Pork Chops with Rub 215

10. Air Fryer Steak with Garlic Mushrooms 216

11. Low Carb Coconut Shrimp..216

12. Tandoori Fish Tikka 217

13. Bharwa Bhindi (Stuffed Okra) 218

14. Greek-Style Chicken Wings...219

15. Air Fryer Garlic Ranch Wings 220

16. Air Fryer Crispy Buffalo Chicken Hot Wings 220

17. Air Fryer Marinated Steak..221

18. Air Fryer Bacon and egg Bite Cups 222

19. Air Fryer Tender Juicy Smoked BBQ Ribs 223

20. Air Fryer Bacon and Cream Cheese Stuffed Jalapeno Poppers 224

21. Air Fryer Italian Herb Pork loin..224

22. Air Fryer Grilled Chicken Kebabs 225

23. Air Fryer Shrimp and Vegetables 226

24. Air Fryer Bratwurst and Vegetables...227

25. Air Fryer Turkey Legs 227

26. Air Fryer Roasted Edamame 228

27. Air Fryer Bulgogi Burgers 228

28. Air Fryer Carne Asada 229

29. Keto Steak Nuggets 230

30. Korean Short BBQ Ribs 231

31. Air Fryer Korean Hot Dogs 231

Chapter 3: Lunch **233**

1. Air Fryer Sweet Chili Chicken Wings 233

2. Air Fryer Fish 234

3. Air Fryer Wonton Mozzarella Sticks 235

4. Air Fryer Steak 235

5. Air Fryer Caramelized Bananas 236

6. Air Fryer Sesame Chicken 237

7. Air Fryer Donuts 237

8. Bang Bang Chicken 238

9. Crispy Air Fryer Eggplant Parmesan 239

10. Air Fryer Shrimp Fajitas 240

11. Honey Glazed Air Fryer Salmon..241

12. Crispy Air Fryer Roasted Brussels Sprouts With Balsamic 241

13. Air Fryer Chicken Nuggets 242

14. Air Fryer Baked Apples 242

15. Air Fryer Fish Tacos 243

16. Air Fryer Dumplings...244

17. Air Fryer Pork Chops 245

18. Air Fryer Chicken Chimichangas...246

19. Simple Chicken Burrito Bowls 247

20. Chicken Soft Tacos 248

21. Ground Pork Tacos - Al Pastor Style 248

22. Air-Fryer Southern-Style Chicken 250

23. Air-Fryer Fish and Fries...251

24. Air-Fryer Ground Beef Wellington...252

25. Air-Fryer Ravioli..253

26. Popcorn Shrimp Tacos with Cabbage Slaw 254

27. Bacon-Wrapped Avocado Wedges..255

28. Air-Fryer Steak Fajitas 255

29. Air-Fryer Sweet and Sour Pork 256

30. Air-Fryer Taco Twists 257

31. Air-Fryer Potato Chips 258

32. Air-Fryer Greek Breadsticks..258

33. Air-Fryer Crumb-Topped Sole...259

34. Air-Fried Radishes 260

35. Air-Fryer Ham and Egg Pockets 260

36. Air-Fryer Eggplant Fries...261

37. Air-Fryer Turkey Croquettes 262

38. Garlic-Herb Fried Patty Pan Squash..262

Conclusion...264

Vegan Air Fryer Cookbook

Introduction..269

What is Cooking Vegan?..271

What advantages would veganism have? 272

Air Fryer 273

Air fryer's Working Process: 275

Tips for using an Air Fryer..277

Outcome...278

CHAPTER 1: Breakfast Recipes..279

1. Toasted French toast 279

2. Vegan Casserole 280

3. Vegan Omelet 282

4. Waffles with Vegan chicken 284

5. Tempeh Bacon 287

6. Delicious Potato Pancakes 289

CHAPTER 2: Air Fryer Main Dishes **291**

1. **Mushroom 'n Bell Pepper Pizza** 292

2. Veggies Stuffed Eggplants 294

3. Air-fried Falafel 296

4. Almond Flour Battered Wings 297

5. Spicy Tofu 298

6. Sautéed Bacon with Spinach 299

7. Garden Fresh Veggie Medley 300

8. Colorful Vegetable Croquettes 301

9. Cheesy Mushrooms 302

10. Greek-style Roasted Vegetables 303

11. Vegetable Kabobs with Simple Peanut Sauce 304

12. Hungarian Mushroom Pilaf 305

13. Chinese cabbage Bake 306

14. Brussels sprouts With Balsamic Oil 308

15. Aromatic Baked Potatoes with Chives 309

16. Easy Vegan "chicken" 309

17. Paprika Vegetable Kebab's 311

18. Spiced Soy Curls 312

19. Cauliflower & Egg Rice Casserole 313

20. Hollandaise Topped Grilled Asparagus 314

21. Crispy Asparagus Dipped In Paprika-garlic Spice 315

22. Eggplant Gratin with Mozzarella Crust 316

23. Asian-style Cauliflower 317

24. **Two-cheese Vegetable Frittata** 318

25. Rice & Beans Stuffed Bell Peppers 319

26. Parsley-loaded Mushrooms 320

27. Cheesy Vegetable Quesadilla 321

28. Creamy 'n Cheese Broccoli Bake 322

29. Sweet & Spicy Parsnips 323

30. Zucchini with Mediterranean Dill Sauce 324

31. Zesty Broccoli 325

32. Chewy Glazed Parsnips 326

33. Hoisin-glazed Bok Choy 327

34. Green Beans with Okra 328

35. Celeriac with some Greek Yogurt Dip 329

36. Wine & Garlic Flavored Vegetables 330

37. Spicy Braised Vegetables 331

CHAPTER 3: Air Fryer Snack Side Dishes and Appetizer Recipes 333

1. Crispy 'n Tasty Spring Rolls 333

2. Spinach & Feta Crescent Triangles 334

3. Healthy Avocado Fries 335

4. Twice-fried Cauliflower Tater Tots 336

5. Cheesy Mushroom & Cauliflower Balls 337

6. Italian Seasoned Easy Pasta Chips 339

7. Thai Sweet Potato Balls 339

8. Barbecue Roasted Almonds 340

9. Croissant Rolls 341

10. Curry' n Coriander Spiced Bread Rolls 342

11. Scrumptiously Healthy Chips 343

12. Kid-friendly Vegetable Fritters 344

13. Avocado Fries 345

14. Crispy Wings with Lemony Old Bay Spice 347

15. Cold Salad with Veggies and Pasta 348

16.   Zucchini and Minty Eggplant Bites...349

17.   Stuffed Potatoes 351

18.   Paneer Cutlet...352

19.   Spicy Roasted Cashew Nuts 352

CHAPTER 4: Deserts **354**

1.   Almond-apple Treat..354

2.   Pepper-pineapple With Butter-sugar Glaze....................................354

3.   True Churros with Yummy Hot Chocolate......................................355

Conclusion **357**

Keto Air Fryer Cookbook with Pictures

Cook and Taste Tens of Low-Carb Fried Recipes. Shed Weight, Kill Hunger, and Regain Confidence Living the Keto Lifestyle

By

Chef Ludovico L'Italiano

Table of Contents

Introduction **20**

Cooking using an Air Fryer 21

Why Use It: 22

Selecting a Custom Air Fryer: 23

Accessories 23

How to clean an Air Fryer 24

Keto Diet 25

Tips for Usage: 25

CHAPTER 1: Breakfast Recipes **26**

1. Loaded Cauliflower Breakfast Bake 26

2. Scrambled Eggs 27

3. "Hard-Boiled" Eggs 28

4. Breakfast Stuffed Poblanos 28

5. Cheesy Cauliflower Hash Browns 29

6. Egg, Cheese, and Bacon Roll-Ups 30

7. Pancake 31

8. Lemon Poppy Seed Cake 32

9. "Banana" Nut Cake 33

10. Bacon Strips 34

11. Pumpkin Spice Muffins 35

12. Veggie Frittata 36

13. Buffalo Egg Cups 37

14. Crispy Southwestern Ham Egg Cups 37

15. Jalapeño Popper Egg Cups 38

16. Crunchy Granola 39

CHAPTER 2: Air Fryer Chicken Main Dishes **40**

1. **Chicken Fajitas** 40

2. **Pepperoni and Chicken Pizza Bake** 40

3.   Almond-Crusted Chicken 41

4.   Southern "Fried" Chicken 42

5.   Spinach and Feta-Stuffed Chicken Breast 43

6.   Blackened Cajun Chicken Tenders 44

7.   Chicken Pizza Crust 45

8.   Chicken Enchiladas 45

9.   Jalapeño Popper Hassel back Chicken 46

10.   Chicken Cordon Bleu Casserole 48

11.   Chicken Parmesan 48

12.   Fajita-Stuffed Chicken Breast 50

13.   Lemon Pepper Drumsticks 50

14.   Cilantro Lime Chicken Thighs 51

15.   Lemon Thyme Roasted Chicken 52

16.   Teriyaki Wings 53

17.   Crispy Buffalo Chicken Tenders 54

CHAPTER 3: Air Fryer Side Dish Recipes **55**

1.   Pita-Style Chips 55

2.   Avocado Fries 56

3.   Flatbread 56

4.   Radish Chips 57

5.   Coconut Flour Cheesy Garlic Biscuits 58

6.   Dinner Rolls 59

7.   Cilantro Lime Roasted Cauliflower 60

8.   Green Bean Casserole 61

9.   Buffalo Cauliflower 62

10.   Kale Chips 62

11.   Roasted Garlic 63

12.   Zucchini Parmesan Chips 64

13.   Crispy Brussels sprouts 65

14.   Cheesy Cauliflower Tots 66

15.   Sausage-Stuffed Mushroom Caps 67

16.   Garlic Herb Butter Roasted Radishes 68

17.   Loaded Roasted Broccoli 68

CHAPTER 4: Air Fryer Snack and Appetizer Recipes **70**

1.   Bacon-Wrapped Brie 70

2.   Crust less Meat Pizza 71

3.   Garlic Cheese Bread 71

4.   Mozzarella Pizza Crust 72

5.   Spicy Spinach Artichoke Dip 73

6.   Mini Sweet Pepper Poppers 74

7.   Bacon-Wrapped Onion Rings 75

8.   Mozzarella Sticks 75

9.   Pork Rind Tortillas 76

10.   Bacon Cheeseburger Dip 77

11.   Pizza Rolls 78

12.   Bacon Jalapeño Cheese Bread 79

13.   Spicy Buffalo Chicken Dip 80

14.   Garlic Parmesan Chicken Wings 81

15.   Bacon-Wrapped Jalapeño Poppers 82

16.   Prosciutto-Wrapped Parmesan Asparagus 83

CHAPTER 5: Desserts **85**

1.   Mini Cheesecake 85

2.   Pecan Brownies 85

3.   Cinnamon Sugar Pork Rinds 86

4.   Almond Butter Cookie Balls 87

Conclusion **88**

Introduction

An air-fryer is a modern kitchen device that cooks food instead of using oil by blowing extremely hot air around it. It provides a low-fat variant of food that in a deep fryer will usually be fried. Consequently, fatty foods such as French fries, fried chicken, and onion rings are usually prepared with no oil or up to 80% less fat relative to traditional cooking techniques.

If you already have an air fryer, you probably know that it's a futuristic gadget designed to save time and help make your life easier. You'll be eager to hear about how soon you'll be addicted to using your air fryer for cooking almost any meal if you've still not taken the jump. What is so unique about air frying, though?

The air fryer will substitute your deep fryer, microwave, oven, and dehydrator and cook tasty meals uniformly in a very small amount of time. Your air fryer is a show stopper if you're trying to help your friends with nutritious food but do not have much time.

With your progress on the ketogenic diet, an air fryer will also aid. The fast cooking time it offers is one of the main advantages of air frying. When you are starving and limited on resources, this is extremely helpful, a formula for cheating on your keto diet. Simple planning of nutritious meals is also linked to long-term progress on a keto diet. That's why during your keto trip, your air fryer can be your best buddy and support you to stay on track, even on days when time is limited for you.

The Air Fryer offers fried foods and nutritious meals, helping you eliminate the calories that come with fried foods and providing you the crunchiness, taste, and flavor you love. By blowing very hot air (up to 400 ° F) uniformly and rapidly around a food ingredient put in an enclosed room, this household appliance works. The heat renders the food part on the outside crispy and brittle, but it is warm and moist on the inside. You can use an air fryer on pretty much everything. You should barbecue, bake and roast in addition to frying. Its choice of cooking choices allows it simpler at any time of the day to eat any food.

Cooking using an Air Fryer

It is as simple to cook with an air fryer as using an oven. Anyone may do it, and then you'll wish that you had turned to this brilliant cooking process earlier after only a few tries. This section will outline air frying choices, optimize your cooking period and juiciness, clarify how to make your air fryer clean and offer some gadgets that will make sure that your air frying experience is even simpler and more pleasant.

Although the fundamentals of using an air fryer would be discussed in this section, the first phase is studying the guide that comes along with the air fryer. Almost all air fryers are distinct, and there are several different versions of the industry with the recent spike in device demand. Knowing how to thoroughly operate your particular air fryer is the secret to victory and can familiarize you with debugging concerns as well as protection features. Until first use, reading through the guide and washing every component with soft, soapy water can make you feel prepared to release your cooking finesse!

Why Use It:

Air frying is widely common because it enables you to cook tasty meals easily and uniformly with very small quantity of oil and very little energy. Here are only a handful of reasons to turn to air frying:

Quick cleanup: You would certainly stain your cooker with every cooking process, but with the smaller frying region of the air fryer and portable basket, comprehensive cleanup is a breeze!

Cooks faster: By rotating heated air throughout the cooking compartment, air frying operates. This contributes to quick and even frying, using a portion of your oven's resources. You can set most air fryers to an extreme temperature of around 350-400°F. Because of which, in an air fryer, you can cook just about everything you can create in a microwave.

Low-Fat Food: The most important feature of the air fryer is the usage of hot-air airflow to cook food products from all directions, removing the need for gasoline. This makes it easier for individuals on a reduced-fat diet to eat deliciously balanced meals safely.

Highly Safe: While tossing chicken or any other ingredients into the deep fryer, do you know how extra cautious you have to be? As it is still really hot, you want to be sure that the hot oil does not spill and damage your face. You wouldn't have to think about brunette skin from hot oil spillage with your air fryer.

Multifunctional Use: Since it can cook many dishes at once, the air fryer helps you multitask. It is your all-in-one gadget that can barbecue, bake, fry and roast the dishes you need! For separate work, you no longer require several appliances.

Healthier Foods: Air fryers are built to operate without fattening oils and up to 80 percent less fat to create healthier foods. This makes it possible to lose weight because you can also enjoy your fried dishes while retaining calories and saturated fat. Through utilizing this appliance, making the transition to a healthy existence is more feasible. The scent that comes with deep-fried items, which also hangs in the room even many hours after deep frying, is also eliminated from your house.

Selecting a Custom Air Fryer:

The dual most significant aspects to concentrate on are scale/size and heat range when picking an air fryer. In general, quart scale air fryers are calculated and vary from around 1.2 quarts size to about 10 quarts or even more. You may be drawn in at a minimum a 5.3-quart fryer which may be used to wonderfully roast a whole chicken if you are trying to prepare meals to serve a group, but if you require a tiny machine owing to the minimal counter room and you are preparing for just one or two, you can certainly crisp up those Fries with a much minor air fryer.

And for the range of temperatures available, many air fryers encourage you to dry out foods and, for a prolonged period, you can fry them at extremely low heat, say about 120 ° F. You'll want to ensure the air fryer takes the necessary cooking power and heat range, based on the functions you use.

Accessories

The cooking chamber of your air fryer is essentially just a wide, open room for the warm air to move. It is a big bonus because it offers you the opportunity to integrate into your kitchen some different accessories. These devices increase the amount of dishes that you can produce using your air fryer and start opening choices that you might never have known was feasible. Below are few of the popular gadgets.

Parchment: In specific, precut parchment may be useful while baking with your air fryer to make cleaning much simpler. Similarly, for quick steaming, you will find parchment paper with precut holes.

Pizza pan: Indeed, using the air fryer, you can make a pizza, and this book contains many recipes for various kinds of keto-friendly pizzas. This is a fantastic alternative to still have the desired form quickly.

Cupcake pan: It typically comes with several tiny cups, and the 5.3-quart size air fryer takes up the whole chamber. For cupcakes, muffins, or even egg plates, these flexible cups are fine. You can still use single silicone baking containers if you would not want to go this path.

Cake pan: For your air fryer, you will find specially designed cake pans that fit perfectly into the inner pot. They even come with a built-in handle so that when your cakes are finished baking, you can quickly take them out.

Skewer rack: This is identical to a holder made of aluminum, except it has built-in skewers of metal that make roasting kebabs a breeze.

Metal holder: To add a layer to your cooking plate, this round rack is used so that you can optimize room and cook several items simultaneously. When you cook meat and vegetables and don't want to stop to cook to get going on the other, this is especially helpful.

How to clean an Air Fryer

Make sure that the air fryer is cold and unhooked before washing it. To wash the air fryer slate, you'll need to follow the steps below:

1. Separate your air fryer plate from its foundation. Fill a tub of worm water and soap for your pan. Let the plate sit in warm water and soap mix for about 10 minutes with your frying bucket inside.

2. Using a brush or sponge, thoroughly clean the bucket.

3. Lift the basket from the frying pan and clean the underneath and exterior surfaces.

4. Now use the same brush or sponge to clean your air-fryer plate.

5. Allow all to air-dry completely and transfer to the foundation of the air fryer.

Simply scrub the exterior with a wet cloth to disinfect the exterior of your air fryer. Then, before starting your next cooking experience, make sure all parts are in there right places.

Keto Diet

A relatively moderate-protein, low-carb, and elevated diet that help the body sustain itself without using sugars or high amounts of carbs is the keto diet or keto. When the system is low on glucose (sugar), ketones are formed by a mechanism called ketosis in the liver from food metabolism. This diet will contribute to some lower blood sugar, weight loss, balanced insulin levels, plus managed cravings, with diligent monitoring, imaginative meals, and self-control.

Your body takes some carbohydrates as you consume high-carb nutrition and converts them into energy to fuel itself. Your liver instead burns fat as you leave out the carbohydrates. A ketogenic régime usually limits carbohydrates to about 0-50 grams a day.

Tips for Usage:

- Preheat your fryer before use
- Always cook in batches. Do not overcrowd your fryer
- Space Your Foods evenly when added to the air fryer
- Keep It Dry
- Use spray oil to oil your food

CHAPTER 1: Breakfast Recipes

If you set your air fryer to work, simple and healthy low-carb breakfasts will soon be the rule in your home! These meals will boot the day in a nutritious way without robbing you of days that should be full of savory fun! It can be not easy to make a nourishing meal for oneself or relatives while you're trying to get out of the house in time. The easiest choice might be to catch a granola bar or microwave pastry, but it will quickly contribute to thoughts of shame and guilt and extreme malnutrition at noon.

This section's meals are full and keto-approved, making you improve your mornings and all your days. Get prepared in a snap for nutritious meals that can be created using your air fryer. You can make meals in advance, such as Cheese Balls, and Sausage and you can put dishes in the air fryer to get ready until you get dressed, such as Quick and Simple Bacon Strips, you'll want to have begun frying your breakfasts earlier!

1. Loaded Cauliflower Breakfast Bake

Preparation time: 15 minutes

Cooking time: 20 minutes

Servings: 4 people

Ingredients:

- 12 slices sugar-free bacon, cooked and crumbled
- 2 scallions, sliced on the bias
- 8 tablespoons full-fat sour cream
- 1 medium avocado, peeled and pitted
- 1 cup shredded medium Cheddar cheese
- 11/2 cups chopped cauliflower
- 1/4 cup heavy whipping cream
- 6 large eggs

Directions:

1. Mix the eggs and milk in a medium dish. Pour it into a circular 4-cup baking tray.
2. Add and blend the cauliflower, and cover it with cheddar. Put your dish in the air-fryer bowl.
3. Change the temperature and set the timer to about 320°F for around 20 minutes.
4. The eggs will be solid once fully baked, and the cheese will be golden brown. Slice it into 4 bits.
5. Cut the avocado and split the bits equally. Put two teaspoons of sliced scallions, sour cream, and crumbled bacon on top of each plate.

2. Scrambled Eggs

Preparation time: 5 minutes

Cooking time: 20 minutes

Servings: 2 people

Ingredients:

- 1/2 cup shredded sharp Cheddar cheese
- 2 tablespoons unsalted butter, melted
- 4 large eggs

Directions:

1. Crack the eggs into a round 2-cup baking pan and whisk them. Put the tray in the air-fryer container.

2. Change the temperature settings and set the timer to about 400°F for around 10 minutes.

3. Mix the eggs after about 5 minutes and add some cheese and butter. Let it cook for another 3 minutes and mix again.

4. Give an extra 2 minutes to finish frying or remove the eggs from flame if they are to your preferred taste.

5. For fluffing, use a fork. Serve it hot.

3. "Hard-Boiled" Eggs

Preparation time: 2 minutes

Cooking time: 20 minutes

Servings: 4 people

Ingredients:

- 1 cup water
- 4 large eggs

Directions:

1. Put the eggs in a heat-proof 4-cup round baking tray and pour some water over your eggs. Put the tray in the air-fryer basket.

2. Set the air fryer's temperature to about 300 ° F and set the clock for about 18-minute.

3. In the fridge, store boiled eggs before ready to consume or peel and serve warmly.

4. Breakfast Stuffed Poblanos

Preparation time: 20 minutes

Cooking time: 15 minutes

Servings: 5 people

Ingredients:

- 1/2 cup full-fat sour cream

- 8 tablespoons shredded pepper jack cheese
- 4 large poblano peppers
- 1/4 cup canned diced tomatoes and green chilies, drained
- 4 ounces full-fat cream cheese, softened
- 4 large eggs
- 1/2 pound spicy ground pork breakfast sausage

Directions:

1. Crumble and brown the cooked sausage in a large skillet over medium-low heat until no red exists. Take the sausage from the skillet and clean the oil. Crack your eggs in the skillet, scramble, and simmer until they are no longer watery.

2. In a wide bowl, add the fried sausage and add in cream cheese. Mix the sliced tomatoes and chilies. Gently fold the eggs together.

3. Cut a 4-5-inch gap at the top of each poblano, separating the white layer and seeds with a tiny knife. In four portions, divide the filling and gently scoop into each pepper. Cover each with 2 teaspoons of cheese from the pepper jack.

4. Drop each pepper into the container of the air fryer.

5. Change the temperature and set the timer to about 350 °F for around 15 minutes.

6. The peppers will be tender, and when prepared, the cheese will be golden brown. Serve instantly with sour cream on top.

5. Cheesy Cauliflower Hash Browns

Preparation time: 20 minutes

Cooking time: 12 minutes

Servings: 4 people

Ingredients:

- 1 cup shredded sharp Cheddar cheese
- 1 large egg
- 1 (12-ounce) steamer bag cauliflower

Directions:

1. Put the bag in the oven and cook as per the directions in the box. To extract excess moisture, leave to cool fully and place cauliflower in a cheesecloth or paper towel and squeeze.

2. Add the cheese and eggs and mash the cauliflower using a fork.

3. Cut a slice of parchment to match the frame of your air fryer. Take 1/4 of the paste and make it into a hash-brown patty shape and mold it. Put it on the parchment and, into your air fryer basket, if required, running in groups.

4. Change the temperature and set the clock to about 400°F for around 12 minutes.

5. Halfway into the cooking process, turn your hash browns. They will be nicely browned when fully baked. Instantly serve.

6. Egg, Cheese, and Bacon Roll-Ups

Preparation time: 20 minutes

Cooking time: 20 minutes

Servings: 4 people

Ingredients:

- 1/2 cup mild salsa for dipping
- 1 cup shredded sharp Cheddar cheese

- 12 slices sugar free bacon
- 6 large eggs
- 1/2 medium green bell pepper, seeded and chopped
- 1/4 cup chopped onion
- 2 tablespoons unsalted butter

Directions:

1. Melt the butter in a small skillet over medium flame. Add the pepper and onion to the skillet and sauté until aromatic, around 3 minutes, and your onions are transparent.

2. In a shallow pot, whisk the eggs and dump them into a skillet. Scramble the pepper and onion with the eggs once fluffy and fully fried after 5 minutes. Remove from the flame and set aside.

3. Put 3 strips of bacon beside each other on the cutting board, overlapping about 1/4. Place 1/4 cup of scrambled eggs on the side nearest to you in a pile and scatter 1/4 cup of cheese on top of your eggs.

4. Wrap the bacon around the eggs securely and, if needed, protect the seam using a toothpick. Put each wrap into the container of the air fryer.

5. Switch the temperature to about 350 ° F and set the clock for around 15 minutes. Midway through the cooking time, turn the rolls.

6. When fully fried, the bacon would be brown and tender. For frying, serve immediately with some salsa.

7. Pancake

Preparation time: 10 minutes

Cooking time: 7 minutes

Servings: 4 people

Ingredients:

- 1/2 teaspoon ground cinnamon

- 1/2 teaspoon vanilla extract

- 1/2 teaspoon unflavored gelatin

- 1 large egg

- 2 tablespoons unsalted butter, softened

- 1/2 teaspoon baking powder

- 1/4 cup powdered erythritol

- 1/2 cup blanched finely ground almond flour

Directions:

1. Combine the erythritol, almond flour, and baking powder in a wide pot. Add some egg, butter, cinnamon, gelatin, and vanilla. Place into a rectangular 6-inch baking tray.

2. Place the tray in the container of your air fryer.

3. Change the temperature to about 300 °F and set the clock for 7 minutes.

4. A toothpick can pop out dry when the dessert is fully baked. Split the cake into four servings and eat.

8. Lemon Poppy Seed Cake

Preparation time: 10 minutes

Cooking time: 14 minutes

Servings: 6 people

Ingredients:

- 1 teaspoon poppy seeds

- 1 medium lemon

- 1 teaspoon vanilla extract

- 2 large eggs

- 1/4 cup unsweetened almond milk

- 1/4 cup unsalted butter, melted

- 1/2 teaspoon baking powder

- 1/2 cup powdered erythritol
- 1 cup blanched finely ground almond flour

Directions:

Mix the erythritol, almond flour, butter, baking powder, eggs, almond milk, and vanilla in a big bowl.

Halve the lime and strain the liquid into a little pot, then transfer it to the mixture.

Zest the lemon with a fine grinder and transfer 1 tbsp. of zest to the mixture and blend.

Add the poppy seeds to your batter.

In the non-stick 6' circular cake tin, add your batter. Put the pan in the container of your air fryer.

Change the temperature and set the clock to about 300°F for around 14 minutes.

A wooden skewer inserted in the middle, if it comes out completely clean, means it's thoroughly fried. The cake will stop cooking and crisp up when it cools. At room temperature, serve.

9. "Banana" Nut Cake

Preparation time: 20 minutes

Cooking time: 30 minutes

Servings: 6-7 people

Ingredients:

- 1/4 cup of chopped walnuts
- 2 large eggs
- 1/4 cup of full-fat sour cream
- 1 teaspoon of vanilla extract
- 21/2 teaspoons of banana extract
- 1/4 cup of unsalted butter, melted
- 1/2 teaspoon of ground cinnamon
- 2 teaspoons of baking powder

- 2 tablespoons of ground golden flaxseed
- 1/2 cup of powdered erythritol
- 1 cup of blanched finely ground almond flour

Directions:

1. Mix the erythritol, almond flour, baking powder, flaxseed, and cinnamon in a big dish.

2. Add vanilla extract, banana extract, butter, and sour cream and mix well.

3. Add your eggs to the combination and whisk until they are fully mixed. Mix in your walnuts.

4. Pour into a 6-inch non-stick cake pan and put in the bowl of your air fryer.

5. Change the temperature and set the clock to about 300°F for around 25 minutes.

6. When fully baked, the cake will be lightly golden, and a toothpick inserted in the middle will come out clean. To prevent cracking, allow it to cool entirely.

10. Bacon Strips

Preparation time: 5 minutes

Cooking time: 12 minutes

Servings: 5 people

Ingredients:

- 10 slices sugar free bacon

Directions:

1. Put slices of bacon into the bucket of your air fryer.

2. Change the temperature and set the timer to about 400°F for around 12 minutes.

3. Turn the bacon after 6 minutes and proceed to cook. Serve hot.

11.Pumpkin Spice Muffins

Preparation time: 10 minutes

Cooking time: 15 minutes

Servings: 6 people

Ingredients:

- 2 large eggs
- 1 teaspoon vanilla extract
- 1/4 teaspoon ground nutmeg
- 1/2 teaspoon ground cinnamon
- 1/4 cup pure pumpkin purée
- 1/4 cup unsalted butter, softened
- 1/2 teaspoon baking powder

- 1/2 cup granular erythritol
- 1 cup blanched finely ground almond flour

Directions:

1. Mix the erythritol, almond flour, butter, baking powder, nutmeg, cinnamon, pumpkin purée, and vanilla in a big dish.
2. Stir in the eggs softly.
3. Add the batter into about six or more silicone muffin cups equally. Put muffin cups in the air fryer basket. If required, make them in groups.
4. Change the temperature and set the clock to about 300°F for around 15 minutes.
5. A wooden skewer inserted in the middle will come out completely clean if thoroughly cooked. Serve hot.

12. Veggie Frittata

Preparation time: minutes

Cooking time: minutes

Servings: people

Ingredients:

- 1/4 cup of chopped green bell pepper
- 1/4 cup of chopped yellow onion
- 1/2 cup of chopped broccoli
- 1/4 cup of heavy whipping cream
- 6 large eggs

Directions:

1. Whisk the heavy whipping cream and eggs in a big bowl. Add in the onion, broccoli, and bell pepper.
2. Load into a 6-inch circular baking dish that is oven-safe. Put the baking tray in the basket of an air fryer.
3. Switch the temperature to about 350 ° F and set the clock for around 12-minute.

4. When the frittata is finished, eggs must be solid and thoroughly cooked. Serve it hot.

13. Buffalo Egg Cups

Preparation time: 12 minutes

Cooking time: 12 minutes

Servings: 3 people

Ingredients:

- 1/2 cup of shredded sharp Cheddar cheese
- 2 tablespoons of buffalo sauce
- 2 ounces of full-fat cream cheese
- 4 large eggs

Directions:

1. In two (4') ramekins, add the eggs.
2. Mix the buffalo sauce, cream cheese, and cheddar in a little, microwave-safe container. For about 20 seconds, microwave and then mix. Put a spoonful on top of each egg within each ramekin.
3. Put the ramekins in the container of an air fryer.
4. Change the temperature and set the timer to about 320°F for around 15 minutes.
5. Serve it hot.

14. Crispy Southwestern Ham Egg Cups

Preparation time: 5 minutes

Cooking time: 14 minutes

Servings: 3 people

Ingredients:

- 1/2 cup of shredded medium Cheddar cheese
- 2 tablespoons of diced white onion
- 2 tablespoons of diced red bell pepper
- 1/4 cup diced of green bell pepper

- 2 tablespoons of full-fat sour cream
- 4 large eggs
- 4 (1-ounce) of slices deli ham

Directions:

1. Put a piece of ham at the bottom of four or more baking cups.

2. Whisk the eggs along with the sour cream in a big bowl. Add the red pepper, green pepper, and onion and mix well.

3. Add the mixture of eggs into baking cups that are ham-lined. Top them with some cheddar cheese. Put the cups in the container of your air fryer.

4. Set the clock for around 12 minutes or till the peaks are golden browned, cook at a temperature of about 320 ° F.

5. Serve it hot.

15. Jalapeño Popper Egg Cups

Preparation time: 10 minutes

Cooking time: 12 minutes

Servings: 3 people

Ingredients:

- 1/2 cup of shredded sharp Cheddar cheese
- 2 ounces of full-fat cream cheese
- 1/4 cup of chopped pickled jalapeños
- 4 large eggs

Directions:

1. Add the eggs to a medium container, and then dump them into 4 silicone muffin cups.

2. Place the cream cheese, jalapeños, and cheddar in a wide, microwave-safe dish. Heat in the microwave for about 30 seconds and mix well. Take a full spoon and put it in

the middle of one of the egg cups, around 1/4 of the paste. Repeat for the mixture left.

3. Put the egg cups in the container of your air fryer.
4. Change the temperature and set the clock for around 10 minutes to about 320 °F.
5. Serve it hot.

16. Crunchy Granola

Preparation time: 10 minutes

Cooking time: 5 minutes

Servings: 6 people

Ingredients:

- 1 teaspoon of ground cinnamon
- 2 tablespoons of unsalted butter
- 1/4 cup of granular erythritol
- 1/4 cup of low-carb, sugar free chocolate chips
- 1/4 cup of golden flaxseed
- 1/3 cup of sunflower seeds
- 1 cup of almond slivers
- 1 cup of unsweetened coconut flakes
- 2 cups of pecans, chopped

Directions:

1. Blend all the ingredients in a big bowl.
2. In a 4-cup circular baking tray, put the mixture into it.
3. Place the tray in the air-fryer container.
4. Change the temperature and set the clock to about 320°F for around 5 minutes.
5. Let it cool absolutely before serving.

CHAPTER 2: Air Fryer Chicken Main Dishes

1. Chicken Fajitas

Preparation time: 10 minutes

Cooking time: 15 minutes

Servings: 2 people

Ingredients:

- 1/2 medium red bell pepper, seeded and sliced
- 1/2 medium green bell pepper, seeded and sliced
- 1/4 medium onion, peeled and sliced
- 1/2 teaspoon garlic powder
- 1/2 teaspoon paprika
- 1/2 teaspoon cumin
- 1 tablespoon chili powder
- 2 tablespoons coconut oil, melted
- 10 ounces boneless, skinless chicken breast, sliced into 1/4" strips

Directions:

1. In a big bowl, mix the chicken and coconut oil and scatter with the paprika, cumin, chili powder, and garlic powder. Toss the chicken with spices until well mixed. Put the chicken in the basket of an air fryer.

2. Set the temperature and adjust the clock to about 350°F for around 15 minutes.

3. When your clock has 7 minutes left, throw in the peppers and onion into the fryer bucket.

4. When frying, flip the chicken at least two to three times. Veggies should be soft; when done, the chicken should be thoroughly cooked to at least 165°F internal temperature. Serve it hot.

2. Pepperoni and Chicken Pizza Bake

Preparation time: 10 minutes

Cooking time: 15 minutes

Servings: 4 people

Ingredients:

- 1/4 cup grated Parmesan cheese
- 1 cup shredded mozzarella cheese
- 1 cup low-carb, sugar-free pizza sauce
- 20 slices pepperoni
- 2 cups cubed cooked chicken

Directions:

1. Add the pepperoni, chicken, and pizza sauce into a 4-cup rectangular baking tray. Stir such that the beef is coated fully in the sauce.
2. Cover with grated mozzarella and parmesan. Put your dish in the air-fryer bucket.
3. Set the temperature and adjust the clock to about 375°F for around 15 minutes.
4. When served, the dish would be brown and bubbly. Instantly serve.

3. Almond-Crusted Chicken

Preparation time: 15 minutes

Cooking time: 25 minutes

Servings: 4 people

Ingredients:

- 1 tablespoon Dijon mustard
- 2 tablespoons full-fat mayonnaise
- 2 (6-ounce) boneless, skinless chicken breasts
- 1/4 cup slivered almonds

Directions:

1. In a food processor, pulse your almonds or cut until finely diced. Put the almonds equally and put them aside on a tray.
2. Completely split each chicken breast lengthwise in part.

3. In a shallow pot, combine the mustard and mayonnaise now, cover the entire chicken with the mixture.

4. Place each piece of chicken completely coated in the diced almonds. Transfer the chicken gently into the bucket of your air fryer.

5. Set the temperature and adjust the clock to about 350°F for around 25 minutes.

6. When it has hit an interior temperature of about 165 ° F or more, the chicken will be cooked. Serve it hot.

4. Southern "Fried" Chicken

Preparation time: 15 minutes

Cooking time: 25 minutes

Servings: 4 people

Ingredients:

- 2 ounces pork rinds, finely ground
- 1/4 teaspoon ground black pepper
- 1/4 teaspoon onion powder
- 1/2 teaspoon cumin

- 1 tablespoon chili powder
- 2 tablespoons hot sauce
- 2 (6-ounce) boneless, skinless chicken breasts

Directions:

1. Longitudinally, split each chicken breast in half. Put the chicken in a big pot and add some hot sauce to coat the chicken completely.

2. Mix the onion powder, cumin, chili powder, and pepper in a shallow container. Sprinkle the mix over your chicken.

3. In a wide bowl, put the seasoned pork rinds and dunk each chicken piece into the container, covering as much as necessary. Put the chicken in the bucket of an air fryer.

4. Set the temperature and adjust the clock to about 350°F for around 25 minutes.

5. Turn the chicken gently midway through the cooking process.

6. The internal temperature will be at most 165 ° F when finished, and the coating of the pork rind will be rich golden brown in color. Serve it hot.

5. Spinach and Feta-Stuffed Chicken Breast

Preparation time: 15 minutes

Cooking time: 25 minutes

Servings: 2 people

Ingredients:

- 1 tablespoon coconut oil
- 2 (6-ounce) boneless, skinless chicken breasts
- 1/4 cup crumbled feta
- 1/4 cup chopped yellow onion
- 1/2 teaspoon salt, divided
- 1/2 teaspoon garlic powder, divided
- 5 ounces frozen spinach, thawed and drained

- 1 tablespoon unsalted butter

Directions:

1. Add some butter to your pan and sauté the spinach for around 3 minutes in a medium-sized skillet over a medium-high flame. Sprinkle the spinach with 1/4 teaspoon salt, 1/4 teaspoon garlic powder now, add your onion to the plate.

2. Sauté for another 3 minutes, then turn off the flame and put it in a medium-sized dish. Fold the feta mixture into the spinach.

3. Lengthwise, carve a nearly 4' cut through the side of each chicken breast. Scoop half of the mix into each portion and seal with a pair of toothpicks shut. Dust with leftover salt and garlic powder outside of your chicken. Drizzle some coconut oil. Put the chicken breasts in the bucket of your air fryer.

4. Set the temperature and adjust the clock to about 350°F for around 25 minutes.

5. The chicken must be golden brown in color and have an internal temperature of at least 165 ° F when fully cooked. Cut and serve hot.

6. Blackened Cajun Chicken Tenders

Preparation time: 10 minutes

Cooking time: 17 minutes

Servings: 4 people

Ingredients:

- 1/4 cup full-fat ranch dressing
- 1 pound boneless, skinless chicken tenders
- 2 tablespoons coconut oil
- 1/8 teaspoon ground cayenne pepper
- 1/4 teaspoon onion powder
- 1/2 teaspoon dried thyme
- 1/2 teaspoon garlic powder
- 1 teaspoon chili powder

- 2 teaspoons paprika

Directions:

1. Mix all the seasonings in a shallow container.

2. Drizzle oil over chicken wings and then cover each tender thoroughly in the mixture of spices. Put tenders in the bucket of your air fryer.

3. Set the temperature and adjust the clock to about 375 °F for around 17 minutes.

4. Tenders, when completely baked, will have a temperature of 165 ° F centrally.

5. For dipping, use some ranch dressing and enjoy.

7. Chicken Pizza Crust

Preparation time: 10 minutes

Cooking time: 25 minutes

Servings: 4 people

Ingredients:

1 pound ground chicken thigh meat

1/4 cup grated Parmesan cheese

1/2 cup shredded mozzarella

Directions:

1. Combine all the ingredients in a wide bowl. Split equally into four portions.

2. Slice out four (6") parchment paper circles and push down the chicken mixture on each one of the circles. Put into the bucket of your air fryer, working as required in groups or individually.

3. Set the temperature and adjust the clock to about 375°F for around 25 minutes.

4. Midway into the cooking process, turn the crust.

5. You can cover it with some cheese and your choice of toppings until completely baked, and cook for 5 extra minutes. Or, you can place the crust in the fridge or freezer and top it later when you are ready to consume.

8. Chicken Enchiladas

Preparation time: 20 minutes

Cooking time: 10 minutes

Servings: 4 people

Ingredients:

- 1 medium avocado, peeled, pitted, and sliced
- Half cup full-fat sour cream
- 1 cup shredded medium Cheddar cheese
- Half cup of torn Monterey jack (MJ) cheese
- 1/2 pound medium-sliced deli chicken
- 1/3 cup low-carb enchilada sauce, divided
- 1 1/2 cups shredded cooked chicken

Directions:

1. Combine the shredded chicken and at least half of the enchilada sauce in a big dish. On a cutting surface, lay pieces of deli chicken and pour 2 teaspoons of shredded chicken mixture on each of your slices.

2. Sprinkle each roll with 2 teaspoons of cheddar cheese. Roll softly to close it completely.

3. Put each roll, seam side down, in a 4-cup circular baking tray. Over the rolls, pour the leftover sauce and top with the Monterey Jack. Put the dish in the air-fryer basket.

4. Set the temperature and adjust the clock to about 370 °F for around 10 minutes.

5. Enchiladas, when baked, would be golden on top and bubbling. With some sour cream and diced avocado, serve hot.

9. Jalapeño Popper Hassel back Chicken

Preparation time: 20 minutes

Cooking time: 20 minutes

Servings: 4 people

Ingredients:

- 2 (6-ounce) boneless, skinless chicken breasts
- 1/4 cup sliced pickled jalapeños
- 1/2 cup shredded sharp Cheddar cheese, divided
- 2 ounces full-fat cream cheese, softened
- 4 slices sugar-free bacon, cooked and crumbled

Directions:

1. Put the fried bacon in a medium-sized dish; add in half of the cheddar, cream cheese, and the jalapeño strips.

1. Using a sharp knife to build slits around 3/4 of the way across the chicken in each of the chicken thighs, being cautious not to go all the way through. You would typically get 6 to 8 per breast, cuts based on the chicken breast's length.

2. Spoon the premade cream cheese mix onto the chicken strips. Toss the leftover shredded cheese over your chicken breasts and put it in the air fryer basket.

3. Set the temperature and adjust the clock to about 350°F for around 20 minutes.

4. Serve it hot.

10. Chicken Cordon Bleu Casserole

Preparation time: 15 minutes

Cooking time: 15 minutes

Servings: 4 people

Ingredients:

- 1-ounce pork rinds, crushed
- 2 teaspoons Dijon mustard
- 2 tablespoons unsalted butter, melted
- 1 tablespoon heavy cream
- 4 ounces full-fat cream cheese, softened
- 2 ounces Swiss cheese, cubed
- 1/2 cup cubed cooked ham
- 2 cups cubed cooked chicken thigh meat

Directions:

1. Put the chicken and ham in a 6-inch circular baking pan and toss to blend the meat uniformly. Scatter on top of the meat some cheese cubes.

2. Add butter, heavy cream, cream cheese, and mustard in a big bowl and then spill the mix over your meat and cheese. Cover with rinds of pork. Put the pan in the bucket of your air fryer.

3. Set the temperature and adjust the clock to about 350°F for around 15 minutes.

4. When finished, the saucepan will be caramelized and bubbling. Serve hot.

11. Chicken Parmesan

Preparation time: 10 minutes

Cooking time: 25 minutes

Servings: 4 people

Ingredients:

- 1-ounce pork rinds, crushed
- 1 cup low-carb, no-sugar-added pasta sauce
- 1/2 cup grated Parmesan cheese, divided
- 2 (6-ounce) boneless, skinless chicken breasts
- 1 cup shredded mozzarella cheese, divided
- 4 tablespoons full-fat mayonnaise, divided
- 1/2 teaspoon dried parsley
- 1/4 teaspoon dried oregano
- 1/2 teaspoon garlic powder

Directions:

1. Cut each chicken breast longitudinally in half and hammer it to pound out a thickness of about 3/4". Sprinkle with parsley, garlic powder, and oregano.
2. On top of each slice of chicken, scatter 1 tablespoon of mayonnaise, then cover each piece with 1/4 cup of mozzarella.
3. Mix the shredded parmesan and pork rinds in a shallow bowl. Sprinkle the surface of the mozzarella with the paste.
4. In a 6' circular baking tray, transfer the sauce and put the chicken on top. Place the pan in the bucket of your air fryer.
5. Set the temperature and adjust the clock to about 320 ° F for around 25 minutes.
6. The cheese will be light browned, and when completely baked, the chicken's internal temperature will be at about 165 ° F. Serve hot.

12. Fajita-Stuffed Chicken Breast

Preparation time: 15 minutes

Cooking time: 25 minutes

Servings: 4 people

Ingredients:

- 1/2 teaspoon garlic powder
- 1 teaspoon ground cumin
- 2 teaspoons chili powder
- 1 tablespoon coconut oil
- 1 medium green bell pepper, seeded and sliced
- 1/4 medium white onion, peeled and sliced
- 2 (6-ounce) boneless, skinless chicken breasts

Directions:

1. "Slice each chicken breast into two equal parts entirely in half longitudinally. Hammer the chicken out until it is around 1/4" thick using a meat mallet.

2. Put out each chicken slice and arrange three onion pieces and four green pepper pieces on end nearest to you. Start to firmly roll the onions and peppers into the chicken. Both with toothpicks or a few strips of butcher's twine protect the roll.

3. Drizzle the chicken with coconut oil. Sprinkle with cumin, chili powder, and garlic powder on either side. Put all the rolls in the bucket of your air fryer.

4. Set the temperature and adjust the clock to about 350°F for around 25 minutes.

5. Serve it hot.

13. Lemon Pepper Drumsticks

Preparation time: 5 minutes

Cooking time: 22 minutes

Servings: 4 people

Ingredients:

- 1 tablespoon lemon pepper seasoning
- 4 tablespoons salted butter, melted
- 8 chicken drumsticks
- 1/2 teaspoon garlic powder
- 2 teaspoons baking powder

Directions:

1. Sprinkle some baking powder over the drumsticks along with some garlic powder and massage it into the chicken skin. Add your drumsticks into the bucket of your air fryer.
2. Set the temperature and adjust the clock to about 375°F for around 25 minutes.
3. Turn your drumsticks midway through the cooking process using tongs.
4. Take out from the fryer when the skin is golden in color, and the inside temperature is at a minimum of 165 ° F.
5. Put lemon pepper seasoning and some butter in a big dish. To the dish, add your fried drumsticks and turn until the chicken is coated. Serve it hot.

14. Cilantro Lime Chicken Thighs

Preparation time: 15 minutes

Cooking time: 22 minutes

Servings: 4 people

Ingredients:

- 1/4 cup chopped fresh cilantro
- 2 medium limes
- 1 teaspoon cumin
- 2 teaspoons chili powder
- 1/2 teaspoon garlic powder
- 1 teaspoon baking powder
- 4 bone-in, skin-on chicken thighs

Directions:

1. Toss some baking powder on your chicken thighs and rinse them.
2. Mix the chili powder, garlic powder, and cumin in a small bowl and sprinkle uniformly over the thighs, rubbing softly on and under the chicken's skin.
3. Halve one lime and squeeze the liquid across the thighs. Place the chicken in the bucket of an air fryer.
4. Set the temperature and adjust the clock to about 380°F for around 22-minute.
5. For serving, split the other lime into four slices and garnish the fried chicken with lemon wedges and some cilantro.

15. Lemon Thyme Roasted Chicken

Preparation time: 10 minutes

Cooking time: 60 minutes

Servings: 6 people

Ingredients:

- 2 tablespoons salted butter, melted
- 1 medium lemon
- 1 teaspoon baking powder
- 1/2 teaspoon onion powder 2 teaspoons dried parsley

- 1 teaspoon garlic powder
- 2 teaspoons dried thyme
- 1 (4-pound) chicken

Directions:

1. Rub the garlic powder, thyme, parsley, onion powder, and baking powder with the chicken.

2. Slice the lemon put four slices using a toothpick on top of the chicken, chest side up, and secure. Put the leftover slices inside your chicken.

3. Put the whole chicken in the bucket of your air fryer, chest side down.

4. Set the temperature and adjust the clock to about 350°F for around 60-minute.

5. Switch the sides of your chicken after 30 minutes, so its breast side is up.

6. The internal temperature should be at about 165 ° F when finished, and the skin should be golden in color and crispy. Pour the melted butter over the whole chicken before serving.

16. Teriyaki Wings

Preparation time: 60 minutes

Cooking time: 45 minutes

Servings: 4 people

Ingredients:

- 2 teaspoons baking powder
- 1/4 teaspoon ground ginger
- 2 teaspoons minced garlic
- 1/2 cup sugar-free teriyaki sauce
- 2 pounds chicken wings

Directions:

1. Put all of your ingredients in a big bowl or bag, excluding the baking powder and leave to marinate in the fridge for at least 1 hour.

2. Bring the wings into the bucket of your air fryer and dust with baking powder. Rub the wings softly.

3. Set the temperature and adjust the clock to about 400°F for around 25 minutes.

4. When frying, rotate the bucket two to three times.

5. Wings, when finished, should be crunchy and cooked internally to a minimum 165 ° F. Instantly serve.

17. Crispy Buffalo Chicken Tenders

Preparation time: 15 minutes

Cooking time: 20 minutes

Servings: 4 people

Ingredients:

- 1 teaspoon garlic powder
- 1 teaspoon chili powder
- 11/2 ounces pork rinds, finely ground
- 1/4 cup hot sauce
- 1 pound boneless, skinless chicken tenders

Directions:

1. Put the chicken tenders in a big bowl and pour them over with hot sauce. In the hot sauce, toss tender, rubbing uniformly.

2. Mix the ground pork rinds with chili powder and garlic powder in a separate, wide bowl.

3. Put each tender, fully coated, in the ground pork rinds. With some water, wet your hands and push down the rinds of pork onto the chicken.

4. Put the tenders in a single layer into the basket of the air fryer.

5. Set the temperature and adjust the clock to about 375°F for around 20 minutes.

6. Serve it hot.

CHAPTER 3: Air Fryer Side Dish Recipes

1. Pita-Style Chips

Preparation time: 10 minutes

Cooking time: 5 minutes

Servings: 4 people

Ingredients:

- 1 large egg
- 1/4 cup blanched finely ground almond flour
- 1/2 ounce pork rinds, finely ground
- 1 cup shredded mozzarella cheese

Directions:

1. Put mozzarella in a wide oven-safe dish and microwave for about 30 seconds or until melted. Add the rest of the ingredients and mix until largely smooth dough shapes into a ball quickly; if your dough is too hard, microwave for an additional 15 seconds.

2. Roll the dough into a wide rectangle among two parchment paper sheets and then use a sharp knife to make the triangle-shaped chips. Put the prepared chips in the bucket of your air fryer.

3. Set the temperature and adjust the clock to about 350°F for around 5 minutes.

4. Chips, when finished, would be golden in color and crunchy. When they cool down, they will become even crispier.

2. Avocado Fries

Preparation time: 15 minutes

Cooking time: 5 minutes

Servings: 4 people

Ingredients:

- 1-ounce pork rinds, finely ground
- 2 medium avocados

Directions:

1. Split each avocado in half. Now have the pit removed. Peel the outer gently and then split the flesh into 1/4'-thick strips.
2. Put the pork rinds in a medium-sized pot and drop each slice of avocado onto your pork rinds to cover it fully. Put the pieces of avocado in the bucket of your air fryer.
3. Set the temperature and adjust the clock to about 350°F for around 5 minutes.
4. Instantly serve.

3. Flatbread

Preparation time: 5 minutes

Cooking time: 7 minutes

Servings: 2 people

Ingredients:

- 1-ounce full-fat cream cheese softened
- 1/4 cup blanched finely ground almond flour
- 1 cup shredded mozzarella cheese

Directions:

1. Meltdown some mozzarella in your microwave for about 30 seconds in a wide oven-safe container. Mix in some almond flour to make it smooth, and add some cream cheese to the mix. Proceed to blend until dough shapes, slowly kneading using wet hands if needed.

2. Split the dough into two parts and roll between two pieces of parchment paper to a thickness of about 1/4". Cut an extra piece of parchment paper to fit in the container of your air fryer.

3. Put a small piece of flatbread; try working in two batches if necessary, on your parchment paper and into the air fryer.

4. Set the temperature and adjust the clock to about 320 ° F for around 7 minutes.

5. Rotate the flatbread midway through the cooking process. Serve it hot.

4. Radish Chips

Preparation time: 10 minutes

Cooking time: 5 minutes

Servings: 4 people

Ingredients:

- 2 tablespoons coconut oil, melted
- 1/2 teaspoon garlic powder
- 1/4 teaspoon paprika
- 1/4 teaspoon onion powder

- 1 pound radishes
- 2 cups water

Directions:

1. Put the water in a medium-sized saucepan and bring the water to a boil.
2. Cut the upper part and bottom of each radish, then cut each radish thinly and evenly using a mandolin. For this stage, you can use the cutting blade in your food processor.
3. For about 5 minutes or until transparent, put the radish pieces in hot water. To trap extra humidity, extract them from the boiling water and put them on a dry paper towel.
4. In a wide pot, combine the radish pieces and the rest of the ingredients until thoroughly covered in oil and seasoned. Put the radish chips in the basket of an air fryer.
5. Set the temperature and adjust the clock to about 320°F for around 5 minutes.
6. During the cooking process, rotate the basket at least two or three times. Serve it hot.

5. Coconut Flour Cheesy Garlic Biscuits

Preparation time: 10 minutes

Cooking time: 12 minutes

Servings: 4 people

Ingredients:

- 1 scallion, sliced
- 1/2 cup shredded sharp Cheddar cheese
- 1/4 cup unsalted butter, melted and divided
- 1 large egg
- 1/2 teaspoon garlic powder
- 1/2 teaspoon baking powder
- 1/3 cup coconut flour

Directions:

1. Combine the baking powder, coconut flour, and garlic powder in a wide dish.

2. Add half the melted butter, some cheddar cheese, egg, and the scallions and mix well. Pour the mixture into a rectangular 6-inch baking tray. Put it in the basket of your air fryer.

3. Set the temperature and adjust the clock to about 320 ° F for around a 12-minute timer.

4. Take out from the pan to enable it to cool thoroughly. Slice into four parts and add leftover melted butter on top of each piece.

6. Dinner Rolls

Preparation time: 10 minutes

Cooking time: 12 minutes

Servings: 6 people

Ingredients:

- 1 large egg
- 1/2 teaspoon baking powder
- 1/4 cup ground flaxseed
- 1 cup blanched finely ground almond flour
- 1-ounce full-fat cream cheese
- 1 cup shredded mozzarella cheese

Directions:

1. In a big oven-safe dish, put the cream cheese, mozzarella, and almond flour. Microwave for about 1 minute. Blend until smooth.

2. When thoroughly mixed and soft, add baking powder, flaxseed, and egg. Suppose the dough is too hard, microwave for an extra 15 seconds.

3. Split your dough into six portions and shape it into small balls. Put the balls into the bucket of your air fryer.

4. Set the temperature and adjust the clock to about 320 ° F for around a 12-minute timer.

5. Let the rolls cool fully before serving.

7. Cilantro Lime Roasted Cauliflower

Preparation time: 10 minutes

Cooking time: 7 minutes

Servings: 4 people

Ingredients:

-   2 tablespoons chopped cilantro
-   1 medium lime
-   1/2 teaspoon garlic powder
-   2 teaspoons chili powder
-   2 tablespoons coconut oil, melted
-   2 cups chopped cauliflower florets

Directions:

1. Toss your cauliflower with coconut oil in a big dish. Dust some garlic powder and chili powder. Put the prepared cauliflower in the bucket of your air fryer.

2. Set the temperature and adjust the clock to about 350°F for around 7 minutes.

3. At the sides, the cauliflower would be soft and starting to become golden. Put in the serving dish.

4. Slice the lime and squeeze the juice over your cauliflower. Garnish using cilantro.

8. Green Bean Casserole

Preparation time: 10 minutes

Cooking time: 15 minutes

Servings: 4 people

Ingredients:

- 1/2 ounce pork rinds, finely ground
- 1 pound fresh green beans, edges trimmed
- 1/4 teaspoon xanthan gum
- 1/2 cup chicken broth
- 1-ounce full-fat cream cheese
- 1/2 cup heavy whipping cream
- 1/2 cup chopped white mushrooms
- 1/4 cup diced yellow onion
- 4 tablespoons unsalted butter

Directions:

1. Melt some butter in a medium-sized skillet over medium flame. Sauté the mushrooms and onion for around 3-5 minutes before they become tender and fragrant.

2. Transfer the cream cheese, heavy whipped cream, and broth. Mix until thick. Bring it to a boil and decrease the flame to let it simmer. Sprinkle your xanthan into the pan and turn off the flame.

3. Cut the green beans into 2-inch pieces and put them in a circular 4-cup baking tray. Pour the combination of sauce over them and swirl until they are covered. Cover the dish with the rinds of ground pork. Place it in the bucket of your air fryer.

4. Set the temperature and adjust the clock to about 320°F for around 15 minutes.

5. When completely baked, the top will be golden brown, and green beans would be fork tender. Serve it hot.

9. Buffalo Cauliflower

Preparation time: 5 minutes

Cooking time: 5 minutes

Servings: 4 people

Ingredients:

- 1/4 cup buffalo sauce
- 1/2 (1-ounce) dry ranch seasoning packet
- 2 tablespoons salted butter, melted
- 4 cups cauliflower florets

Directions:

1. Toss the cauliflower with the butter and dry the ranch in a wide pot. Place it in the bucket of your air fryer.

2. Set the temperature and adjust the clock to about 400°F for around 5 minutes.

3. During frying, rotate the basket at least two to three times. Take out the cauliflower from the fryer basket when soft, and then toss in the buffalo sauce. Serve it hot.

10. Kale Chips

Preparation time: 5 minutes

Cooking time: 5 minutes

Servings: 4 people

Ingredients:

- 1/2 teaspoon salt
- 2 teaspoons avocado oil
- 4 cups stemmed kale

Directions:

1. Toss the kale in some avocado oil in a wide bowl and dust it with some salt. Put it in the bucket of your air fryer.
2. Set the temperature and adjust the clock to about 400°F for around 5 minutes.
3. Kale, when cooked completely, would be crisp. Instantly serve.

11. Roasted Garlic

Preparation time: 5 minutes

Cooking time: 20 minutes

Servings: 12 people

Ingredients:

- 2 teaspoons avocado oil
- 1 medium head garlic

Directions:

1. Remove the garlic from any remaining excess peel. However, keep the cloves protected. Slice 1/4 of the garlic head off, showing the tops of the cloves.
2. Add your avocado oil to it. In a small layer of aluminum foil, put the garlic head, tightly enclosing it. Put it in the bucket of your air fryer.
3. Set the temperature and adjust the clock to about 400 °F for around 20 minutes. Monitor it after about 15 minutes if the garlic head is a little shorter.
4. Garlic should be nicely browned when finished and very tender.

5. Cloves can pop out to eat and be scattered or sliced quickly. Up to 2 - 5 in an airtight jar store in the fridge. You can even freeze individual cloves on a baking tray, and then put them together in a fridge-safe storage bag when frozen completely.

12. Zucchini Parmesan Chips

Preparation time: 10 minutes

Cooking time: 10 minutes

Servings: 4 people

Ingredients:

- 1/2 cup grated Parmesan cheese
- 1 large egg
- 1-ounce pork rinds
- 2 medium zucchini

Directions:

1. "Cut zucchini into thick slices of about 1/4 ". To extract excess water, put on a dry kitchen towel or two paper towels for around 30 minutes.
2. Put pork rinds and process until finely ground in the food processor. Dump into a medium-sized bowl and blend with parmesan.
3. In a shallow bowl, beat your egg.
4. Add the egg into pork rind mixture; soak zucchini pieces in it, covering as thoroughly as possible. Put each piece gently in a thin layer in the air fryer bucket, working as required in groups or individually.
5. Set the temperature and adjust the clock to about 320 degrees F for around 10 minutes.
6. Midway through the cooking process, turn your chips. Serve hot.

13. Crispy Brussels sprouts

Preparation time: 5 minutes

Cooking time: 10 minutes

Servings: 4 people

Ingredients:

- 1 tablespoon unsalted butter, melted
- 1 tablespoon coconut oil
- 1 pound Brussels sprouts

Directions:

1. Please remove all of the loose leaves from the Brussels sprouts and break them in half.

2. Sprinkle the sprouts with some coconut oil and placed them in the bowl of your air fryer.

3. Set the temperature and adjust the clock to about 400 ° F and for around10 minutes. Based on how they tend to cook, you might want to softly mix midway through the cooking period.

4. They should be soft with deeper caramelized spots when fully baked. Take out from the bucket of fryers and drizzle some melted butter. Serve instantly.

14. Cheesy Cauliflower Tots

Preparation time: 15 minutes

Cooking time: 12 minutes

Servings: 4 people

Ingredients:

- 1/8 teaspoon onion powder
- 1/4 teaspoon dried parsley
- 1/4 teaspoon garlic powder
- 1 large egg
- 1/2 cup grated Parmesan cheese
- 1 cup shredded mozzarella cheese
- 1 large head cauliflower

Directions:

1. Fill a big pot with 2 cups of water on the cooktop and put a steamer in the pot. Bring the water to a boil. Chop the cauliflower into florets and put it on a steamer bowl. Close the pot with a lid.

2. Enable cauliflower to steam for around 7 minutes before they are tender fork. Take out your cauliflower from the steamer basket and put it in a cheesecloth or dry kitchen towel, and leave it to cool down. Squeeze over the sink and extract as much extra moisture as necessary. If not all the moisture is extracted, the mixture would be too fragile to shape into tots. Crush to a smooth consistency using a fork.

3. Add in some parmesan, mozzarella, parsley, garlic powder, egg, and onion powder and place the cauliflower in a big mixing dish. Stir when thoroughly mixed. The paste should be sticky but hard to shape.

4. Roll into tot form by taking 2 teaspoons of the mix. Repeat for the remaining mixture. Put in the bucket of your air fryer.

5. Set the temperature and Adjust the clock to about 320 ° F for around 12-minute.

6. Switch tots midway through the cooking period. When fully baked, cauliflower tots should be crispy. Serve hot.

15. Sausage-Stuffed Mushroom Caps

Preparation time: 10 minutes

Cooking time: 8 minutes

Servings: 2 people

Ingredients:

- 1 teaspoon minced fresh garlic
- 1/4 cup grated Parmesan cheese
- 2 tablespoons blanched finely ground almond flour
- 1/4 cup chopped onion
- 1/2 pound Italian sausage
- 6 large Portobello mushroom caps

Directions:

1. Using a spoon, voiding scrapings, to hollow out each mushroom shell.

2. Brown the sausage for approximately 10 minutes or until thoroughly baked, and no red exists in a small-sized skillet over medium flame. Drain and then add some reserved mushroom scrapings, parmesan, almond flour, onion, and garlic. Fold ingredients softly together and proceed to cook for an extra minute, and then remove from flame.

3. Pour the mixture uniformly into mushroom caps and put the caps in a circular 6-inch pot. Put the pan in the bucket of your air fryer.

4. Set the temperature and adjust the clock to about 375 °F for around 8 minutes.

5. The tops would be browned and fizzing when it is cooked completely. Serve it hot.

16. Garlic Herb Butter Roasted Radishes

Preparation time: 10 minutes

Cooking time: 10 minutes

Servings: 4 people

Ingredients:

- black pepper
- 1/4 teaspoon ground
- 1/4 teaspoon dried oregano
- 1/2 teaspoon dried parsley
- 1/2 teaspoon garlic powder
- 2 tablespoons unsalted butter, melted
- 1 pound radishes

Directions:

1. Remove the radish roots and split them into quarters.
2. Put seasonings and butter in a shallow dish. In the herb butter, turn the radishes and put them in your air-fryer basket.
3. Set the temperature and adjust the clock to about 350°F for around 10 minutes.
4. Simply throw the radishes in the air fryer basket midway through the cooking time. Keep cooking until the edges start to turn dark brown.
5. Serve it hot.

17. Loaded Roasted Broccoli

Preparation time: 10 minutes

Cooking time: 10 minutes

Servings: 3 people

Ingredients:

- 1 scallion, sliced on the bias
- 4 slices sugar-free bacon, cooked and crumbled

- 1/4 cup full-fat sour cream
- 1/2 cup shredded sharp Cheddar cheese
- 1 tablespoon coconut oil
- 3 cups fresh broccoli florets

Directions:

1. In the air fryer basket, put the broccoli and drizzle with some coconut oil.

2. Set the temperature and adjust the clock to about 350°F for around 10 minutes.

3. During frying, turn the basket at least two to three times to prevent burning.

4. Remove from the fryer as the broccoli continues to crisp at the ends. Garnish with some scallion slices and finish with sour cream, melted cheese, and crumbled bacon.

CHAPTER 4: Air Fryer Snack and Appetizer Recipes

1. Bacon-Wrapped Brie

Preparation time: 5 minutes

Cooking time: 10 minutes

Servings: 8 people

Ingredients:

- 1 (8-ounce) round Brie
- 4 slices sugar-free bacon

Directions:

1. To shape an X, position two bacon strips. Put the third bacon strip over the middle of the X sideways. Position vertically over the X a fourth slice of bacon. On top of your X, it could appear like an addition sign (+). Position the Brie in the middle of the bacon.

2. Tie the bacon from around Brie, using several toothpicks to hold it. To suit your air-fryer container, take a piece of parchment paper and put your bacon-wrapped Brie on it. Put it in the container of your air fryer.

3. Set the temperature and set the clock to about 400°F for around 10 minutes.

4. When there are only 3 minutes left on the clock, rotate Brie gently.

5. The bacon will be crispy when grilled, and the cheese will be smooth and melted. Cut into eight pieces to serve.

2. Crust less Meat Pizza

Preparation time: 5 minutes

Cooking time: 5 minutes

Servings: 1 people

Ingredients:

- 2 tablespoons low-carb, sugar-free pizza sauce for dipping
- 1 tablespoon grated or cutup Parmesan cheese
- 2 slices sugar-free bacon, cooked and crumbled
- 1/4 cup cooked ground sausage
- 7 slices pepperoni
- 1/2 cup shredded mozzarella cheese

Directions:

1. Line the bottom of a mozzarella 6' cake tray. Put on top of your cheese some sausage, pepperoni, and bacon and cover with parmesan. Put the pan in the bowl of your air fryer.

2. Set the temperature and set the clock to about 400°F for around 5 minutes.

3. Remove from the flame once the cheese is fizzing and lightly golden. Serve hot with some pizza sauce as dipping.

3. Garlic Cheese Bread

Preparation time: 10 minutes

Cooking time: 10 minutes

Servings: 2 people

Ingredients:

- 1/2 teaspoon garlic powder
- 1 large egg1 large egg
- 1/4 cup grated Parmesan cheese
- 1 cup shredded mozzarella cheese1 cup shredded mozzarella cheese

Directions:

1. In a big bowl, combine all the ingredients. To fit your air fryer bowl cut a piece of parchment paper. Add the blend onto the parchment paper to form a circle and put it in the air fryer basket.
2. Set the temperature and adjust the timer to about 350°F for around 10 minutes.
3. Serve it hot.

4. Mozzarella Pizza Crust

Preparation time: 5 minutes

Cooking time: 10 minutes

Servings: 1 people

Ingredients:

- 1 large egg white
- 1 tablespoon full-fat cream cheese
- 2 tablespoons blanched finely ground almond flour
- 1/2 cup shredded whole-milk mozzarella cheese

Directions:

1. In a small oven-safe bowl, put almond flour, mozzarella, and cream cheese. Microwave for about 30 seconds. Mix until the mixture becomes a softball. Add egg white and mix until fluffy, circular dough forms.
2. Shape into 6 round crust pizza.

3. To suit your air fryer container, take a piece of parchment paper and put each crust on the parchment paper. Place it in the basket of your air fryer.

4. Set the temperature and adjust the clock to about 350°F for around 10 minutes.

5. Switch sides after 5 minutes and put any preferred toppings on your crust at this stage. Keep cooking until lightly golden. Immediately serve.

5. Spicy Spinach Artichoke Dip

Preparation time: 10 minutes

Cooking time: 10 minutes

Servings: 6 people

Ingredients:

- 1 cup shredded pepper jack cheese
- 1/4 cup grated Parmesan cheese
- 1/2 teaspoon garlic powder
- 1/4 cup full-fat sour cream
- 1/4 cup full-fat mayonnaise
- 8 ounces full-fat cream cheese, softened
- 1/4 cup chopped pickled jalapeños
- 1 (14-ounce) can artichoke hearts, drained and chopped
- 10 ounces frozen spinach, drained and thawed

Directions:

1. In a 4-cup baking dish, combine all your ingredients. Put it in the basket of your air fryer.

2. Set the temperature and adjust the timer for around 10 minutes to about 320 °F.

3. When dark brown and sizzling, remove from flame. Serve it hot.

6. Mini Sweet Pepper Poppers

Preparation time: 18 minutes

Cooking time: 8 minutes

Servings: 4 people

Ingredients:

- 1/4 cup shredded pepper jack cheese
- 4 slices sugar-free bacon, cooked and crumbled
- 4 ounces full-fat cream cheese, softened
- 8 mini sweet peppers

Directions:

1. Cut the tops of your peppers and lengthwise cut each one in the quarter. Remove the seeds and cut the membranes with a tiny knife.
2. Toss the bacon, cream cheese, and pepper jack in a tiny bowl.
3. Put each sweet pepper with 3 tsp. of the mixture and push down smoothly. Put it in the air fryer basket.
4. Set the temperature and adjust the clock to about 400°F for around 8 minutes.

5. Serve it hot.

7. Bacon-Wrapped Onion Rings

Preparation time: 5 minutes

Cooking time: 10 minutes

Servings: 4 people

Ingredients:

- 8 slices sugar-free bacon
- 1 tablespoon sriracha
- 1 large onion, peeled

Directions:

1. Cut your onion into large 1/4-inch pieces. Sprinkle the sriracha on the pieces of your onion. Take two pieces of onion and cover the circles with bacon. Redo with the rest of the onion and bacon. Put in the container of your air fryer.

2. Set the temperature and adjust the clock to about 350°F for around 10 minutes.

3. To rotate the onion rings midway through the frying period, use tongs. The bacon would be crispy once completely fried. Serve hot.

8. Mozzarella Sticks

Preparation time: 60 minutes

Cooking time: 10 minutes

Servings: 4 people

Ingredients:

- 2 big eggs
- 1 teaspoon dried parsley
- 1/2 ounce pork rinds, finely ground
- 1/2 cup of grated Parmesan or any other kind of cheese
- 6 (1-ounce) mozzarella string cheese sticks

Directions:

1. Put mozzarella sticks on a chopping board and slice in half. Freeze for about 45 minutes or till solid. Remove your frozen sticks after an hour if freezing overnight, then put them in a sealed zip-top plastic bag and put them back for potential usage in the freezer.

2. Mix the ground pork rinds, parmesan, and parsley in a wide dish.

3. Whisk the eggs together in a medium dish separately.

4. Soak a stick of frozen mozzarella into whisked eggs and then cover in Parmesan mixture. Repeat for the leftover sticks. Put the sticks of mozzarella in the basket of your air fryer.

5. Set the temperature to about 400 degrees F and adjust the clock for around 10 minutes or till it turns golden.

6. Serve it hot.

9. Pork Rind Tortillas

Preparation time: 10 minutes

Cooking time: 5 minutes

Servings: 4 people

Ingredients:

- 1 large egg
- 2 tablespoons full-fat cream cheese
- 3/4 cup shredded mozzarella cheese
- 1-ounce pork rinds

Directions:

1. Put pork rinds and pulses into the food processor pulse till finely ground.

2. Put mozzarella in a big oven-safe bowl. Cut the cream cheese into tiny bits and transfer them to the bowl. Microwave for about 30 seconds or so; all cheeses are molten and can be combined into a ball quickly. To the cheese mixture, add some ground pork rinds and eggs.

3. Keep mixing until the combination forms a ball. If it cools too fast and the cheese hardens, microwave for another 10 seconds.

4. Divide the dough into four tiny balls. Put each dough ball among 2 pieces of parchment paper and roll into a 1/4" flat layer.

5. Put the tortilla chips in a thin layer in your air fryer basket, operating in groups if required.

6. Set the temperature and adjust the clock to about 400°F for around 5 minutes.

7. Tortillas, when thoroughly baked, would be crispy and solid.

8. Instantly serve.

10. Bacon Cheeseburger Dip

Preparation time: 20 minutes

Cooking time: 10 minutes

Servings: 6 people

Ingredients:

- 2 large pickle spears, chopped
- 6 slices sugar-free bacon, cooked and crumbled
- 1/2 pound cooked 80/20 ground beef
- 11/4 cups shredded medium Cheddar cheese, divided
- 1 tablespoon Worcestershire sauce
- 1 teaspoon garlic powder
- 1/4 cup chopped onion
- 1/4 cup full-fat sour cream
- 1/4 cup full-fat mayonnaise
- 8 ounces full-fat cream cheese

Directions:

1. Put the cream cheese in a big, oven-safe dish and microwave for about 45 seconds. Add the Worcestershire sauce, sour cream, mayonnaise, garlic powder, onion, and

1 cup of Cheddar and mix well. Add fried ground beef and your bacon to it. Sprinkle the leftover Cheddar on top of the mixture.

2. Put in a 6-inch bowl and dump into the basket of your air fryer.

3. Set the temperature and adjust the clock to about 400°F for around 10 minutes.

4. When the surface is golden brown and bubbling, dipping is cooked. Scatter pickles over the dish. Serve hot.

11. Pizza Rolls

Preparation time: 18 minutes

Cooking time: 10 minutes

Servings: 8 people

Ingredients:

- 2 tablespoons grated Parmesan cheese
- 1/2 teaspoon dried parsley
- 1/4 teaspoon garlic powder
- 2 tablespoons unsalted butter, melted

- 8 (1-ounce) mozzarella string cheese sticks, cut into 3 pieces each
- 72 slices pepperoni
- 2 large eggs
- 1/2 cup almond flour
- 2 cups shredded mozzarella cheese

Directions:

1. Put almond flour and mozzarella in a big oven-safe bowl. Microwave for a minute. Withdraw the bowl and blend until a ball of dough forms. If required, microwave for an extra 30 seconds.

2. Crack the eggs into your bowl and blend until the ball becomes soft dough. Wet your hands with some water and gently knead your dough.

3. Rip off two wide pieces of parchment paper and brush with nonstick cooking spray on each side. Put your dough ball between the 2 pieces, facing dough with coated sides. To roll dough to a thickness of 1/4', use a rolling pin.

4. To cut into 24 rectangles, use a cutter. Put three pepperoni pieces and 1 strip of stringed cheese on each one of your rectangle.

5. Fold the rectangle in two, lining the filling with cheese and pepperoni. Ends closed by squeeze or roll. To suit your air-fryer bowl, take a piece of parchment paper and put it in the basket. On the parchment paper, place the rolls.

6. Set the temperature and adjust the clock to about 350°F for around 10 minutes.

7. Open your fryer after 5 minutes and rotate the rolls of pizza. Resume the fryer and proceed to cook until the rolls of pizza are golden brown.

8. Put the garlic powder, butter, and parsley in a tiny bowl. Brush the mix over the rolls of fried pizza and scatter the pizza with parmesan. Serve it hot.

12. Bacon Jalapeño Cheese Bread

Preparation time: 10 minutes

Cooking time: 18 minutes

Servings: 4 people

Ingredients:

- 4 slices sugar-free bacon, cooked and chopped
- 2 large eggs
- 1/4 cup chopped pickled jalapeños
- 1/4 cup of grated Parmesan cheese
- 2 cups shredded mozzarella cheese

Directions:

1. In a wide bowl, combine all your ingredients. Cut a slice of parchment to match the basket of your air fryer.

2. With a touch of water, dampen both of your hands and spread the mix out into a disk. Depending on the fryer's scale, you would need to split this into 2 small cheese bread.

3. Put the parchment paper and your cheese bread into the basket of the air fryer.

4. Set the temperature and adjust the clock to about 320°F for around 15 minutes.

5. Turn the bread gently once you have 5 minutes remaining.

6. The top would be golden brown when completely baked. Serve it hot.

13. Spicy Buffalo Chicken Dip

Preparation time: 10 minutes

Cooking time: 10 minutes

Servings: 4 people

Ingredients:

- 2 scallions, sliced on the bias
- 11/2 cups shredded medium Cheddar cheese, divided
- 1/3 cup chopped pickled jalapeños
- 1/3 cup full-fat ranch dressing
- 1/2 cup buffalo sauce

- 8 ounces full-fat cream cheese, softened
- 1 cup cooked, diced chicken breast

Directions:

1. Put the chicken in a spacious bowl. Add some ranch dressing, cream cheese, and buffalo sauce. Mix until the sauces are fully blended and completely soft. Fold the jalapeños along with 1 cup of Cheddar in it.

2. Transfer the mixture into a circular 4-cup baking dish and put the leftover Cheddar on top. Put the dish in your air-fryer basket.

3. Set the temperature and adjust the clock to about 350°F for around 10 minutes.

4. When cooked, it'll be brown at the top, and the dip will bubble. Serve it hot with some cut-up scallions on top.

14. Garlic Parmesan Chicken Wings

Preparation time: 4 minutes

Cooking time: 25 minutes

Servings: 4 people

Ingredients:

- 1/4 teaspoon dried parsley
- 1/3 cup grated Parmesan cheese
- 4 tablespoons unsalted butter, melted
- 1 tablespoon baking powder
- 1/2 teaspoon garlic powder
- 1 teaspoon pink Himalayan salt
- 2 pounds raw chicken wings

Directions:

1. Put the chicken wings, 1/2 teaspoon of garlic powder, salt, and baking powder in a wide bowl, then toss. Put the wings in the basket of your air fryer.

2. Set the temperature and adjust the clock to about 400°F for around 25 minutes.

3. During the cooking period, rotate the bowl two to three times to ensure even cooking.

4. Mix the parmesan, butter, and parsley in a shallow dish.

5. Please take out your wings from the fryer and put them in a big, clean dish. Over your wings, pour the butter mixture and toss until covered completely. Serve it hot.

15. Bacon-Wrapped Jalapeño Poppers

Preparation time: 16 minutes

Cooking time: 12 minutes

Servings: 5 people

Ingredients:

- 12 slices sugar-free bacon
- 1/4 teaspoon garlic powder
- 1/3 cup shredded medium Cheddar cheese
- 3 ounces full-fat cream cheese
- 6 jalapeños (about 4" long each)

Directions:

1. Slice off the tops of the jalapeños and cut lengthwise down the middle into two sections. Using a knife to gently detach the white membrane and seeds from the peppers.

2. Put the Cheddar, cream cheese, and garlic powder in a big, oven-proof dish. Stir in the microwave for about 30 seconds. Spoon the blend of cheese into your hollow jalapeño.

3. Place a bacon slice over each half of the jalapeño, totally covering the pepper. Place it in the basket of an air fryer.

4. Set the temperature and adjust the clock to about 400°F for around 12 minutes.

5. Flip the peppers halfway into the cooking period. Serve it hot.

16. Prosciutto-Wrapped Parmesan Asparagus

Preparation time: 10 minutes

Cooking time: 10 minutes

Servings: 4 people

Ingredients:

- 2 tablespoons salted butter, melted

- 1/3 cup grated Parmesan cheese

- 1/8 teaspoon red pepper flakes

- 2 teaspoons lemon juice

- 1 tablespoon coconut oil, melted

- 12 (0.5-ounce) slices prosciutto

- 1 pound asparagus

Directions:

1. Put an asparagus spear on top of a slice of prosciutto on a clean cutting board.

2. Drizzle with coconut oil and lemon juice. Sprinkle the asparagus with parmesan and red pepper flakes. Roll prosciutto across a spear of asparagus. Put it in the basket of your air fryer.

3. Set the temperature and adjust the clock to about 375 °F for around 10 minutes or so.

4. Dribble the asparagus roll with some butter before serving.

CHAPTER 5: Desserts

1. Mini Cheesecake

Preparation time: 10 minutes

Cooking time: 15-18 minutes

Servings: 2 people

Ingredients:

- 1/8 cup powdered erythritol
- 1/2 teaspoon vanilla extract
- 1 large egg
- 4 ounces full-fat cream cheese, softened
- 2 tablespoons granular erythritol
- 2 tablespoons salted butter
- 1/2 cup walnuts

Directions:

1. In a food mixer, put the butter, walnuts, and granular erythritol. Pulse until the items bind together to shape the dough.
2. Push the dough into a 4-inch spring form pan and put the pan in the bucket of your air fryer.
3. Set the temperature and adjust the clock to about 400°F for around 5 minutes.
4. Pick the crust when the timer dings, and let it cool.
5. Mix your cream cheese with the vanilla extract, egg, and powdered erythritol in a medium-sized bowl until creamy.

2. Pecan Brownies

Preparation time: 10 minutes

Cooking time: 20 minutes

Servings: 6 people

Ingredients:

- 1/4 cup low-carb, sugar-free chocolate chips
- 1/4 cup chopped pecans
- 1 large egg
- 1/4 cup unsalted butter, softened
- 1/2 teaspoon baking powder
- 2 tablespoons unsweetened cocoa powder
- 1/2 cup powdered erythritol
- 1/2 cup blanched finely ground almond flour

Directions:

1. Mix the almond flour, chocolate powder, erythritol, and baking powder in a big bowl. Stir in the egg and butter.
2. "Fold in the chocolate chips and pecans. Pour the mixture into a 6" circular baking tray. Place the pan in the bucket of your air fryer.
3. Set the temperature and adjust the clock to about 300°F for around 20 minutes.
4. A toothpick placed in the middle will fall out clean once completely fried. Please enable it to cool off entirely and firm up for about 20 minutes.

3. Cinnamon Sugar Pork Rinds

Preparation time: 5 minutes

Cooking time: 5 minutes

Servings: 2 people

Ingredients:

- 1/4 cup powdered erythritol
- 1/2 teaspoon ground cinnamon
- 2 tablespoons unsalted butter, melted
- 2 ounces pork rinds

Directions:

1. Toss the pork rinds and butter into a wide pan. Sprinkle some erythritol and cinnamon, and toss to cover uniformly.

2. Put the pork rinds into the bucket of your air fryer.

3. Set the temperature and adjust the clock to about 400°F for around 5 minutes.

4. Instantly serve.

4. Almond Butter Cookie Balls

Preparation time: 5 minutes

Cooking time: 10 minutes

Servings: 10 people

Ingredients:

- 1/2 teaspoon ground cinnamon
- 1/4 cup low-carb, sugar-free chocolate chips
- 1/4 cup shredded unsweetened coconut
- 1/4 cup powdered erythritol
- 1/4 cup low-carb protein powder
- 1 teaspoon vanilla extract
- 1 large egg
- 1 cup almond butter

Directions:

1. Mix the almond butter with the egg in a big pot. Add protein powder, vanilla, and erythritol to it.

2. Fold in the coconut, chocolate chips, and cinnamon. Roll into 1" spheres. Put the balls in a 6' circular baking tray and place them in the bucket of your air fryer.

3. Set the temperature and adjust the clock to about 10 minutes to around 320 °F.

4. Please enable it to cool fully. Up to 4 days in an airtight jar placed in the fridge.

Conclusion

These times, air frying is one of the most common cooking techniques and air fryers have become one of the chef's most impressive devices. In no time, air fryers can help you prepare nutritious and tasty meals! To prepare unique dishes for you and your family members, you do not need to be a master in the kitchen!

Everything you have to do is buy an air fryer and this wonderful cookbook for air fryers! Soon, you can make the greatest dishes ever and inspire those around you.

Cooked meals at home with you! Believe us! Get your hands on an air fryer and this handy set of recipes for air fryers and begin your new cooking experience! Have fun!

The Complete Air Fryer Cookbook with Pictures

70+ Perfectly Portioned Air Fryer Recipes for Busy People on a Budget

By

Chef Ludovico L'Italiano

Table of Contents

INTRODUCTION: 93

Chapter # 1: 94

An Overview & Benefits of an Air Fryer 94

  Introduction: 94

  The Air Fryer Usability: 94

  The Air Fryer Works as: 94

  What necessary to Search for in an Air Fryer? 95

  Most Common - Five Guidelines for an Air Fryer usage: 95

    1. Shake the food. 95

    2. Do not overload. 95

    3. Slightly spray to food. 95

    4. Retain an Air fry dry. 95

    5. Other Most Dominant cooking techniques. 96

  An Air Fryer Helps to reduce fat content 96

  Air Fryer provides an Aid in Weight Loss 96

  Air Fried food may reduce the potentially harmful chemicals 96

Chapter # 2: 98

70 Perfectly Portioned Air Fryer Recipes for Busy People in Minimum Budget 98

  1. Air fried corn, zucchini and haloumi fritters 98

  2. Air fryer fried rice 99

  3. Air fried banana muffins 100

  4. Air fried Nutella brownies 101

  5. Air fried celebration bites 101

  6. Air fried nuts and bolts 102

  7. Air fried coconut shrimps 103

  8. Air fried Roasted Sweet and Spicy Carrots 104

  9. Air fried Chicken Thighs 105

  10. Air fried French Fries 106

  11. Air fried Mini Breakfast Burritos 107

  12. Air fried Vegan Tator Tots 108

13. Air fried Roasted Cauliflower 109

14. Air fried Cinnamon-Sugar Doughnuts 110

15. Air Fried Broiled Grapefruit 111

16. Air Fried Brown Sugar and Pecan Roasted Apples 112

17. Air Fried Breaded Sea Scallops 113

18. Air Fried Crumbed Fish...114

19. Air Fried Cauliflower and Chickpea Tacos 115

20. Air Fried Roasted Salsa 116

21. Air Fried Flour Tortilla Bowls 117

22. Air Fried Cheese and Mini Bean Tacos 118

23. Air Fried Lemon Pepper Shrimp 119

24. Air Fried Shrimp a la Bang Bang..120

25. Air Fried Spicy Bay Scallops 121

26. Air Fried Breakfast Fritatta...122

27. Air Fried Roasted Okra..123

28. Air Fried Rib-Eye Steak 124

29. Air Fried Potato Chips 125

30. Air Fried Tofu 126

31. Air Fried Acorn Squash Slices 127

32. Air Fried Red Potatoes 128

33. Air Fried Butter Cake 129

34. Air Fried Jelly and Peanut Butter S'mores 130

35. Air Fried Sun-Dried Tomatoes 131

36. Air Fried Sweet Potatoes Tots 132

37. Air Fried Banana Bread 133

38. Air Fried Avocado Fries...134

39. "Strawberry Pop Tarts" in an Air Fryer 135

40. Lighten up Empanadas in an Air Fryer 136

41. Air Fried Calzones..138

42. Air Fried Mexican Style Corns 139

43. Air Fryer Crunchy & Crispy Chocolate Bites 140

44. Doritos-Crumbled Chicken tenders in an Air fryer 141

46. Air Fryer Lemonade Scones 143

47. Air Fryer Baked Potatoes...144

48. Air Fryer Mozzarella Chips 145

49. Air Fryer Fetta Nuggets 146

50. Air Fryer Japanese Chicken Tender..147

51. Whole-Wheat Pizzas in an Air Fryer 148

52. Air Fryer Crispy Veggie Quesadillas...149

53. Air Fried Curry Chickpeas 150

54. Air Fried Beet Chips 151

55. Double-Glazed Air Fried Cinnamon Biscuits 152

56. Lemon Drizzle Cake in an Air Fryer..153

57. Air Fryer dukkah-Crumbed chicken 154

58. Air Fryer Vietnamese-style spring roll salad................................155

59. Air Fryer Pizza Pockets..157

60. Air Fryer Popcorn Fetta with Maple Hot Sauce 158

61. Air fryer Steak Fajitas...159

62. Air-Fryer Fajita-Stuffed Chicken 160

63. Nashvilla Hot Chicken in an Air Fryer 161

64. Southern-style Chicken...163

65. Chicken Parmesan in an Air Fryer...163

66. Lemon Chicken Thigh in an Air Fryer 164

67. Salmon with Maple-Dijon Glaze in air fryer 165

68. Air Fryer Roasted Beans 166

69. Air Fried Radishes 167

70. Air Fried Catfish Nuggets..168

CONCLUSION: 170

INTRODUCTION:

The aim of this cookbook is to provide the easiness for those who are professional or doing job somewhere. But with earning, it is also quite necessary to cook food easily & timely instead of ordering hygienic or costly junk food. As we know, after doing office work, no one can cook food with the great effort. For the ease of such people, there are a lot of latest advancements in kitchen accessories. The most popular kitchen appliances usually helps to make foods or dishes like chicken, mutton, beef, potato chips and many other items in less time and budget. There are a lot of things that should be considered when baking with an air fryer. One of the most important tips is to make sure you have all of your equipment ready for the bake. It is best to be prepared ahead of time and this includes having pans, utensils, baking bags, the air fryer itself, and the recipe book instead of using stove or oven. With the help of an air fryer, you can make various dishes for a single person as well as the entire family timely and effortlessly. As there is a famous proverb that "Nothing can be done on its own", it indicates that every task takes time for completion. Some tasks take more time and effort and some requires less time and effort for their completion. Therefore, with the huge range of advancements that come to us are just for our ease. By using appliances like an air fryer comes for the comfort of professional people who are busy in earning their livelihood. In this book, you can follow the latest, delicious, and quick, about 70 recipes that will save your time and provide you healthy food without any great effort.

Chapter # 1:
An Overview & Benefits of an Air Fryer

Introduction:

The most popular kitchen appliance that usually helps to make foods or dishes like chicken, mutton, beef, potato chips and many other items in less time and budget.

Today, everything is materialistic, every person is busy to earn great livelihood. Due to a huge burden of responsibilities, they have no time to cook food on stove after doing hard work. Because, traditionally cooking food on the stove takes more time and effort. Therefore, there are a vast variety of Kitchen appliances. The kitchen appliances are so much helpful in making or cooking food in few minutes and in less budget. You come to home from job, and got too much tired. So, you can cook delicious food in an Air Fryer efficiently and timely as compared to stove. You can really enjoy the food without great effort and getting so much tired.

The Air Fryer Usability:

Be prepared to explore all about frying foods that you learned. To crisp, golden brown excellence (yes, French-fried potatoes and potato chips!), air fryers will fry your favourite foods using minimum or no oil. You can not only make commonly fried foods such as chips and French fries of potatoes, however it is also ideal for proteins, vegetables such as drummettes and chicken wings, coquettes & feta triangles as well as appetizers. And cookies are perfectly cooked in an air fryer, such as brownies and blondies.

The Air Fryer Works as:

- Around 350-375°F (176-190°C) is the ideal temperature of an Air Fryer
- To cook the surface of the food, pour over a food oil at the temperature mentioned above. The oil can't penetrate because it forms a type of seal.
- Simultaneously, the humidity within the food turns into steam that helps to actually cook the food from the inside. It is cleared that the steam helps to maintain the oil out of the food.
- The oil flows into the food at a low temperature, rendering it greasy.
- It oxidizes the oil and, at high temperatures, food will dry out.

On the other hand, an air fryer is similar to a convection oven, but in a diverse outfit, food preparation done at very high temperatures whereas, inside it, dry air circulates around the food at the same time, while making it crisp without putting additional fat, it makes it possible for cooking food faster.

What necessary to Search for in an Air Fryer?

As we know, several different sizes and models of air fryers are available now. If you're cooking for a gathering, try the extra-large air fryer, that can prepare or fry a whole chicken, other steaks or six servings of French fries.

Suppose, you've a fixed counter space, try the Large Air Fryer that uses patented machinery to circulate hot air for sufficient, crispy results. The latest air fryer offers an extra compact size with identical capacity! and tar equipment, which ensures that food is cooking evenly (no further worries of build-ups). You will be able to try all the fried foods you enjoy, with no embarrassment.

To increase the functionality of an air fryer, much more, you can also purchase a wide range of different accessories, including a stand, roasting pan, muffin cups, and mesh baskets. Check out the ingredients of our air fryer we created, starting from buttermilk with black pepper seasoning to fry chicken or Sichuan garlic seasoning suitable for Chinese cuisine.

We will read about the deep fryer, with tips and our favourite recipes like burgers, chicken wings, and many more.

Most Common - Five Guidelines for an Air Fryer usage:

1. Shake the food.

Open the air fryer and shake the foods efficiently because the food is to "fry" in the machine's basket—Light dishes like Sweet French fries and Garlic chips will compress. Give Rotation to the food every 5-10 mins for better performance

2. Do not overload.

Leave enough space for the food so that the air circulates efficiently; so that's gives you crunchy effects. Our kitchen testing cooks trust that the snacks and small batches can fry in air fryer.

3. Slightly spray to food.

Gently spray on food by a cooking spray bottle and apply a touch of oil on food to make sure the food doesn't stick to the basket.

4. Retain an Air fry dry.

Beat food to dry before start cooking (even when marinated, e.g.) to prevent splashing & excessive smoke. Likewise, preparing high-fat foods such as chicken steaks or wings, be assured to remove the grease from the lower part of machine regularly.

5. Other Most Dominant cooking techniques.

The air fryer is not just for deep frying; It is also perfect for further safe methods of cooking like baking, grilling, roasting and many more. Our kitchen testing really loves using the unit for cooking salmon in air fryer!

An Air Fryer Helps to reduce fat content

Generally, food cooked in deep fryer contains higher fat level than preparing food in other cooking appliances. For Example; a fried chicken breast contains about 30% more fat just like a fat level in roasted chicken

Many Manufacturers claimed, an Air fryer can reduce fat from fried food items up-to 75%. So, an air fryer requires less amount of fat than a deep fryer. As, many dishes cooked in deep fryer consume 75% oil (equal to 3 cups) and an air fryer prepare food by applying the oil in just about 1 tablespoon (equal to 15ml).

One research tested the potato chips prepared in air fryer characteristics then observed: the air frying method produces a final product with slightly lower fat but same moisture content and color. So, there is a major impact on anyone's health, an excessive risk of illnesses such as inflammation, infection and heart disease has been linked to a greater fat intake from vegetable oils.

Air Fryer provides an Aid in Weight Loss

The dishes prepared deep fryer are not just having much fat but also more in calories that causes severe increase in weight. Another research of 33,542 Spanish grown-ups indicates that a greater usage of fried food linked with a higher occurrence of obesity. Dietetic fat has about twice like many calories per gram while other macro-nutrients such as carbohydrates, vitamins and proteins, averaging in at 9 calories throughout each and every gram of oil or fat.

By substituting to air fryer is an easy way to endorse in losing weight and to reduce calories and it will be done only by taking food prepared in air fryer.

Air Fried food may reduce the potentially harmful chemicals

Frying foods can produce potentially hazardous compounds such as acrylamide, in contrast to being higher in fat and calories. An acrylamide is a compound that is formed in carbohydrate- rich dishes or foods during highly-heated cooking methods such as frying. Acrylamide is known as a "probable carcinogen" which indicates as some research suggests that it could be associated with the development of cancer. Although the findings are conflicting, the link between dietary acrylamide and a greater risk of kidney, endometrial and ovarian cancers has been identified in some reports. Instead of cooking food in a deep fryer, air frying your food may aid the acrylamide content. Some researches indicates that air-frying method may cut the acrylamide by 90% by comparing deep frying method. All other extremely harmful chemicals produced by high-heat cooking are polycyclic aromatic hydrocarbons, heterocyclic amines and aldehydes and may be associated with a greater risk of cancer. That's why, the air fried food may help to reduce the chance of extremely dangerous chemicals or compounds and maintain your health.

Chapter # 2:

70 Perfectly Portioned Air Fryer Recipes for Busy People in Minimum Budget

1. Air fried corn, zucchini and haloumi fritters

Ingredients

- Coarsely grated block haloumi - 225g
- Coarsely grated Zucchini - 2 medium sized
- Frozen corn kernels - 150g (1 cup)
- Lightly whisked eggs - 2
- Self-raising flour - 100g
- Extra virgin olive oil - to drizzle
- Freshly chopped oregano leaves - 3 tablespoons
- Fresh oregano extra sprigs - to serve
- Yoghurt - to serve

Method

1. Use your palms to squeeze out the extra liquid from the zucchini and place them in a bowl. Add the corn and haloumi and stir for combining them. Then add the eggs, oregano and flour. Add seasoning and stir until fully mixed.
2. Set the temperature of an air fryer to 200 C. Put spoonsful of the mixture of zucchini on an air fryer. Cook until golden and crisp, for 8 minutes. Transfer to a dish that is clean. Again repeat this step by adding the remaining mixture in 2 more batches.

3. Take a serving plate and arrange soft fritters on it. Take yoghurt in a small serving bowl. Add seasoning of black pepper on the top of yoghurt. Drizzle with olive oil. At the end, serve this dish with extra oregano.

2. Air fryer fried rice

Ingredients

- Microwave long grain rice - 450g packet
- Chicken tenderloins - 300g
- Rindless bacons - 4 ranchers
- Light Soy sauce - 2 tablespoons
- Oyster sauce - 2 tablespoons
- Sesame oil - 1 tablespoon
- Fresh finely grated ginger - 3 tablespoons
- Frozen peas - 120g (3/4 cup)
- Lightly whisked eggs - 2
- Sliced green shallots - 2
- Thin sliced red chilli - 1
- Oyster sauce - to drizzle

Method
1. Set the 180°C temperature of an air fryer. Bacon and chicken is placed on the rack of an air fryer. Cook them until fully cooked for 8-10 minutes. Shift it to a clean plate and set this plate aside to cool. Then, slice and chop the bacon and chicken.
2. In the meantime, separate the rice grains in the packet by using your fingers. Heat the rice for 60 seconds in a microwave. Shift to a 20cm ovenproof, round high-sided pan or dish. Apply the sesame oil, soy sauce, ginger, oyster sauce and 10ml water and mix well.

3. Put a pan/dish in an air fryer. Cook the rice for 5 minutes till them soft. Then whisk the chicken, half of bacon and peas in the eggs. Completely cook the eggs in 3 minutes. Mix and season the top of half shallot with white pepper and salt.

4. Serve with the seasoning of chilli, remaining bacon and shallot and oyster sauce.

3. Air fried banana muffins

Ingredients
- Ripe bananas - 2
- Brown sugar - 60g (1/3 cup)
- Olive oil - 60ml (1/4 cup)
- Buttermilk - 60ml (1/4 cup)
- Self-raising flour - 150g (1 cup)
- Egg - 1
- Maple syrup - to brush or to serve

Method
1. Mash the bananas in a small bowl using a fork. Until needed, set aside.

2. In a medium cup, whisk the flour and sugar using a balloon whisk. In the middle, make a well. Add the buttermilk, oil and egg. Break up the egg with the help of a whisk. Stir by using wooden spoon until the mixture is mixed. Stir the banana through it.

3. Set the temperature of an air fryer at 180C. Splits half of the mixture into 9 cases of patties. Remove the rack from the air fryer and pass the cases to the rack carefully. Switch the rack back to the fryer. Bake the muffins completely by cooking them for 10 minutes. Move to the wire rack. Repeat this step on remaining mixture to produce 18 muffins.

4. Brush the muffin tops with maple syrup while they're still warm. Serve, if you like, with extra maple syrup.

4. Air fried Nutella brownies

Ingredients
- Plain flour - 150g (1 cup)
- Castor white sugar - 225g (1 cup)
- Lightly whisked eggs - 3
- Nutella - 300g (1 cup)
- Cocoa powder - to dust

Method
1. Apply butter in a 20cm circular cake pan. Cover the base by using baking paper.
2. Whisk the flour and sugar together in a bowl by using balloon whisk. In the middle, make a well. Add the Nutella and egg in the middle of bowl by making a well. Stir with a large metal spoon until mixed. Move this mixture to the previously prepared pan and smooth the surface of the mixture by using metal spoon.
3. Pre - heat an air fryer to 160C. Bake the brownie about 40 minutes or until a few crumbs stick out of a skewer inserted in the middle. Fully set aside to cool.
4. Garnish the top of the cake by dusting them with cocoa powder, and cut them into pieces. Brownies are ready to be served.

5. Air fried celebration bites

Ingredients
- Frozen shortcrust partially thawed pastry - 4 sheets
- Lightly whisked eggs - 1
- Unrapped Mars Celebration chocolates - 24
- Icing sugar - to dust
- Cinnamon sugar - to dust
- Whipped cream - to serve

Method

1. Slice each pastry sheet into 6 rectangles. Brush the egg gently. One chocolate is placed in the middle of each rectangular piece of pastry. Fold the pastry over to cover the chocolate completely. Trim the pastry, press and seal the sides. Place it on a tray containing baking paper. Brush the egg on each pastry and sprinkle cinnamon sugar liberally.

2. In the air-fryer basket, put a sheet of baking paper, making sure that the paper is 1 cm smaller than the basket to allow airflow. Put six pockets in the basket by taking care not to overlap. Cook for 8-9 minutes at 190°C until pastries are completely cooked with golden color. Shift to a dish. Free pockets are then used again.

3. Sprinkle Icing sugar on the top of tasty bites. Serve them with a whipped cream to intensify its flavor.

6. Air fried nuts and bolts

Ingredients

- Dried farfalle pasta - 2 cups
- Extra virgin olive oil - 60ml (1/4th cup)
- Brown sugar - 2 tablespoons
- Onion powder - 1 tablespoon
- Smoked paprika - 2 tablespoons
- Chili powder - 1/2 tablespoon
- Garlic powder - 1/2 tablespoon
- Pretzels - 1 cup
- Raw macadamias - 80g (1/2 cup)
- Raw cashews - 80g (1/2 cup)
- Kellog's Nutri-grain cereal - 1 cup
- Sea salt - 1 tablespoon

Method

1. Take a big saucepan of boiling salted water, cook the pasta until just ready and soft. Drain thoroughly. Shift pasta to a tray and pat with a paper towel to dry. Move the dried pasta to a wide pot.

2. Mix the sugar, oil, onion, paprika, chili and garlic powders together in a clean bowl. Add half of this mixture in the bowl containing pasta. Toss this bowl slightly for the proper coating of mixture over pasta.

3. Set the temperature at 200C of an Air Fryer. Put the pasta in air fryer's pot. After cooking for 5 minutes, shake the pot and cook for more 5-7 minutes, until they look golden and crispy. Shift to a wide bowl.

4. Take the pretzels in a bowl with the nuts and apply the remaining mixture of spices. Toss this bowl for the proper coating. Put in air fryer's pot and cook at 180C for 3-4 minutes. Shake this pot and cook for more 2-3 minutes until it's golden in color. First add pasta and then add the cereal. Sprinkle salt on it and toss to mix properly. Serve this dish after proper cooling.

7. Air fried coconut shrimps

Ingredients

- Plain flour - 1/2 cup
- Eggs - 2
- Bread crumbs - 1/2 cup
- Black pepper powder - 1.5 teaspoons
- Sweetless flaked coconut - 3/4 cup
- Uncooked, deveined and peeled shrimp - 12 ounces
- Salt - 1/2 teaspoon
- Honey - 1/4 cup
- Lime juice - 1/4 cup
- Finely sliced serrano chili - 1

- Chopped cilantro - 2 teaspoons
- Cooking spray

Method
1. Stir the pepper and flour in a clean bowl together. Whisk the eggs in another bowl and h panko and coconut in separate bowl.   Coat the shrimps with flour mixture by holding each shrimp by tail and shake off the extra flour.   Then coat the floured shrimp with egg and allow it to drip off excess. Give them the final coat of coconut mixture and press them to stick. Shift on a clean plate. Spray shrimp with cooking oil.
2. Set the temperature of the air-fryer to 200C. In an air fryer, cook half of the shrimp for 3 minutes. Turn the shrimp and cook further for more 3 minutes until color changes in golden. Use 1/4 teaspoon of salt for seasoning.   Repeat this step for the rest of shrimps.
3. In the meantime, prepare a dip by stirring lime juice, serrano chili and honey in a clean bowl.
4. Serve fried shrimps with sprinkled cilantro and dip.

8. Air fried Roasted Sweet and Spicy Carrots

Ingredients
- Cooking oil
- Melted butter - 1 tablespoon
- Grated orange zest - 1 teaspoon
- Carrots - 1/2 pound

- Hot honey - 1 tablespoon
- Cardamom powder - 1/2 teaspoon
- Fresh orange juice - 1 tablespoon
- Black pepper powder - to taste
- Salt - 1 pinch

Method
1. Set the temperature of an air to 200C. Lightly coat its pot with cooking oil.
2. Mix honey, cardamom and orange zest in a clean bowl. Take 1 tablespoon of this sauce in another bowl and place aside. Coat carrots completely by tossing them in remaining sauce. Shift carrots to an air fryer pot.
3. Air fry the carrots and toss them after every 6 minutes. Cook carrots for 15-20 minutes until they are fully cooked and roasted. Combine honey butter sauce with orange juice to make sauce. Coat carrots with this sauce. Season with black pepper and salt and serve this delicious dish.

9. Air fried Chicken Thighs

Ingredients
- Boneless chicken thighs - 4
- Extra virgin olive oil - 2 teaspoons
- Smoked paprika - 1 teaspoon
- Salt - 1/2 teaspoon
- Garlic powder - 3/4 teaspoon
- Black pepper powder - 1/2 teaspoon

Method

1. Set the temperature of an air fryer to 200C.
2. Dry chicken thighs by using tissue paper. Brush olive oil on the skin side of each chicken thigh. Shift the single layer of chicken thighs on a clean tray.
3. Make a mixture of salt, black pepper, paprika and garlic powder in a clean bowl. Use a half of this mixture for the seasoning of 4 chicken thighs on both sides evenly. Then shift single layer of chicken thighs in an air fryer pot by placing skin side up.
4. Preheat the air fryer and maintain its temperature to 75C. Fry chicken for 15-18 minutes until its water become dry and its color changes to brown. Serve immediately.

10. Air fried French Fries

Ingredients
- Peeled Potatoes - 1 pound
- Vegetable oil - 2 tablespoon
- Cayenne pepper - 1 pinch
- Salt - 1/2 teaspoon

Method

1. Lengthwise cut thick slices of potato of 3/8 inches.

2. Soak sliced potatoes for 5 minutes in water. Drain excess starch water from soaked potatoes after 5 minutes. Place these potatoes in boiling water pan for 8-10 minutes.

3. Remove water from the potatoes and dry them completely. Cool them for 10 minutes and shift in a clean bowl. Add some oil and fully coat the potatoes with cayenne by tossing.

4. Set the temperature of an air fryer to 190C. Place two layers of potatoes in air fryer pot and cook them for 10-15 minutes. Toss fries continuously and cook for more 10 minutes until their color changes to golden brown. Season fries with salt and serve this appetizing dish immediately.

11. Air fried Mini Breakfast Burritos

Ingredients

- Mexican style chorizo - 1/4 cup
- Sliced potatoes - 1/2 cup
- Chopped serrano pepper - 1
- 8-inch flour tortillas - 4
- Bacon grease - 1 tablespoon
- Chopped onion - 2 tablespoon
- Eggs - 2
- Cooking avacado oil - to spray
- Salt - to taste
- Black pepper powder - to taste

Method

1. Take chorizo in a large size pan and cook on medium flame for 8 minutes with continuous stirring until its color change into reddish brown. Shift chorizo in a clean plate and place separate.

2. Take bacon grease in same pan and melt it on medium flame. Place sliced potatoes and cook them for 10 minutes with constant stirring. Add serrano pepper and onion meanwhile. Cook for more 2-5 minutes until potatoes are fully cooked, onion and serrano pepper become soften. Then add chorizo and eggs and cook for more 5 minutes until potato mixture is fully incorporated. Use pepper and salt for seasoning.

3. In the meantime, heat tortillas in a large pan until they become soft and flexible. Put 1/3 cup of chorizo mixture at the center of each tortilla. Filling is covered by rolling the upper and lower side of tortilla and give shape of burrito. Spray cooking oil and place them in air fryer pot.

4. Fry these burritos at 200C for 5 minutes. Change the side'scontinuously and spray with cooking oil. Cook in air fryer for 3-4 minutes until color turns into light brown. Shift burritos in a clean dish and serve this delicious dish.

12. Air fried Vegan Tator Tots

Ingredients

- Frozen potato nuggets (Tator Tots) - 2 cups
- Buffalo wing sauce - 1/4 cup
- Vegan ranch salad - 1/4 cup

Method

1. Set the temperature of an air fryer to 175C.
2. Put frozen potato nuggets in air fryer pot and cook for 6-8 minutes with constant shake.
3. Shift potatoes to a large-sized bowl and add wing sauce. Combine evenly by tossing them and place them again in air fryer pot.
4. Cook more for 8-10 minutes without disturbance. Shift to a serving plate. Serve with ranch dressing and enjoy this dish.

13. Air fried Roasted Cauliflower

Ingredients
- Cauliflower florets - 4 cups
- Garlic - 3 cloves
- Smoked paprika - 1/2 teaspoon
- Peanut oil - 1 tablespoon
- Salt - 1/2 teaspoon

Method
1. Set the temperature of an air fryer to 200C.
2. Smash garlic cloves with a knife and mix with salt, oil and paprika. Coat cauliflower in this mixture.
3. Put coated cauliflower in air fryer pot and cook around 10-15 minutes with stirring after every 5 minutes. Cook according to desired color and crispiness and serve immediately.

14. Air fried Cinnamon-Sugar Doughnuts

Ingredients
- White sugar - 1/2 cup
- Brown sugar - 1/4 cup
- Melted butter - 1/4 cup
- Cinnamon powder - 1 teaspoon
- Ground nutmeg - 1/4 TEASPOON
- Packed chilled flaky biscuit dough - 1 (16.3 ounce)

Method

1. Put melted butter in a clean bowl. Add brown sugar, white sugar, nutmeg and cinnamon and mix.
2. Divide and cut biscuit dough into many single biscuits and give them the shape of doughnuts using a biscuit cutter. Shift doughnuts in an air fryer pot.
3. Air fry the doughnuts for 5-6 minutes at 175C until color turns into golden brown. Turn the side of doughnuts and cook for more 1-3 minutes.
4. Shift doughnuts from air fryer to a clean dish and dip them in melted butter. Then completely coat these doughnuts in sugar and cinnamon mixture and serve frequently.

15. Air Fried Broiled Grapefruit

Ingredients

- Chilled red grapefruit - 1
- Melted butter - 1 tablespoon
- Brown sugar - 2 tablespoon
- Ground cinnamon - 1/2 teaspoon
- Aluminium foil

Method

1. Set the temperature of an air fryer to 200C.
2. Cut grapefruit crosswise to half and also cut a thin slice from one end of grapefruit for sitting your fruit flat on a plate.
3. Mix brown sugar in melted butter in a small sized bowl. Coat the cut side of the grapefruit with this mixture. Dust the little brown sugar over it.
4. Take 2 five inch pieces of aluminium foil and put the half grapefruit on each piece. Fold the sides evenly to prevent juice leakage. Place them in air fryer pot.
5. Broil for 5-7 minutes until bubbling of sugar start in an air fryer. Before serving, sprinkle cinnamon on grapefruit.

16. Air Fried Brown Sugar and Pecan Roasted Apples

Ingredients

- Apples - 2 medium
- Chopped pecans - 2 tablespoons
- Plain flour - 1 teaspoon
- Melted butter - 1 tablespoon
- Brown sugar - 1 tablespoon
- Apple pie spice - 1/4 teaspoon

Method
1. Set the temperature of an air fryer to 180C.
2. Mix brown sugar, pecan, apple pie spice and flour in a clean bowl. Cut apples in wedges and put them in another bowl and coat them with melted butter by tossing. Place a single layer in an air fryer pot and add mixture of pecan on the top.
3. Cook apples for 12-15 minutes until they get soft.

17. Air Fried Breaded Sea Scallops

Ingredients
- Crushed butter crackers - 1/2 cup
- Seafood seasoning - 1/2 teaspoon
- Sea scallops - 1 pound
- Garlic powder - 1/2 teaspoon
- Melted butter - 2 tablespoons
- Cooking oil - for spray

Method

1. Set the temperature of an air fryer to 198C.

2. Combine garlic powder, seafood seasoning and cracker crumbs in a clean bowl. Take melted butter in another bowl.

3. Coat each scallop with melted butter. Then roll them in breading until completely enclose. Place them on a clean plate and repeat this step with rest of the scallops.

4. Slightly spray scallops with cooking oil and place them on the air fryer pot at equal distance. You may work in 2-3 batches.

5. Cook them for 2-3 minutes in preheated air fryer. Use a spatula to change the side of each scallop. Cook for more 2 minutes until they become opaque. Dish out in a clean plate and serve immediately.

18. Air Fried Crumbed Fish

Ingredients

- Flounder fillets - 4
- Dry bread crumbs - 1 cup
- Egg - 1
- Sliced lemon - 1
- Vegetable oil - 1/4 cup

Method

1. Set the temperature of an air fryer to 180C.
2. Combine oil and bread crumbs in a clean bowl and mix them well.
3. Coat each fish fillets with beaten egg, then evenly dip them in the crumbs mixture.
4. Place coated fillets in preheated air fryer and cook for 10-12 minutes until fish easily flakes by touching them with fork. Shift prepared fish in a clean plate and serve with lemon slices.

19. Air Fried Cauliflower and Chickpea Tacos

Ingredients

- Cauliflower - 1 small
- Chickpeas - 15 ounce
- Chili powder - 1 teaspoon
- Cumin powder - 1 teaspoon
- Lemon juice - 1 tablespoon
- Sea salt - 1 teaspoon
- Garlic powder - 1/4 teaspoon
- Olive oil - 1 tablespoon

Method

1. Set the temperature of an air fryer to 190C.

2. Mix lime juice, cumin, garlic powder, salt, olive oil and chili powder in a clean bowl. Now coat well the cauliflower and chickpeas in this mixture by constant stirring.

3. Put cauliflower mixture in an air fryer pot. Cook for 8-10 minutes with constant stirring. Cook for more 10 minutes and stir for final time. Cook for more 5 minutes until desired crispy texture is attained.

5. Place cauliflower mixture by using spoon and serve.

20. Air Fried Roasted Salsa

Ingredients

- Roma tomatoes - 4
- Seeded Jalapeno pepper - 1
- Red onion - 1/2
- Garlic - 4 cloves
- Cilantro - 1/2 cup
- Lemon juice - 1
- Cooking oil - to spray

- Salt - to taste

Method

1. Set the temperature of an air fryer to 200C.

2. Put tomatoes, red onion and skin side down of jalapeno in an air fryer pot. Brush lightly these vegetables with cooking oil for roasting them easily.

3. Cook vegetables in an air fryer for 5 minutes. Then add garlic cloves and again spray with cooking oil and fry for more 5 minutes.

4. Shift vegetables to cutting board and allow them to cool for 8-10 minutes.

5. Separate skins of jalapeno and tomatoes and chop them with onion into large pieces. Add them to food processor bowl and add lemon juice, cilantro, garlic and salt. Pulsing for many times until all the vegetables are evenly chopped. Cool them for 10-15 minutes and serve this delicious dish immediately.

21. Air Fried Flour Tortilla Bowls

Ingredients

- Flour tortilla - 1 (8 inch)
- Souffle dish - 1 (4 1/2 inch)

Method

1. Set the temperature of an air fryer to 190C.

2. Take tortilla in a large pan and heat it until it become soft. Put tortilla in the souffle dish by patting down side and fluting up from its sides of dish.

3. Air fry tortilla for 3-5 minutes until its color change into golden brown.

4. Take out tortilla bowl from the dish and put the upper side in the pot. Air fry again for more 2 minutes until its color turns into golden brown. Dish out and serve.

22. Air Fried Cheese and Mini Bean Tacos

Ingredients

- Can Refried beans - 16 ounce
- American cheese - 12 slices
- Flour tortillas - 12 (6 inch)
- Taco seasoning mix - 1 ounce
- Cooking oil - to spray

Method

1. Set the temperature of an air fryer to 200C.

2. Combine refried beans and taco seasoning evenly in a clean bowl and stir.

3. Put 1 slice of cheese in the center of tortilla and place 1 tablespoon of bean mixture over cheese. Again place second piece of cheese over this mixture. Fold tortilla properly from upper side and press to enclose completely. Repeat this step for the rest of beans, cheese and tortillas.

4. Spray cooking oil on the both sides of tacos. Put them in an air fryer at equal distance. Cook the tacos for 3 minutes and turn it side and again cook for more 3 minutes. Repeat this step for the rest of tacos. Transfer to a clean plate and serve immediately.

23. Air Fried Lemon Pepper Shrimp

Ingredients

- Lemon - 1
- Lemon pepper - 1 teaspoon
- Olive oil - 1 tablespoon
- Garlic powder - 1/4 teaspoon
- Paprika - 1/4 teaspoon
- Deveined and peeled shrimps - 12 ounces
- Sliced lemon – 1

Method

1. Set the temperature of an air fryer to 200C.

2. Mix lemon pepper, garlic powder, and olive oil, paprika and lemon juice in a clean bowl. Coat shrimps by this mixture by tossing.

3. Put shrimps in an air fryer and cook for 5-8 minutes until its color turn to pink. Dish out cooked shrimps and serve with lemon slices.

24. Air Fried Shrimp a la Bang Bang

Ingredients

- Deveined raw shrimps - 1 pound
- Sweet chili sauce - 1/4 cup
- Plain flour - 1/4 cup
- Green onions - 2
- Mayonnaise - 1/2 cup
- Sriracha sauce - 1 tablespoon
- Bread crumbs - 1 cup
- Leaf lettuce - 1 head

Method

1. Set the temperature of an air fryer to 200C

2. Make a bang bang sauce by mixing chili sauce, mayonnaise and sriracha sauce in a clean bowl. Separate some sauce for dipping in a separate small bowl.

3. Place bread crumbs and flour in two different plates. Coat shrimps with mayonnaise mixture, then with flour and then bread crumbs. Set coated shrimps on a baking paper.

4. Place them in an air fryer pot and cook for 10-12 minutes. Repeat this step for the rest of shrimps. Transfer shrimps to a clean dish and serve with green onions and lettuce.

25. Air Fried Spicy Bay Scallops

Ingredients

- Bay scallops - 1 pound
- Chili powder - 2 teaspoons
- Smoked paprika- 2 teaspoons
- Garlic powder - 1 teaspoon
- Olive oil - 2 teaspoons
- Black pepper powder - 1/4 teaspoon
- Cayenne red pepper - 1/8 teaspoon

Method

1. Set the temperature of an air fryer to 200C

2. Mix smoked paprika, olive oil, bay scallops, garlic powder, pepper, chili powder and cayenne pepper in a clean bowl and stir properly. Shift this mixture to an air fryer.

3. Air fry for 6-8 minutes with constant shaking until scallops are fully cooked. Transfer this dish in a clean plate and serve immediately.

26. Air Fried Breakfast Fritatta

Ingredients

- Fully cooked breakfast sausages - 1/4 pound
- Cheddar Monterey Jack cheese - 1/2 cup
- Green onion - 1
- Cayenne pepper - 1 pinch
- Red bell pepper - 2 tablespoons
- Eggs - 4
- Cooking oil - to spray

Method

1. Set the temperature of an air fryer to 180C.

2. Mix eggs, sausages, Cheddar Monterey Jack cheese, onion, bell pepper and cayenne in a clean bowl and stir to mix properly.

3. Spray cooking oil on a clean non-stick cake pan. Put egg mixture in the cake pan. Air fry for 15-20 minutes until fritatta is fully cooked and set. Transfer it in a clean plate and serve immediately.

27. Air Fried Roasted Okra

Ingredients

- Trimmed and sliced Okra - 1/2 pound
- Black pepper powder - 1/8 teaspoon
- Olive oil - 1 teaspoon
- Salt - 1/4 teaspoon

Method

1. Set the temperature of an air fryer to 175C.

2. Mix olive oil, black pepper, salt and okra in a clean bowl and stir to mix properly.

3. Make a single layer of this mixture in an air fryer pot. Air fry for 5-8 minutes with constant stirring. Cook for more 5 minutes and again toss. Cook for more 3 minutes and dish out in a clean plate and serve immediately.

28. Air Fried Rib-Eye Steak

Ingredients

- Rib-eye steak - 2 (1 1/2 inch thick)
- Olive oil - 1/4 cup
- Grill seasoning - 4 teaspoons
- Reduced sodium soy sauce - 1/2 cup

Method

1. Mix olive oil, soy sauce, seasoning and steaks in a clean bowl and set aside meat for marination.

2. Take out steaks and waste the remaining mixture. Remove excess oil from steak by patting.

3. Add 1 tablespoon water in an air fryer pot for the prevention from smoking during cooking of steaks.

3. Set the temperature of an air fryer to 200C. Place steaks in an air fryer pot. Air fry for 7-8 minutes and turn its side after every 8 minutes. Cook for more 7 minutes until it is rarely medium. Cook for final 3 minutes for a medium steak and dish out in a clean plate and serve immediately.

29. Air Fried Potato Chips

Ingredients

- Large potatoes - 2
- Olive oil - to spray
- Fresh parsley - optional
- Sea salt - 1/2 teaspoon

Method

1. Set the temperature of an air fryer to 180C.

2. Peel off the potatoes and cut them into thin slices. Shift the slices in a bowl containing ice chilled water and soak for 10 minutes. Drain potatoes, again add chilled water and soak for more 15 minutes.

3. Remove water from potatoes and allow to dry by using paper towel. Spray potatoes with cooking oil and add salt according to taste.

4. Place a single layer of potatoes slices in an oiled air fryer pot and cook for 15-18 minutes until color turns to golden brown and crispy. Stir constantly and turn its sides after every 5 minutes.

5. Dish out these crispy chips and serve with parsley.

30. Air Fried Tofu

Ingredients

- Packed tofu - 14 ounces
- Olive oil - 1/4 cup
- Reduced sodium soy sauce - 3 tablespoons

- Crushed red pepper flakes - 1/4 teaspoon
- Green onions - 2
- Cumin powder - 1/4 teaspoon
- Garlic - 2 cloves

Method

1. Set the temperature of an air fryer to 200C.

2. Mix olive oil, soy sauce, onions, garlic, cumin powder and red pepper flakes in a deep bowl to make marinade mixture.

3. Cut 3/8 inches' thick slices of tofu lengthwise and then diagonally. Coat tofu with marinade mixture. Place them in refrigerate for 4-5 minutes and turn them after every 2 minutes.

4. Place tofu in buttered air fryer pot. Put remaining marinade over each tofu. Cook for 5-8 minutes until color turns to golden brown. Dish out cooked tofu and serve immediately.

31. Air Fried Acorn Squash Slices

Ingredients

- Medium sized acorn squash - 2
- Soft butter - 1/2 cup
- Brown sugar - 2/3 cup

Method

1. Set the temperature of an air fryer to 160C.

2. Cut squash into two halves from length side and remove seeds. Again cut these halves into half inch slices.

3. Place a single layer of squash on buttered air fryer pot. Cook each side of squash for 5 minutes.

4. Mix butter into brown sugar and spread this mixture on the top of every squash. Cook for more 3 minutes. Dish out and serve immediately.

32. Air Fried Red Potatoes

Ingredients

- Baby potatoes - 2 pounds
- Olive oil - 2 tablespoons
- Fresh rosemary - 1 tablespoon
- Garlic - 2 cloves
- Salt - 1/2 teaspoon
- Black pepper - 1/4 teaspoon

Method

1. Set the temperature of an air fryer to 198C.

2. Cut potatoes into wedges. Coat them properly with minced garlic, rosemary, black pepper and salt.

3. Place coated potatoes on buttered air fryer pot. Cook potatoes for 5 minutes until golden brown and soft. Stir them at once. Dish out in a clean plate and serve immediately.

33. Air Fried Butter Cake

Ingredients

- Melted butter - 7 tablespoons
- White sugar - 1/4 cup & 2 tablespoons
- Plain flour - 1 & 2/3 cup
- Egg - 1
- Salt - 1 pinch
- Milk - 6 tablespoons
- Cooking oil - to spray

Method

1. Set the temperature of an air fryer to 180C and spray with cooking oil.

2. Beat white sugar, and butter together in a clean bowl until creamy and light. Then add egg and beautiful fluffy and smooth. Add salt and flour and stir. Then add milk and mix until batter is smooth. Shift batter to an preheated air fryer pot and level its surface by using spatula.

3. Place in an air fryer and set time of 15 minutes. Bake and check cake after 15 minutes by inserting toothpick in the cake. If toothpick comes out clean it means cake has fully baked.

4. Take out cake from air fryer and allow it to cool for 5-10 minutes. Serve immediately and enjoy.

34. Air Fried Jelly and Peanut Butter S'mores

Ingredients

- Chocolate topping peanut butter cup - 1
- Raspberry jam (seedless) - 1 teaspoon
- Marshmallow - 1 large
- Chocolate cracker squares – 2

Method

1. Set the temperature of an air fryer to 200C.

2. Put peanut butter cup on one cracker square and topped with marshmallow and jelly. Carefully transfer it in the preheated air fryer.

3. Cook for 1 minute until marshmallow becomes soft and light brown. Remaining cracker squares is used for topping.

4. Shift this delicious in a clean plate and serve immediately.

35. Air Fried Sun-Dried Tomatoes

Ingredients

- Red grape tomatoes - 5 ounces
- Olive oil - 1/4 teaspoon
- Salt - to taste

Method

1. Set the temperature of an air fryer to 115C.

2. Combine tomatoes halves, salt and olive oil evenly in a clean bowl. Shift tomatoes in an air fryer pot by placing skin side down.

3. Cook in air fryer for 45 minutes. Smash tomatoes by using spatula and cook for more 30 minutes. Repeat this step with the rest of tomatoes.

4. Shift this delicious dish in a clean plate and allow it to stand for 45 minutes to set. Serve this dish and enjoy.

36. Air Fried Sweet Potatoes Tots

Ingredients:

- Peeled Sweet Potatoes - 2 small (14oz.total)
- Garlic Powder - 1/8 tsp
- Potato Starch - 1 tbsp
- Kosher Salt, Divided - 11/4 tsp
- Unsalted Ketchup - 3/4 Cup
- Cooking Oil for spray

Method:

1. Take water in a medium pan and give a single boil over high flame. Then, add the sweet potatoes in the boiled water & cook for 15 minutes till potatoes becomes soft. Move the potatoes to a cooling plate for 15 minutes.

2. Rub potatoes using the wide hole's grater over a dish. Apply the potato starch, salt and garlic powder and toss gently. Make almost 24 shaped cylinders (1-inch) from the mixture.

3. Coat the air fryer pot gently with cooking oil. Put single layer of 1/2 of the tots in the pot and spray with cooking oil. Cook at 400 °F for about 12 to 14 minutes till lightly browned and flip tots midway. Remove from the pot and sprinkle with salt. Repeat with rest of the tots and salt left over. Serve with ketchup immediately.

37. Air Fried Banana Bread

Ingredients:

- White Whole Wheat Flour - 3/4 cup (3 oz.)
- Mashed Ripe Bananas - 2 medium or (about 3/4th cup)
- Cinnamon powder– 4 pinches
- Kosher Salt - 1/2 tsp
- Baking Soda - 1/4 tsp
- Large Eggs, Lightly Beaten - 2
- Regular Sugar - 1/2 cup
- Vanilla Essence - 1 tsp
- Vegetable Oil - 2 tbsp
- Roughly Chopped and toasted Walnuts - 2 table-spoons (3/4 oz.)
- Plain Non-Fat Yogurt - 1/3 cup

- Cooking Oil for Spray - as required

Method:

1. Cover the base of a 6-inches round cake baking pan with baking paper and lightly brush with melted butter. Beat the flour, baking soda, salt, and cinnamon together in a clean bowl and let it reserve.

2. Whisk the mashed bananas, eggs, sugar, cream, oil and vanilla together in a separate bowl. Stir the wet ingredients gently into the flour mixture until everything is blended. Pour the mixture in the prepared pan and sprinkle with the walnuts.

3. Set the temperature of an air fryer to 310 °F and put the pan in the air fryer. Cook until browned, about 30 to 35 minutes. Rotate the pan periodically until a wooden stick put in it and appears clean. Before flipping out & slicing, move the bread to a cooling rack for 15 minutes.

38. Air Fried Avocado Fries

Ingredients:

- Avocados --. 2 - Cut each into the 8 pieces
- All-purpose flour - 1/2 cup (about 2 1/8 oz.)
- Panko (Japanese Style Breadcrumbs) - 1/2 cup
- Large Eggs - 2
- Kosher Salt - 1/4 tsp
- Apple Cider - 1 tbsp
- Sriracha Chilli Sause - 1 tbsp

- Black pepper - 11/2 tsp
- Water - 1 tbsp
- Unsalted Ketchup - 1/2 cup
- Cooking spray

Method:

1. Mix flour and pepper collectively in a clean bowl. Whip eggs & water gently in another bowl. Take panko in a third bowl. Coat avocado slices in flour and remove extra flour by shaking. Then, dip the slices in the egg and remove any excess. Coat in panko by pushing to stick together. Spray well the avocado slices with cooking oil.

2. In the air fryer's basket, put avocado slices & fry at 400 ° F until it turns into golden for 7-8 minutes. Turn avocado wedges periodically while frying. Take out from an air fryer and use salt for sprinkling.

3. Mix the Sriracha, ketchup, vinegar, and mayonnaise together in a small bowl. Put two tablespoons of sauce on each plate with 4 avocado fries before serving.

39. "Strawberry Pop Tarts" in an Air Fryer

Ingredients:

- Quartered Strawberries - (about 13/4 cups equal to 8 ounces)
- White/Regular Sugar - 1/4 cup
- Refrigerated Piecrusts - 1/2(14.1-oz)
- Powdered Sugar - 1/2 cup (about 2-oz)

- Fresh Lemon Juice - 11/2 tsp
- Rainbow Candy Sprinkles - 1 tbsp(about 1/2 ounce)
- Cooking Spray

Method:

1. Mix strawberries & white sugar and stay for 15 minutes with periodically stirring. Air fryer them for 10 minutes until glossy and reduced with constant stirring. Let it cool for 30 minutes.

2. Use the smooth floured surface to roll the pie crust and make 12-inches round shape. Cut the dough into 12 rectangles of (2 1/2- x 3-inch), re-rolling strips if necessary. Leaving a 1/2-inch boundary, add the spoon around 2 tea-spoons of strawberry mixture into the middle of 6 of dough rectangles. Brush the edges of the rectangles of the filled dough with water. Then, press the edges of rest dough rectangles with a fork to seal. Spray the tarts very well with cooking oil.

3. In an air fryer pot, put 3 tarts in a single layer and cook them at 350 ° F for 10 minutes till golden brown. With the rest of the tarts, repeat the process. Set aside for cooling for 30 minutes.

4. In a small cup, whip the powdered sugar & lemon juice together until it gets smooth. Glaze the spoon over the cooled tarts and sprinkle equally with candy.

40. Lighten up Empanadas in an Air Fryer

Ingredients:

- Lean Green Beef - 3 ounces
- Cremini Mushrooms - Chopped finely - 3 ounces
- White onion - Chopped finely - 1/4th cup
- Garlic – Chopped finely - 2 tsp.
- Pitted Green Olives - 6
- Olive Oil - 1 table-spoon
- Cumin - 1/4th tsp
- Cinnamon - 1/8th tsp
- Chopped tomatoes - 1/2 cup
- Paprika - 1/4 tea-spoon
- Large egg lightly Beaten - 1
- Square gyoza wrappers - 8

Method:

1. In a medium cooking pot, let heat oil on the medium/high temperature. Then, add beef & onion; for 3 minutes, cook them, mixing the crumble, until getting brown. Put the mushrooms; let them cook for 6 mins, till the mushrooms start to brown, stirring frequently. Add the paprika, olives, garlic, cinnamon, and cumin; cook for three minutes until the mushrooms are very tender and most of the liquid has been released. Mix in the tomatoes and cook, turning periodically, for 1 minute. Put the filling in a bowl and let it cool for 5 minutes.

2. Arrange 4 wrappers of gyoza on a worktop. In each wrapper, put around 1 1/2 tablespoons of filling in the middle. Clean the edges of the egg wrappers; fold over the

wrappers and pinch the edges to seal. Repeat with the remaining wrappers and filling process.

3. Place the 4 empanadas in one single layer in an air-fryer basket and cook for 7 minutes at 400 °F until browned well. Repeat with the empanadas that remain.

41. Air Fried Calzones

Ingredients:

- Spinach Leaves --> 3 ounces (about 3 cups)
- Shredded Chicken breast --> 2 ounces (about 1/3 cup)
- Fresh Whole Wheat Pizza Dough --> 6 ounces
- Shredded Mozzarella Cheese --> 11/2 ounces (about 6 tbsp)
- Low Sodium Marinara Sauce --> 1/3 cup

Method:

1. First of all, in a medium pan, let heat oil on medium/high temperature. Include onion & cook, continue mixing then well efficiently, for two min, till get soft. After that, add the spinach; then cover & cook it until softened. After that, take out the pan from the heat; mix the chicken & marinara sauce.

2. Divide the dough in to the four identical sections. Then, roll each section into a 6-inches circle on a gently floured surface. Place over half of each dough circular shape with one-fourth of the spinach mixture. Top with one-fourth of the cheese each. Fold the dough

to make half-moons and over filling, tightening the edges to lock. Coat the calzones well with spray for cooking

3. In the basket of an air fryer, put the calzones and cook them at 325 ° F until the dough becomes nicely golden brown, in 12 mins, changing the sides of the calzones after 8 mins.

42. Air Fried Mexican Style Corns

Ingredients:

- Unsalted Butter - 11/2 tbsp.
- Chopped Garlic -2 tsp
- Shucked Fresh Corns - 11/2 lb
- Fresh Chopped Cilantro - 2 tbsp.
- Lime zest - 1 tbsp.
- Lime Juice - 1 tsp
- Kosher Salt - 1/2 tsp
- Black Pepper - 1/2 tsp

Method:

1. Coat the corn delicately with the cooking spray, and put the corn in the air fryer's basket in one single layer. Let it Cooking for 14 mins at 400 °F till tender then charred gently, changing the corn half the way via cooking.

2. In the meantime, whisk together all the garlic, lime juice, butter, & lime zest in the microwaveable pot. Let an air fryer on Fast, about 30 seconds, until the butter melts and

the garlic is aromatic. Put the corn on the plate and drop the butter mixture on it. Using the salt, cilantro, and pepper to sprinkle. Instantly serve this delicious recipe.

43. Air Fryer Crunchy & Crispy Chocolate Bites

Ingredients:

- Frozen Shortcrust Pastry - Partially thawed -- 4
- Cinnamon for dusting -- as required
- Icing Sugar for dusting -- as required
- Mars Celebration Chocolates -- 24
- Whipped Cream - as required

Method:

1. First of all, cut each pastry sheet into 6 equal rectangles. Brush the egg finely. In the centre of each piece of the pastry, place one chocolate. Fold the pastry over to seal the chocolate. Trim the extra pastry, then press and lock the corners. Put it on a tray lined with baking sheet. Brush the tops with an egg. Use the mixture of cinnamon and sugar to sprinkle liberally.

2. In the air-fryer basket, put a layer of the baking paper, ensuring that the paper is 1 cm smaller than that of the basket to permit air to circulate well. Place the 6 pockets in basket, taking care that these pockets must not to overlap. Then, cook them for 8-9 mins at 190 ° C till they become golden and the pastry are prepared thoroughly. As the pockets cooked, transfer them into a dish. Repeat the process with the pockets that remain.

3. After taking out from the air fryer, dust the Icing sugar and at last with whipped cream. Serve them warm.

44. Doritos-Crumbled Chicken tenders in an Air fryer

Ingredients:

- Buttermilk -- 1 cup (about 250ml)
- Doritos Nacho Cheese Corn Chips -- 170g Packet
- Halved Crossways Chicken Tenderloins -- 500g
- Egg -- 1
- Plain Flour -- 50g
- Mild Salsa -- for serving

Method:

1.Take a ceramic bowl or glass and put the chicken in it. Then, c over the buttermilk with it. Wrap it and put it for 4 hours or may be overnight in the refrigerator to marinate.

2. Let Preheat an air fryer at 180C. Then, cover a Baking tray with grease-proof paper.

3. In a Chopper, add the corn chips then pulse them until the corn chips become coarsely chopped. Then, transfer the chopped chips to a dish. In a deep cup, put the egg and beat it. On another plate, put the flour.

4. Remove the unnecessary water from the chicken, and also discard the buttermilk. Then, dip the chicken in the flour mixture and wipe off the extra flour. After that, dip in the beaten egg and then into the chips of corn, press it firmly to coat well. Transfer it to the tray that made ready to next step.

5. In the air fryer, put half of the chicken and then, fry for 8 to 10 mins until they are golden as well as cooked completely. Repeat the process with the chicken that remain.

Transfer the chicken in the serving dish. Enjoy this delicious recipe with salsa.

45. Air Fryer Ham & Cheese Croquettes

Ingredients:

- Chopped White Potatoes -- 1 kg
- Chopped Ham -- 100g
- Chopped Green Shallots -- 2
- Grated Cheddar Cheese -- 80g (about 1 cup)
- All-purpose flour -- 50g
- eggs -- 2
- Breadcrumbs -- 100g
- Lemon Slices -- for serving
- Tonkatsu Sause -- for serving

Method:

1. In a large-sized saucepan, put the potatoes. Cover with chill water. Carry it over high temperature to a boil. Boil till tender for 10 to 12 minutes. Drain thoroughly. Return over low heat to pan. Mix until it is smooth and has allowed to evaporate the certain water. Withdraw from the sun. Switch to a tub. Fully set aside to chill.

2. Then, add the shallot, Ham and cheese in the mashed potatoes also season with kosher salt. Mix it well. Take the 2 tablespoons of the mixture and make its balls. And repeat process for the rest of mixture.

3. Take the plain flour in a plate. Take another small bowl and beat the eggs. Take the third bowl and add the breadcrumbs in it. Toss the balls in the flour. Shake off the extra flour then in eggs and coat the breadcrumbs well. Make the balls ready for frying. Take all the coated balls in the fridge for about 15 minutes.

4. Preheat an air fryer at 200 ° C. Then, cook the croquettes for 8 to10 mints until they become nicely golden, in two rounds. Sprinkle the tonkatsu sauce and serve the croquettes with lemon slices.

46. Air Fryer Lemonade Scones

Ingredients:

- Self-raising flour -- 525g (about 3 1/2 cups)
- Thickened Cream -- 300ml
- Lemonade -- 185ml (about 3/4 cup)
- Caster Sugar -- 70g (1/3 cup)
- Vanilla Essence -- 1 tsp
- Milk -- for brushing
- Raspberry Jam -- for serving
- Whipped Cream -- for serving

Method:

1. In a large-sized bowl, add the flour and sugar together. Mix it well. Add lemonade, vanilla and cream. In a big bowl, add the flour and sugar. Just make a well. Remove milk, vanilla and lemonade. Mix finely, by using a plain knife, till the dough comes at once.

2. Take out the dough on the flat surface and sprinkle the dry flour on the dough. Knead it gently for about 30 secs until the dough get smooth. On a floured surface, roll out the dough. Politely knead for thirty seconds, until it is just smooth. Form the dough into a round shape about 2.5 cm thick. Toss around 5.5 cm blade into the flour. Cut the scones out. Push the bits of remaining dough at once gently and repeat the process to make Sixteen scones.

3. In the air fryer bucket, put a layer of baking paper, ensuring that the paper is 1 cm shorter than the bucket to allow air to flow uniformly. Put 5 to 6 scones on paper in the bucket, even hitting them. Finely brush the surfaces with milk. Let cook them for about 15 mins at 160 ° C or when they tapped on the top, until become golden and empty-sounding. Move it safely to a wire or cooling rack. Repeat the same process with the rest of scones and milk two more times.

4. Serve the lemonade scones warm with raspberry jam & whipped cream.

47. Air Fryer Baked Potatoes

Ingredients:

- Baby Potatoes -- Halved shape -- 650g
- Fresh rosemary sprigs-- 2 large
- Sour Cream -- for serving

- Sweet Chilli Sauce -- for serving
- Salt -- for seasoning

Method:

1. Firstly, at 180C, pre-heat the air fryer. In an air fryer, put the rosemary sprigs & baby potatoes. Use oil for spray and salt for seasoning. Then, cook them for fifteen min until become crispy and cooked completely, also turning partially.

2. Serve the baked potatoes sweet chilli Sause & sour cream to enhance its flavour.

48. Air Fryer Mozzarella Chips

Ingredients:

- All-purpose flour -- 1 tbsp
- Breadcrumbs -- 2/3 cup
- Garlic Powder -- 3 tbsp
- Lemon Juice -- 1/3 cup
- Avocado -- 1
- Basil Pesto -- 2 tbsp
- Plain Yogurt -- 1/4 cup
- Chopped Green Onion --1
- Cornflakes crumbs -- 1/4 cup
- Mozzarella block -- 550g
- Eggs – 2
- Olive Oil for spray

Method:

1. Start making Creamy and fluffy Avocado Dipped Sauce: In a small-sized food processor, put the yogurt, avocado, lemon juice, onion, and pesto. Also add the pepper & salt, blend properly. Process it well until it get mixed and smooth. Switch the batter to a bowl. Cover it. Place in the fridge, until It required.

2. Take a large-sized tray and place a baking sheet. In a large bowl, add the garlic powder & plain flour together. Also add the salt and season well. Take another medium bowl, whisk the eggs. Mix the breadcrumbs well in bowl.

3. Make the 2 cm thick wedges of mozzarella, then put them into the sticks. For coating, roll the cheese in the flour. Shake off the extra flour. Then, coat the sticks in the egg fusion, then in the breadcrumbs, operating in rounds. Place the prepared plate on it. Freeze till solid, or even for around 1 hour.

4. Spray the oil on the mozzarella lightly. Wrap the air fryer bucket with baking sheet, leaving an edge of 1 cm to enable air to flow. Then, cook at 180C, for 4 to 4 1/2 mins until the sticks become crispy & golden. Serve warm with sauce to dip.

49. Air Fryer Fetta Nuggets

Ingredients:

- All-purpose flour -- 1 tbsp.
- Chilli flakes -- 1 tsp
- Onion powder -- 1 tsp
- Sesame Seeds -- 1/4 cup
- Fetta Cheese Cubes -- Cut in 2 cm 180g
- Fresh Chives -- for serving

- Breadcrumbs -- 1/4 cup

BARBECUE SAUSE:

- apple cider -- 11/2 tsp
- Chilli Flakes -- 1/2 tsp
- Barbecue Sause -- 1//4 cup

Method:

1. Mix the onion powder, flour and chilli flakes in a medium-sized bowl. Use pepper for seasoning. Take another bowl, and beat an egg. Take one more bowl and mix sesame seeds and breadcrumbs. Then, toss the fetta in the chilli flakes, onion powder & flour mixture. Dip the fetta in egg, and toss again in breadcrumbs fusion. Put them on a plate.

2. Pre- heat the air fryer at 180 °C. Put the cubes of fetta in a baking tray, in the basket of the air fryer. cook till fetta cubes become golden, or may be for 6 mins.

3. In the meantime, mix all the wet ingredients and create the Barbecue sauce.

4. Sprinkle the chives on the fetta and serve with Barbecue Sause.

50. Air Fryer Japanese Chicken Tender

Ingredients:

- McCormick Katsu Crumb for seasoning -- 25g
- Pickled Ginger -- 1 tbsp.
- Japanese-Style Mayonnaise -- 1/3 cup
- Chicken Tenderloins -- 500g

- Oil for spray

Method:

1. Put the chicken on tray in the form of single layer. Sprinkle the half seasoning on chicken. Then, turn chicken and sprinkle the seasoning again evenly. Use oil for spray on it.

2. Pre-heat at 180°C, an air fryer. Let the chicken cooking for about 12 - 14 mins until it becomes golden & cooked completely.

3. In the meantime, take a small-sized bowl, mix the mayonnaise and the remaining pickling sauce.

4. Serve the chicken with white sauce and put the ginger on the side, in a platter.

51. Whole-Wheat Pizzas in an Air Fryer

Ingredients:

- Low-sodium Marinara Sauce -- 1/4 cup
- Spinach leaves -- 1 cup
- Pita Breads -- 2
- Shredded Mozzarella Cheese -- 1/4 cup
- Parmigiano- Reggiano Cheese -- 1/4 ounces (about 1 tbsp.)
- Tomato slices -- 8
- Sliced Garlic Clove -- 1

Method:

1. Spread the marinara sauce on 1 side of each pita bread uniformly. Cover the cheese spinach leaves, tomato slices and garlic, with half of each of these.

2. Put one pita bread in an air fryer pot, then cook it at 350°F till the cheese becomes melted and pita becomes crispy, 4 - 5 mins. Repeat the process with the pita leftover.

52. Air Fryer Crispy Veggie Quesadillas

Ingredients:

- 6 inches Whole Grain Flour Tortillas -- 4
- Full fat Cheddar Cheese -- 4 ounces (about 1 cup)
- Sliced Zucchini -- 1 cup
- Lime Zest -- 1 tbsp.
- Lime Juice -- 1 tsp.
- Fresh Cilantro -- 2 tbsp.
- Chopped Red Bell Pepper -- (about 1 cup)
- Cumin -- 1/4 tsp.
- Low-fat Yoghurt -- 2 ounces
- Refrigerated Pico de Gallo -- 1/2 cup
- Oil for spray

Method:

1. Put tortillas on the surface of the work. Sprinkle onto half of each tortilla with 2 tbsp. of grated cheese. Cover each tortilla with 1/4 cup of chopped red bell pepper, zucchini chunks & the black beans on the top of the cheese. Sprinkle finely with 1/2 cup of cheese left. Fold over the tortillas to create quesadillas form like half-moons. Coat the quesadillas slightly with a cooking spray, & lock them with match picks or toothpicks.

2. Lightly brush a bucket of air fryer with cooking oil spray. Place 2 quesadillas carefully in the basket. Cook at 400°F till the tortillas become golden brown & gently crispy. Melt the cheese & gradually tender the vegetables for ten mins, tossing the quesadillas partially throughout the cooking period. Repeat the process with leftover quesadillas.

3. Mix together lime zest, yogurt, cumin, & lime juice, in a small-sized bowl since the quesadillas getting prepare. Break each quesadilla in-to the pieces to serve and then sprinkle the coriander. With one tbsp. of cumin cream and two tablespoons of pico de gallo, and serve each.

53. Air Fried Curry Chickpeas

Ingredients:

- Drained & Rinsed Un-Salted Chickpeas -- 11/2 cups (15-oz.)
- Olive Oil -- 2 tbsp.
- Curry Powder -- 2 tsp.
- Coriander -- 1/4 tsp.
- Cumin -- 1/4 tsp.
- Cinnamon -- 1/4 tsp.
- Turmeric -- 1/2 tsp.
- Aleppo Pepper -- 1/2 tsp.

- Red Wine Vinegar -- 2 tbsp.
- Kosher Salt -- 1/4 tsp.
- Sliced Fresh Cilantro -- as required

Method:

1. Break the chickpeas lightly in a medium-sized bowl with your hands (don't crush them); and then remove the skins of chickpea.

2. Add oil & vinegar to the chickpeas, and stir to coat. Then, add curry powder, turmeric, coriander, cumin, & cinnamon; mix gently to combine them.

3. In the air fryer bucket, put the chickpeas in one single layer & cook at 400°F temperature until becoming crispy, for about 15 min, stirring the chickpeas periodically throughout the cooking process.

4. Place the chickpeas in a dish. Sprinkle the salt, cilantro and Aleppo pepper on chickpeas; and cover it.

54. Air Fried Beet Chips

Ingredients:

- Canola Oil -- 1 tsp.
- Medium-sized Red Beets -- 3
- Black Pepper -- 1/4 tsp.
- Kosher Salt -- 3/4 tsp.

Method:

1. Cut and Peel the red beets. Make sure each beet cutted into 1/8-inch-thick slices. Take a large-sized bowl and toss the beets slices, pepper, salt and oil well.

2. Put half beets in air fryer bucket and then cook at the 320°F temperature about 25 - 30 mins or until they become crispy and dry. Flip the bucket about every 5 mins. Repeat the process for the beets that remain.

55. Double-Glazed Air Fried Cinnamon Biscuits

Ingredients:

- Cinnamon -- 1/4 tsp.
- Plain Flour -- 2/3 cup (about 27/8 oz.)
- Whole-Wheat Flour -- 2/3 cup (about22/3 oz.)
- Baking Powder -- 1 tsp.
- White Sugar -- 2 tbsp.
- Kosher Salt -- 1/4 tsp.
- Chill Salted Butter -- 4 tbsp.
- Powdered Sugar -- 2 cups (about 8-oz.)
- Water -- 3 tbsp.
- Whole Milk -- 1/3 cup
- Oil for spray -- as required

Method:

1. In a medium-sized bowl, stir together salt, plain flour, baking powder, white sugar cinnamon and butter. Use two knives or pastry cutter to cut mixture till butter becomes well mixed with the flour and the mixture seems to as coarse cornmeal. Add the milk, then mix well until the dough becomes a ball. Place the dough on a floury surface and knead for around 30 seconds until the dough becomes smooth. Break the dough into 16 identical parts. Roll each part carefully into a plain ball.

2. Coat the air fryer pot well with oil spray. Put 8 balls in the pot, by leaving the space between each one; spray with cooking oil. Cook them until get browned & puffed, for 10 - 12 mins at 350°F temperature. Take out the doughnut balls from the pot carefully and put them on a cooling rack having foil for five mins. Repeat the process with the doughnut balls that remain.

3. In a medium pot, mix water and powdered sugar together until smooth. Then, spoon half of the glaze carefully over the doughnut balls. Cool for five mins and let it glaze once and enabling to drip off extra glaze.

56. Lemon Drizzle Cake in an Air Fryer

Ingredients:

- Grated Lemon rind -- 2 tsp.
- Cardamom -- 1 tsp.
- Softened Butter -- 150g
- Eggs -- 3
- Honey-flavoured Yoghurt -- 3/4 cup
- Self-raising flour -- 11/2 cups
- Caster Sugar -- 2/3 cup (150g)
- Lemon Zest -- for serving

LEMON ICING:

- Icing Sugar -- 1 cup
- Lemon Juice -- 11/2 tbsps.
- Softened Butter -- 10g

Method:

1. First, grease a 20 cm cake baking pan of round shape having butter paper. Take an electric beater and beat cardamom, sugar, lemon rind, and butter until the mixture becomes smooth & pale. Then, add the eggs one by one and beat well. Put the eggs in the flour and yoghurt. Fold by spatula and make the surface very smooth.

2. Pre-heat the air fryer at 180 C temperature. Put the pan in air fryer's pot. Bake it for about 35 mins. Check it by putting skewer in it that comes out clean without any sticky batter. Reserve it in the pan for 5 minutes to become cool before shifting it to a cooling rack.

3. Make the lemon glaze, add butter and icing sugar in a bowl. By adding lemon juice as required and form a smooth paste.

4. Put the cake on a plate to serve. Sprinkle the lemon zest and lemon icing to serve.

57. Air Fryer dukkah-Crumbed chicken

Ingredients:

- Chicken Thigh Fillets -- 8
- Herb or dukkah -- 45g packet
- Plain Flour -- 1/3 cup (about 50g)
- Kaleslaw kit -- 350g Packet
- Breadcrumbs -- 1 cup (about 80g)
- Eggs -- 2

Method:

1. Put half of the chicken within 2 sheets of cling paper. Gently beat until it remains 2 cm thick by using a meat hammer or rolling pin. Repeat the process with the chicken that remains.

2. In a deep bowl, mix breadcrumbs and dukkah together. Beat an egg in medium bowl., Put the flour and all the seasoning on a tray. Coat chicken pieces one by one in the flour and shake off the extra. Dip chicken pieces into the egg, then in breadcrumbs for coating. Move them to a dish. Cover them with the plastic wrapper & leave it to marinate for 30 mins in the fridge.

3. Pre-heat air fryer at 200°C temperature. Use olive oil to spray the chicken pieces. Put half of the chicken in one single layer in the air fryer pot. Cook them for about 16 mins and turning partially until they become golden & get cooked completely. Move to a plate & wrap them with foil to stay warm. Repeat the process with the chicken pieces that remains.

4. After that, place the kaleslaw kit in a serving bowl by following instructions mentioned in the packets.

5. Divide the prepared chicken & the kaleslaw between serving platters, and season it.

58. Air Fryer Vietnamese-style spring roll salad

Ingredients:

- Rice Noodles -- 340g
- Crushed Garlic -- 1 clove
- Grated Ginger -- 2 tsp.
- Pork Mince -- 250g

- Lemongrass paste -- 1 tsp
- Cutted into matchsticks the Peeled Carrots -- 2
- Sliced Spring onion -- 3
- Fish sauce -- 2 tsp.
- Spring roll pastries -- 10 sheets
- Coriander -- 1/2 cup
- Sliced Red Chilli - 1 long
- Vietnamese-style Salad -- for dressing
- Mint Leaves -- 1/2
- Bean Sprouts -- 1 cup

Method:

1. Take a large-sized saucepan and cook the noodles for about 4 mins until get soft. Take the cold water and discharge thoroughly. Cutting 1 cup of the boiled noodles into the short lengths, with the leftover noodles reserved.

2. Take a large-sized bowl, add the mince, lemongrass, ginger, garlic, half carrot, spring onion, and fish sauce together and mix them well.

3. On a clean surface, put one pastry paper. Add two tablespoons across 1 side of the mince fusion diagonally. With just a little spray, brush its opposite side. Fold and roll on the sides to completely cover the mince filling. Repeat the process with the sheets of pastry and fill the thin layer of mince mixture, that remain.

4. Pre-heat at 200°C, an air fryer. Use olive oil, spray on the spring rolls. Put in the bucket of air fryer and cook the spring rolls for fifteen mins until cooked completely. Change the sides half-way during cooking.

5. After that, equally split reserved noodles in the serving bowls. Place coriander, bean sprouts, mint and the remaining spring onion and carrots at the top of the serving bowl.

6. Then, break the spring rolls in the half and place them over the mixture of noodles. Sprinkle the chili and serve with Vietnamese-style salad dressing according to your taste.

59. Air Fryer Pizza Pockets

Ingredients:

- Olive oil - 2 tsp.
- Sliced Mushrooms - 6 (about 100g)
- Chopped Leg Ham - 50g
- Crumbled Fetta - 80g
- White Wraps - 4
- Basil Leaves - 1/4 cup
- Baby Spinach - 120g
- Tomato Paste - 1/3 cup
- Chopped Red Capsicum - 1/2
- Dried Oregano - 1/2 tsp
- Olive oil - for spray
- Green Salad - for serving

Method:

1. Heat oil on medium temperature in an air fryer. Cook capsicum for about five minutes until it starts to soften. Add mushrooms and cook them for another five mins until

mushrooms become golden and evaporating any water left in the pan. Move mushrooms to another bowl. Leave them to cool for 10 mins.

2. Take a heatproof bowl and put spinach in it. Cover it with boiling water. Wait for 1 min until slightly wilted. Drain water and leave it to cool for about 10 mins.

3. Excessive spinach moisture is squeezed and applied to the capsicum mixture. Add the oregano, basil, ham and fetta. Season it with both salt & pepper. Mix it well to combine properly.

4. Put one wrapper on the smooth surface. Add 1 tbsp of tomato paste to the middle of the wrap. Cover it with a combination of 1-quarter of the capsicum. Roll up the wrap to completely enclose the filling, give it as the shape of parcel and folding the sides. To build four parcels, repeat the procedure with the remaining wraps, mixture of capsicum & tomato paste. Use oil spray on the tops.

5. Pre-heat the air fryer at 180 C temperature. Cook the parcels for 6 - 8 mins until they become golden & crispy, take out them and move to 2 more batches. Serve along with the salad.

60. Air Fryer Popcorn Fetta with Maple Hot Sauce

Ingredients:

- Marinated Fetta cubes - 265g
- Cajun for seasoning - 2 tsp.
- Breadcrumbs - 2/3 cups
- Corn flour - 2 tbsp.
- Egg - 1
- Chopped Fresh Coriander - 1 tbsp.
- Coriander leaves - for serving

Maple hot sauce:

- Maple syrup - 2 tbsp.
- Sriracha - 1 tbsps.

Method:

1. Drain the fetta, then reserve 1 tbsp of oil making sauce.

2. Take a bowl, mix the cornflour and the Cajun seasoning together. Beat the egg in another bowl. Take one more bowl and combine the breadcrumbs & cilantro in it. Season it with salt & pepper. Work in batches, coat the fetta in cornflour mixture, then dip in the egg. After that, toss them in breadcrumb mixture for coating. Place them on the plate and freeze them for one hour.

3. Take a saucepan, add Sriracha, reserved oil and maple syrup together and put on medium low heat. Stir it for 3 - 4 minutes continuously until sauce get start to thicken. Then, remove the maple sauce from heat.

4. Pre-heat the air fryer at 180C. Place the cubes of fetta in a single layer in the air fryer's pot. Cook them for 3 - 4 mins until just staring softened, and fettas become golden. Sprinkled with extra coriander leaves and serve them with the maple hot sauce.

61. Air fryer Steak Fajitas

Ingredients:

- Chopped tomatoes - 2 large
- Minced Jalapeno pepper - 1
- Cumin - 2 tsp.
- Lime juice - 1/4 cup
- Fresh minced Cilantro - 3 tbsp.
- Diced Red Onion - 1/2 cup
- 8-inches long Whole-wheat tortillas - 6

- Large onion - 1 sliced
- Salt - 3/4 tsp divided
- Beef steak - 1

Method:

1. Mix first 5 ingredients in a clean bowl then stir in cumin and salt. Let it stand till before you serve.

2. Pre-heat the air fryer at 400 degrees. Sprinkle the cumin and salt with the steak that remain. Place them on buttered air-fryer pot and cook the steak until the meat reaches the appropriate thickness (a thermometer should read 135 ° for medium-rare; 140 °; moderate, 145 °), for 6 to 8 mins per side. Remove from the air fryer and leave for five min to stand.

3. Then, put the onion in the air-fryer pot. Cook it until get crispy-tender, stirring once for 2 - 3 mins. Thinly slice the steak and serve with onion & salsa in the tortillas. Serve it with avocado & lime slices if needed.

62. Air-Fryer Fajita-Stuffed Chicken

Ingredients:

- Boneless Chicken breast - 4
- Finely Sliced Onion - 1 small
- Finely Sliced Green pepper - 1/2 medium-sized
- Olive oil - 1 tbsp.
- Salt - 1/2 tsp.
- Chilli Powder - 1 tbsp.
- Cheddar Cheese - 4 ounces
- Cumin - 1 tsp.
- Salsa or jalapeno slices - optional

Method:

1. Pre-heat the air fryer at the 375 degrees. In the widest part of every chicken breast, cut a gap horizontally. Fill it with green pepper and onion. Combine olive oil and the seasonings in a clean bowl and apply over the chicken.

2. Place the chicken on a greased dish in the form of batches in an air-fryer pot. Cook it for 6 minutes. Stuff the chicken with cheese slices and secure the chicken pieces with toothpicks. Cook at 165° until for 6 to 8 minutes. Take off the toothpicks. Serve the delicious chicken with toppings of your choosing, if wanted.

63. Nashvilla Hot Chicken in an Air Fryer

Ingredients:

- Chicken Tenderloins - 2 pounds
- Plain flour - 1 cup
- Hot pepper Sauce - 2 tbsp.
- Egg - 1 large

- Salt - 1 tsp.
- Pepper - 1/2 tsp.
- Buttermilk - 1/2 cup
- Cayenne Pepper - 2 tbsp.
- Chilli powder - 1 tsp.
- Pickle Juice - 2 tbsp.
- Garlic Powder - 1/2 tsp.
- Paprika - 1 tsp.
- Brown Sugar - 2 tbsp.
- Olive oil - 1/2 cup
- Cooling oil for spray

Method:

1. Combine pickle juice, hot sauce and salt in a clean bowl and coat the chicken on its both sides. Put it in the fridge, cover it, for a minimum 1 hour. Throwing away some marinade.

2. Pre-heat the air fryer at 375 degrees. Mix the flour, the remaining salt and the pepper in another bowl. Whisk together the buttermilk, eggs, pickle juice and hot sauce well. For coating the both sides, dip the chicken in plain flour; drip off the excess. Dip chicken in egg mixture and then again dip in flour mixture.

3. Arrange the single layer of chicken on a greased air-fryer pot and spray with cooking oil. Cook for 5 to 6 minutes until it becomes golden brown. Turn and spray well. Again, cook it until golden brown, for more 5-6 minutes.

4. Mix oil, brown sugar, cayenne pepper and seasonings together. Then, pour on the hot chicken and toss to cover. Serve the hot chicken with pickles.

64. Southern-style Chicken

Ingredients:

- Crushed Crackers - 2 cups (about 50)
- Fresh minced parsley - 1 tbsp.
- Paprika - 1 tsp.
- Pepper - 1/2 tsp.
- Garlic salt - 1 tsp.
- Fryer Chicken - 1
- Cumin - 1/4 tsp.
- Egg - 1
- Cooking Oil for spray

Method:

1. Set the temperature of an air fryer at 375 degrees. Mix the first 7 ingredients in a deep bowl. Beat an egg in deep bowl. Soak the chicken in egg, then pat in the cracker mixture for proper coat. Place the chicken in a single layer on the greased air-fryer pot and spray with cooking oil.

2. Cook it for 10 minutes. Change the sides of chicken and squirt with cooking oil spray. Cook until the chicken becomes golden brown & juices seem to be clear, for 10 - 20 minutes longer.

65. Chicken Parmesan in an Air Fryer

Ingredients:

- Breadcrumbs - 1/2 cup

- Pepper - 1/4 tsp.
- Pasta Sauce - 1 cup
- Boneless Chicken breast - 4
- Mozzarella Cheese - 1 cup
- Parmesan Cheese - 1/3 cup
- Large Eggs - 2
- Fresh basil - Optional

Method:

1. Set the temperature of an air-fryer at 375 degrees. In a deep bowl, beat the eggs gently. Combine the breadcrumbs, pepper and parmesan cheese in another bowl. Dip the chicken in beaten egg and coat the chicken parmesan with breadcrumbs mixture.

2. In an air-fryer pot, put the chicken in single layer. Cook the chicken for 10 to 12 mins with changing the sides partially. Cover the chicken with cheese and sauce. Cook it for 3 to 4 minutes until cheese has melted. Then, sprinkle with basil leaves and serve.

66. Lemon Chicken Thigh in an Air Fryer

Ingredients:

- Bone-in Chicken thighs- 4
- Pepper - 1/8 tsp.
- Salt - 1/8 tsp.
- Pasta Sauce - 1 cup
- Lemon Juice - 1 tbsp.
- Lemon Zest - 1 tsp.
- Minced Garlic - 3 cloves
- Butter - 1/4 cup

- Dried or Fresh Rosemary - 1 tsp.
- Dried or Fresh Thyme - 1/4 tsp.

Method:

1. Pre-heat the air fryer at 400 degrees. Combine the butter, thyme, rosemary, garlic, lemon juice & zest in a clean bowl. Spread a mixture on each of the thigh's skin. Use salt and pepper to sprinkle.

2. Place the chicken, then side up the skin, in a greased air-fryer pot. Cook for 20 mins and flip once. Switch the chicken again (side up the skin) and cook it for about 5 mins until the thermometer will read 170 degrees to 175 degrees. Then, place in the serving plate and serve it.

67. Salmon with Maple-Dijon Glaze in air fryer

Ingredients:

- Salmon Fillets - 4 (about ounces)
- Salt - 1/4 tsp.
- Pepper - 1/4 tsp.
- Butter - 3 tbsp.
- Mustard - 1 tbsp.
- Lemon Juice - 1 medium-sized
- Garlic clove - 1 minced
- Olive oil

Method:

1. Pre-heat the air fryer at 400 degrees. Melt butter in a medium-sized pan on medium temperature. Put the mustard, minced garlic, maple syrup & lemon juice. Lower the heat and cook for 2 - 3 minutes before the mixture thickens significantly. Take off from the heat and set aside for few mins.

2. Brush the salmon with olive oil and also sprinkle the salt and pepper on it.

3. In an air fryer bucket, put the fish in a single baking sheet. Cook for 5 to 7 mins until fish is browned and easy to flake rapidly with help of fork. Sprinkle before to serve the salmon with sauce.

68. Air Fryer Roasted Beans

Ingredients:

- Fresh Sliced Mushrooms - 1/2 pounds
- Green Beans cut into 2-inch wedges - 1 pound
- Italian Seasoning - 1 tsp.
- Pepper - 1/8 tsp.
- Salt - 1/4 tsp.
- Red onion - 1 small
- Olive oil - 2 tbsp.

Method:

1. Pre-heat the air fryer at 375 degrees. Merge all of the ingredients in the large-sized bowl by tossing.

2. Assemble the vegetables on the greased air-fryer pot. Cook for 8 -10 minutes until become tender. Redistribute by tossing and cook for 8-10 minutes until they get browned.

69. Air Fried Radishes

Ingredients:

- Quartered Radishes - (about 6 cups)
- Fresh Oregano - 1 tbsp.
- Dried Oregano - 1 tbsp.
- Pepper - 1/8 tsp.
- Salt - 1/4 tsp.
- Olive Oil - 3 tbsp.

Method:

1. Set the temperature of an air fryer to 375 degrees. Mix the rest of the ingredients with radishes. In an air-fryer pot, put the radishes on greased dish.

2. Cook them for 12-15 minutes until they become crispy & tender with periodically stirring. Take out from the air fryer and serve the radishes in a clean dish.

70. Air Fried Catfish Nuggets

Ingredients

- Catfish fillets (1 inch) - 1 pound
- Seasoned fish fry coating - 3/4 cup
- Cooking oil - to spray

Method

1. Set the temperature of an air fryer to 200C.

2. Coat catfish pieces with seasoned coating mix by proper mixing from all sides.

3. Place nuggets evenly in an oiled air fryer pot. Spray both sides of nuggets with cooking oil. You can work in batches if the size of your air fryer is small.

4. Air fry nuggets for 5-8 minutes. Change sides of nuggets with the help of tongs and cook for more 5 minutes. Shift these delicious nuggets in a clean plate and serve immediately.

CONCLUSION:

This manual served you the easiest, quick, healthy and delicious foods that are made in an air fryer. It is also very necessary to cook food easily and timely without getting so much tired. We've discussed all the 70 easy, short, quick, delicious and healthy foods and dishes. These recipes can be made within few minutes. This manual provides the handiest or helpful cooking recipes for the busy people who are performing their routine tasks. Instead of ordering the costly or unhealthy food from hotels, you will be able to   make the easy, tasty and healthy dishes with minimum cost. By reading this the most informative handbook, you can learn, experience or make lots of recipes in an air with great taste because cooking food traditionally on the stove is quite difficult for the professional persons. With the help of an air fryer, you can make various dishes for a single person as well as the entire family timely and effortlessly. We conclude that this cook book will maintain your health and it would also be the source of enjoying dishes without doing great effort in less and budget.

Breville Smart Air Fryer Oven Cookbook

250+ Quick | Affordable | Mouth-watering Recipes

for Smart People on a Budget

By

Chef Ludovico L'Italiano

Table of Contents

Introduction..176

Chapter 1: Health Benefits of Air and Deeply Fried Meals............................180

1.1 Statistics of Deeply Fried Foods..180

1.2 Comparison of Deeply Fried and Air Fried Meals...181

Chapter 2: Breakfast & Main Dishes...182

1. Ninja Foodi Low-Carb Breakfast Casserole...182

2. Air Fryer Breakfast Sausage..183

3. Air Fryer Avocado Boats...184

4. Air Fryer Breakfast Stuffed Peppers...184

5. Air Fryer Breakfast Pockets...185

6. Air Fryer Bacon and Egg Breakfast Biscuit Bombs..186

7. Air Fryer Breakfast Potatoes..187

8. Breakfast Egg Rolls..187

9. Air Fryer Sausage Breakfast Casserole...188

10. Air Fryer Egg in Hole..190

11. Air Fryer Baked Egg Cups with Spinach & Cheese...191

12. Air Fryer French Toast Sticks..191

13. Air Fryer Apple Fritters...192

14. Air Fryer French Toast Sticks..193

15. Air Fryer Breakfast Toad-in-the-Hole Tarts..194

16. Air Fryer Churros...196

17. Air Fryer Hard Boiled Eggs...197

18. Air Fryer Omelette..197

19. Air Fryer McDonald's Copycat Egg McMuffin...198

20. Air Fryer Breakfast Pizza...198

21. Air Fryer Cherry and Cream Cheese Danish...199

22. Air-Fryer Southern Bacon, Egg, and Cheese Breakfast Sandwich.......................200

23. Air-Fried Breakfast Bombs...201

24. Air Fryer Breakfast Biscuit Bombs 201

25. Air Fryer Stuffed Breakfast Bombs with Eggs & Bacon 202

26. Air Fryer Breakfast Burritos 203

27. Air Fryer Breakfast Frittata 203

28. Air Fryer Crispy Bacon 204

29. Air Fryer Raspberry Muffins 204

30. Air Fryer Tofu 205

31. Air Fryer Brussel Sprouts 205

Air Fryer Main Dishes **207**

1. Parmesan Breaded Air Fryer Chicken Tenders 207

2. Air Fryer Garlic Mushrooms Steaks 207

3. Air Fryer Falafels 209

4. Air Fryer Pita Bread Pizza 210

5. Air Fryer Chicken Quesadilla 210

6. Crispy Golden Air Fryer Fish 212

7. Air Fryer Chicken Fried Rice 213

8. Air Fryer Steak Bites and Mushrooms 213

9. Juicy Air Fryer Pork Chops with Rub 215

10. Air Fryer Steak with Garlic Mushrooms 216

11. Low Carb Coconut Shrimp 216

12. Tandoori Fish Tikka 217

13. Bharwa Bhindi (Stuffed Okra) 218

14. Greek-Style Chicken Wings 219

15. Air Fryer Garlic Ranch Wings 220

16. Air Fryer Crispy Buffalo Chicken Hot Wings 220

17. Air Fryer Marinated Steak 221

18. Air Fryer Bacon and egg Bite Cups 222

19. Air Fryer Tender Juicy Smoked BBQ Ribs 223

20. Air Fryer Bacon and Cream Cheese Stuffed Jalapeno Poppers 224

21. Air Fryer Italian Herb Pork loin..224

22. Air Fryer Grilled Chicken Kebabs 225

23. Air Fryer Shrimp and Vegetables 226

24. Air Fryer Bratwurst and Vegetables 227

25. Air Fryer Turkey Legs 227

26. Air Fryer Roasted Edamame 228

27. Air Fryer Bulgogi Burgers 228

28. Air Fryer Carne Asada...229

29. Keto Steak Nuggets 230

30. Korean Short BBQ Ribs 231

31. Air Fryer Korean Hot Dogs 231

Chapter 3: Lunch..**233**

1. Air Fryer Sweet Chili Chicken Wings 233

2. Air Fryer Fish 234

3. Air Fryer Wonton Mozzarella Sticks 235

4. Air Fryer Steak 235

5. Air Fryer Caramelized Bananas...236

6. Air Fryer Sesame Chicken 237

7. Air Fryer Donuts 237

8. Bang Bang Chicken..238

9. Crispy Air Fryer Eggplant Parmesan 239

10. Air Fryer Shrimp Fajitas 240

11. Honey Glazed Air Fryer Salmon 241

12. Crispy Air Fryer Roasted Brussels Sprouts With Balsamic 241

13. Air Fryer Chicken Nuggets 242

14. Air Fryer Baked Apples..242

15. Air Fryer Fish Tacos...243

16. Air Fryer Dumplings 244

17. Air Fryer Pork Chops...245

18. Air Fryer Chicken Chimichangas..246

19. Simple Chicken Burrito Bowls 247

20. Chicken Soft Tacos 248

21. Ground Pork Tacos - Al Pastor Style 248

22. Air-Fryer Southern-Style Chicken 250

23. Air-Fryer Fish and Fries...251

24. Air-Fryer Ground Beef Wellington 252

25. Air-Fryer Ravioli 253

26. Popcorn Shrimp Tacos with Cabbage Slaw 254

27. Bacon-Wrapped Avocado Wedges 255

28. Air-Fryer Steak Fajitas...255

29. Air-Fryer Sweet and Sour Pork 256

30. Air-Fryer Taco Twists 257

31. Air-Fryer Potato Chips...258

32. Air-Fryer Greek Breadsticks...258

33. Air-Fryer Crumb-Topped Sole 259

34. Air-Fried Radishes 260

35. Air-Fryer Ham and Egg Pockets 260

36. Air-Fryer Eggplant Fries..261

37. Air-Fryer Turkey Croquettes...262

38. Garlic-Herb Fried Patty Pan Squash...262

Conclusion..**264**

Introduction

A convenient way to prepare tasty, nutritious meals is the Breville Air Fryer Cooker. The system uses powerful warm air to flow around and cook foods, instead of cooking in a hot and oil fat meal. Which makes it easier to be crispy on the surface of the food to ensure sure the inner layers are cooked thru. The Breville Air Fryer Oven helps us to cook several dishes and almost everything. The Breville Air Fryer Oven may be used for frying beef, seafood, herbs, berries, poultry, and a broad selection of desserts. All your meals, ranging from appetizers to main meals and desserts, can be packed. Homemade or even tasty desserts and cakes are even permitted in the Breville Air Fryer Oven. Benefits of the Breville Air Fryer Oven:- Cleaner, oil-free foods- By inner filters of air, it removes cooking odors- Allows cleaning simpler free of oil- Air Fryers can bake, barbecue, roast more choices- A better cooking process opposed to frying with exposed warm oil- seems to have the potential to put and quit than other versions and provides a digital time.

To cook and crisp food that people put in a basket within the unit, air fryers use rotating warm air and oil. People might want to suggest introducing the fryer to their kitchen equipment collection. It is a relatively modern appliance that helps make healthy versions of the fried foods you love, from French fries to chicken nuggets, and is common. "Robin Plotkin, a licensed dietitian and culinary nutritionist located in Dallas, says, "The appeal is that it is a modern way to be 'healthier.' "This is a pleasant new way to achieve the objectives they are seeking to attain without getting depressed, particularly for people adopting low-carb diets."

The air fryer operates and lies on the countertop like a conventional oven. To cook and crisp the food in the basket inside, it uses swirling hot air and some oil. Without adding some gasoline, you can do it, or you can put a bit, which Plotkin says usually enhances the taste. "If people don't consume the food, diet doesn't matter, because people just want the food to taste good, and that's where I'd suggest you need some oil to appreciate the meal," she says. Either way, lowering the amount of oil consumed can decrease fat and calorie consumption. Instead of cooking meat, the Cleveland Clinic reports that air frying can help you reduce your calorie consumption by 80 - 85%. Jane Pelcher, RDN, a Mountain View, California-based recipe creation and fitness writer, claims it is one of the finest kitchen appliances. "It's simple to use and in far less than halves the time that it takes in the oven, I can air-fried my rice," she says. According to the Cleveland Clinic, the consequence is food that is crispy on the outside and juicy on the ground. Keeping things safe is about the meals you produce. "It depends on what you placed in there, whether the air fryer is safe or not," Pelcher says. Quite certainly, frozen ready - to - cook fish sticks, chips, and wings is thoroughly fried in advance, but warming them high in an air fryer would not make them good. The nutritious way to go is to roast new tomatoes and broccoli, air fried raw proteins, and produce fries from scratch.

A better option to deep frying is the air fryer, although that does not render it the healthful form of cooking anywhere. The Cleveland Clinic warns that air frying can cause people to believe it's fine to eat fried food as often as they should. "If you consume this kind of meal over and over again, it would not be as good for you as you initially meant it to be," says Plotkin. "Eat it from time to time, play with it, prepare with that as well, and make it part of your toolbox for food."

Like those from brands such as Cuisinart, Philips, and NuWave, many air fryers are on the market. 6 They vary from around $60 to $360 in volume. For individuals living in tiny spaces with no oven or stove, such as college students living in dorms, Pelcher says they can be fantastic. The quantity of counter room you have is one factor you will want to remember since they come in multiple sizes. When picking the best air fryer, also remember life. e.g., a tiny one, whether you would like to support a family, maybe challenging, Plotkin says. According to the Cleveland Clinic, most people will cook around 2 - 3 lbs. at a time. Conclude, Plotkin claims that hers is quick and clear to scrub. Pelcher says there is typically a flexible basket bottom for the higher-end fryers that helps wash and extract food from each inch of the air fryer basket. Many lacking a flexible base are often more challenging to scrub, but the key should be to soak it for a prolonged amount of time in hot soapy water.

In recent years, air fryer is becoming a common addition to kitchen utensils and does not indicate slowing or stopping. Whether you still spotted one below Christmas tree, bought either from a sale on Cyber Monday, or treated yourself to your party, then you are in fortune. This air fryer can give you the capacity or cook tasty meals by producing a crispy coating with minimal or oil free meal. It will free up your place to a completely different era of recipes, and you will get a grasp of how to operate an air fryer. While you can believe that the air fryer is restricted to fried classics such as Fries or chicken nuggets, a broad range of dishes can be made. Whip up some freshly made mini apple pies, challenge your beloved Italian restaurant's eggplant Parmesan, or even replicate equal foods such as fried pickles.

If people want to make a crunchy meal, it is time for the air fryer to heat up and start cooking. In each group, we have combined up 5-6 of our favorite meals, so you have got a baseline to start your air frying adventure. These meals will expose to the strengths of the appliance, and you will soon be able to play with a large variety of air-fried foods.

With these unforgettable air fryer meals in the air fryer, launch the day off. These Breakfast Frittata or Scotch Eggs could hit the flavor if savory is what crave early in the morning. But if the taste is sweeter, stay with the Sugar Doughnuts or Simple French Toast Sticks. Many of these meals include components that can be cooked in the afternoon unless you are in a hurry around breakfast time.

When bad weather helps prevent from cooking outdoors, Steak is perfect. Both and Breaded Pork Chops and Crumbled Chicken are made in the oven quicker than frying. Plus, every time they fall out wet and delicate. If you want to surf more than turf, the famous seafood recipes are Coconut Shrimp and Salmon. Parmesan Eggplant is a guaranteed crowd-pleaser for a full vegetarian Air Fryer oven.

When cooking dinner, save the stovetop room by tossing a side meal into the air fryer. Ratatouille Italian-Style and Green Beans (spicy) both are recipes that, if overcooked, will quickly turn soggy, suggesting they are ideal for the air fryer. With this process, making Baked Potatoes guarantees a crispy, fluffy coating of skin, but every time, French fries do not have all the fun. If you are trying to make picky eater-friendly veggies, frying Roasted Cauliflower and Okra makes crunchy and tasty vegetables in the air fryer. Corn in the air fryer on the Cob offers it the perfect feel, although the grilled flavor can be added with a splashing of paprika.

If someone is preparing treats for a Movie evening or looking for appetizers or snacks to serve at a picnic, the latest take-to for finger foods would be the air fryer. French Fries are the main food that most people attempt in an air fryer, and with valid reason: with a little oil usually used; hence, get crunchy and golden fries. Cheese and Sausage Filled Chicken Wings or small Peppers are also sophisticated enough to function as hors d'oeuvres, but still low-key enough as to serve at your next tailgate. Because people are hoping to bend fast food cravings, it's sure to please cooking up a bowl of Onion Rings, Mozzarella Sticks, or Fried Pickles.

And sweets, when it happens to an air fryer, work out delicious. Take typically deep-fried meals such as Beignets, or Fried chocolate bars or Apple pies to get crispy outside and tender indoors for a turn in the air fryer. For a moister product, producing baked products, such as Butter and Banana Cake, Roasted bananas served with a splashing of cinnamon or confectioner's sugar is a perfect way to finish your meal if you want to serve a nutritious dessert.

Chapter 1: Health Benefits of Air and Deeply Fried Meals

Air frying is, on certain standards, easier than frying in grease. It decreases calories by 60 to 90% and has a ton of fat. This form of cooking may also minimize any of the other adverse consequences of oil processing when you fried potatoes or other starchy foods, the reaction that occurs creates the organic acrylamide, which literature ties to higher cancer risks. One research reveals that acrylamide volume in fried potatoes is decreased by 89 percent by air frying. Any air-frying stuff might not be good. Air frying of fish improved the quantity of a material labeled 'cholesterol oxidation products' (COPs) in one report. COPs develop as, during frying, the cholesterol in fish or meat breaks down. Studies relate these compounds to cardiovascular disease, cancer, artery hardening and other diseases.

The study reveals that one way to reduce the number of COPs when you air-fried fish is to incorporate chives, parsley, or a combination of the two. Analysis reveals that these herbs function in air-fried foods as antioxidants. It also suggests that air frying curbs the saturated omega-3 fats in trout. These "healthy fats" help reduce blood pressure and increase the amounts of "healthy" HDL cholesterol, protecting the core.

The batter consumes the oil that is used to prepare it when fried the rice. This makes fried foods on the outside their happy crunch while holding the inward soft. Frying often adds a deep, dark coloring to foods that are appealing to the eyes. You can get a crunch with air frying, but it doesn't produce the same look or sound of the mouth like oil frying. One research contrasting oil frying with air frying showed that the two approaches contributed to foods with varying textures and sensory properties, but with a similar color and moisture content.

1.1 Statistics of Deeply Fried Foods

Generally, deep-fried foods are rich in calories than foods cooked with other types of frying. For instance, about 30 percent more fat is contained in a chicken breast that has been frying than an equivalent amount of roasted chicken. Some manufacturers say that fried foods' saturated fat can be decreased by up to 75% using an air fryer. It is due to air fryers need considerably reduced fat than conventional deep fryers. Although many recipes need up to 3 cups of oil for deeply fried dishes, just around 1 tablespoon of air-fried food is required. This indicates that deep fryers require up to 49 times much more oil than air fryers, and although the product consumes not all of the oil, the total fat content of the meal will be decreased when utilizing an air fryer.

1.2 Comparison of Deeply Fried and Air Fried Meals

One research contrasted the properties of deeply fried & air-fried fries said that a finished product of considerably reduced fat but a higher color and water absorption rate resulted from air-frying. As a larger consumption of fatty acids from vegetable oils has also been linked with a higher risk of conditions such as heart failure and arthritis, this may have a direct influence on your wellbeing. Not only are deeply fried meals rich in calories, but they are often higher in fat, which causes weight gain. Dietary fat produces almost twice as much energy per serving as other essential nutrients such as carbohydrates and protein, weighing in at 8.9 calories throughout. Since air-fried meals are low in saturated fat than deeply fried items, it can be a convenient way to reduce calories and facilitate weight reduction by converting to an electric oven.

Frying meals may produce toxic compounds such as acrylamide and become rich in calories and fats. Acrylamide is a substance produced during higher heating and cooking procedures such as frying in carbohydrate-rich meals. Acrylamide is listed as a 'probable carcinogen,' as per the International Organization for Testing on Cancer, indicating that certain research suggests that acrylamide could be related to cancer growth. Rather than using a deep fryer, wind frying food can help reduce acrylamide content in fried foods. It's important to note, though, that other hazardous substances can also be produced during the air-frying process.

Chapter 2: Breakfast & Main Dishes

1. Ninja Foodi Low-Carb Breakfast Casserole

Ingredients

- ❖ Ground Sausage 1 LB
- ❖ Shredded Cheese 1/2 Cup
- ❖ Green Bell Pepper 1 Diced
- ❖ Eggs 8 Whole
- ❖ Diced White Onion 1/4 Cup
- ❖ Garlic Salt 1/2 Tsp
- ❖ Fennel Seed 1 Tsp

Steps

1. Add the pepper and onion and steam till the vegetables are soft and the sausage is fried, along with the ground sausage.

2. Spray it with non-stick cooking spray using the Air Fryer pan.

3. Position the bottom part with the ground sausage mixture.

4. Marinade equally with cheese.

5. Over the cheese and bacon, place the pounded eggs equally.

6. Similarly, sprinkle fennel seed and garlic salt to the chickens.

7. In the Ninja Foodi, put the rack in the low spot and put the pan on top.

8. Set at 390 degrees for 15 minutes on Air Crisp.

9. If you use an air fryer, put the dish directly in the air fryer's basket and cook at 390 degrees for 15 minutes.

10. Remove carefully and serve.

2. Air Fryer Breakfast Sausage

Ingredients

- ❖ Pork 1 lb.
- ❖ Fennel seeds 2 tsp
- ❖ Turkey 1 lb. ground
- ❖ Paprika 1 tsp
- ❖ Rubbed sage 2 tsp
- ❖ Sea salt 1 tsp
- ❖ Maple syrup 1 tbsp
- ❖ Dried thyme 1 tsp
- ❖ Garlic powder 2 tsp

Steps

1. Start by combining in a wide bowl the pork and turkey together. Mix the remaining ingredients in a shallow bowl: sage, fennel, ground garlic, paprika, thyme, and cinnamon. Add spices into the meat and keep combining until the spices are thoroughly added.

2. Spoon into balls and flatten into patties (about 2-3 tbsp of meat).

3. At 370 degrees, set the temperature and heat for 10 minutes. Remove and repeat for the leftover sausage from the air fryer.

3. Air Fryer Avocado Boats

Ingredients

- ❖ Avocados 2
- ❖ Plum tomatoes 2
- ❖ Lime juice 1 tbsp
- ❖ Red onion ¼ cup
- ❖ Black pepper ¼ tsp
- ❖ Jalapeno 1 tbsp
- ❖ Fresh sliced cilantro 2 tbsp
- ❖ Eggs 4 medium
- ❖ Salt ½ teaspoon

Steps

1. Squeeze the avocado pulp out from the skin with a spoon, leaving the shell intact. Dice the avocado and put it in a medium dish. Combine the peppers, onion, lime juice, cilantro, salt, and jalapeno, if needed. Cover and refrigerate the combination of avocado until fit for usage.
2. Heat the air fryer to 350 degrees Fahrenheit.
3. Put them on a foil ring to make sure the avocado shells wouldn't rock when frying. Simply wrap two 3-inch-wide strips of aluminum foil into rope shaped to build them, and form each into a 3-inch circle. In an air fryer bowl, put every avocado shell on a foil frame. Break 1 egg into each avocado shell and fried for 5 to 7 minutes or until the doneness is needed.
4. Remove from the basket; cover with salsa with avocado and eat.

4. Air Fryer Breakfast Stuffed Peppers

Ingredients

- ❖ Bell pepper 1
- ❖ Olive oil 1 tsp
- ❖ Salt 1 pinch
- ❖ Eggs 4

Steps

1. Lengthwise, split bell peppers in half and discard the seeds and base, keeping the sides as bowls intact.

2. Rub a little of olive oil only on the raw edges using your finger.

3. Crack 2 eggs into each half of the bell pepper. Sprinkle with the spices you desire.

4. Set them within your Ninja Foody on a trivet.

5. Close the cover (the one attached to your Ninja Foody machine) on the air fryer.

6. Switch on the computer, click the air crisper button for 13 minutes at 390 degrees.

7. Add the bell pepper and less brown egg on the exterior, add just one egg to the pepper and set the air fryer for 15 minutes to 330 degrees. (for consistency over hard eggs)

5. Air Fryer Breakfast Pockets

Ingredients

- ❖ Pastry sheets 1 box
- ❖ Sausage crumbles ½ cup
- ❖ Cheddar cheese ½ cup
- ❖ Bacon ½ cup
- ❖ Eggs 5

Steps

1. Eggs should be cooked like regular scrambled eggs. If needed, add meat to the egg mixture as you cook.
2. On a cutting board, lay out puff pastry sheets and slice out rectangles with a cookie blade, make sure they are all standardized enough to come together well.
3. On half of the pastry rectangles, Spoon chose a mixture of beef, milk, and cheese.
4. Cover the mixture with a pastry rectangle and press the sides together with a fork to cover.
5. Put breakfast pockets in an air-fryer basket and cook at 370 degrees for 8-10 minutes.
6. Monitor closely and test for ideal every 2-3 minutes.

6. Air Fryer Bacon and Egg Breakfast Biscuit Bombs

Ingredients

- ❖ Eggs 2
- ❖ Biscuit bombs
- ❖ Bacon 4 pieces
- ❖ Butter 1 tablespoon
- ❖ Pillsbury 1 can
- ❖ Pepper 1 teaspoon
- ❖ Egg 1
- ❖ Water 1 tablespoon
- ❖ Cheddar cheese 2 oz

Steps

1. Break the cooking parchment paper into two 8-inch rounds. Set one round at the bottom of the basket of the air fryer. Spray with spray for frying.

2. Cook the bacon over medium-high heat in a 10-inch nonstick skillet until crisp. Put on a paper towel, extract from the sauce. Wipe the pan gently with a paper towel. To the skillet, add butter; melt over medium heat. Add 2 pounded eggs and pepper to the skillet; boil until the eggs are thickened, stirring regularly, yet still moist. Remove from the heat; add bacon and swirl. Cool for five minutes.

3. Meanwhile, divide the dough into five biscuits; divide each biscuit into two layers. Push into a 4-inch round each. Spoon 1 into the middle of each circular heaping tablespoonful of the egg mixture. Cover it with one of the cheese bits. Fold the sides

carefully up and over the filling, press to seal. Beat most of the egg and water in a shallow cup. Rub the biscuits with egg wash on both ends.

4. Put 5 of the biscuit bombs on the parchment in the air fryer bowl, seam side down. With cooking water, water all sides of the second round of parchment. Cover the second parchment round biscuit bombs in the bowl, then cover it with the leftover 5 biscuit bombs.

5. Set to 325 degrees F; cook for 8 minutes. Remove the circular parchment; use tongs to carefully transform the biscuits and position them in a single layer in the basket. Cook 5 minutes longer or (at least 165 ° F) before cooked through.

7. Air Fryer Breakfast Potatoes

Ingredients

- ❖ Potatoes 1 1/2 pounds
- ❖ Onion ¼ sliced
- ❖ Garlic cloves 2
- ❖ Green bell pepper 1
- ❖ Olive oil 1 Tablespoon
- ❖ Paprika 1/2 teaspoon
- ❖ Pepper 1/4 teaspoon
- ❖ Salt 1/2 teaspoon

Steps

1. Clean the potatoes and bell pepper.

2. Dice the potatoes and boil them for 30 minutes in water. Pat dry after 30 minutes.

3. Chop the mushrooms, cabbage, and bell pepper. Garlic is minced.

4. In a bowl, put all the ingredients and combine them. Put it into an air-fryer.

5. Cook in an air fryer for 10 minutes at 390-400 degrees. Move the bowl and cook for another 10 minutes, then lift the bowl again and cook for another 5 minutes, for a total of 25 minutes.

6. Only serve.

8. Breakfast Egg Rolls

Ingredients

- ❖ Salt and pepper
- ❖ Milk 2 T
- ❖ Eggs 2
- ❖ Cheddar cheese ½ cup
- ❖ Olive oil 1 tablespoon
- ❖ Egg rolls 6
- ❖ Sausage patties 2
- ❖ Water

Steps

1. Cook the sausage in a small skillet or replace it according to the packet. Remove and cut into bite-sized bits from the skillet.
2. Combine the chickens, sugar, and a touch of salt and pepper. Over medium / low flame adds a teaspoon of oil or a little butter to a plate. Pour in the egg mixture and fry, stirring regularly to render scrambled eggs for a few minutes. Stir the sausage in. Only put back.
3. Put the egg roll wrapper on a working surface to create a diamond formation with points. Position roughly 1 T of the cheese on the bottom third of the wrapper. Comb with a blend of chickens.
4. Water the finger or pastry brush and rub all the egg roll wrapper's sides, allowing it to close.
5. Fold the egg roll up and over the filling at the bottom stage, attempting to keep it as close as you can. Then, fold the sides together to make an envelope-looking form. Last, tie the whole wrapping around the top. Put the seam side down and begin the remaining rolls to assemble.
6. Heat the fryer for 5 minutes to 400 F.
7. Rub rolls with grease or spray them. Placed the hot oven bowl in place. Set for 8 minutes to 400 F.
8. Flip over the egg rolls after 5 minutes. For a further 3 minutes, return the egg rolls to the air fryer.

9. Air Fryer Sausage Breakfast Casserole

Ingredients

- ❖ Onion ¼ cup
- ❖ Red Bell pepper 1
- ❖ Green Bell pepper 1

- ❖ Breakfast sausage 1 lb.
- ❖ Hash Browns 1 lb.
- ❖ Eggs 4
- ❖ Yellow Bell pepper 1

Steps

1. Foil fills the air fryer's basket.
2. Cover the uncooked sausage with it.
3. Put the peppers and onions uniformly on top.
4. Cook for 10 minutes at 355 *.
5. Open an air fryer and, if necessary, blend the casserole a little.
6. In a bowl, crack every egg, then pour it right in the middle of the casserole.
7. Cook for another 10 minutes on 355 *.
8. To try, mix with salt and pepper.

10. Air Fryer Egg in Hole

Ingredients

- ❖ Egg 1
- ❖ Salt and pepper
- ❖ Toast piece 1

Steps

1. Spray the safe pan of the air fryer with nonstick oil spray.

2. Put a slice of bread in a healthy pan inside the air fryer.

3. Create a spot, then slice the bread with a cup.

4. Into the hole, crack the egg.

5. Fry for 6 minutes at 330 degrees, then use a large spoon and rotate the egg and fry for another 4 minutes.

11. Air Fryer Baked Egg Cups with Spinach & Cheese

Ingredients

- ❖ Milk 1 tablespoon
- ❖ Cheese 1-2 teaspoons
- ❖ Egg 1 large
- ❖ Frozen spinach 1 tablespoon
- ❖ Cooking spray
- ❖ Salt and black pepper

Steps

1. Spray with oil spray inside the silicone muffin cups.

2. In a muffin cup, incorporate the cream, potato, spinach, and cheese.

3. Gently combine the egg whites with the liquids without separating the yolk and salt and pepper to taste.

4. For around 6-12 minutes, Air Fried at 330 ° F (single egg cups typically take about 5 minutes-several or doubled cups require as many as 12.

5. It may take a bit longer to cook in a ceramic ramekin. Cook for less time if you like runny yolks. After 5 minutes, regularly check the eggs to make sure the egg is of your desired texture.

12. Air Fryer French Toast Sticks

Ingredients

- ❖ Butter 2 tablespoon
- ❖ Salt 1 pinch
- ❖ Eggs 2
- ❖ Bread pieces 4
- ❖ Cinnamon 1 pinch
- ❖ Ground cloves 1 pinch
- ❖ Nutmeg 1 pinch
- ❖ Icing sugar 1 teaspoon

Steps

1. Heat the air fryer at 180 degrees centigrade.

2. Two eggs, a sprinkle of salt, a few hard-cinnamon shakes, and tiny pinches of both nutmeg and ground cloves are softly pounded together in a cup.

3. Butter all sides of the pieces of bread and break them into segments.

4. In the egg mixture, dredge-strip and place it in an air fryer.

5. After 2 minutes of frying, stop the air fryer, remove the pan, make sure you put the pan on a heat-safe surface and sprinkle the bread with cooking spray.

6. Flip and spray the second side till you have adequately sprayed the strips, as well.

7. Return the pan to the fryer and cook for another 4 minutes, testing after a few minutes to ensure that they are uniformly fried and not burnt.

8. Remove from the air fryer until the egg is fried, and the bread is golden brown and eat immediately.

9. Sprinkle with icing sugar for garnishing and serving, finish with ice cream, drizzle with maple syrup, or represent a little dipping cup of syrup.

13. Air Fryer Apple Fritters

Ingredients

- ❖ Cooking spray
- ❖ Flour 1-1/2 cups

❖ Sugar 1/4 cup

❖ Baking powder 2 teaspoons

❖ Cinnamon 1-1/2 teaspoons

❖ Salt 1/2 teaspoon

❖ 2% Milk 2/3 cup

❖ Eggs 2 large

❖ 1 tablespoon lemon juice

❖ Honey Crisp apples 2 medium sliced

❖ Butter 1/4 cup

❖ Confectioners' sugar 1 cup

❖ 2% Milk 1 tablespoon

❖ Vanilla extract 1-1/2 teaspoons

Steps

1. Heat an air-fryer at 410 degrees.

2. Integrate the sugar, starch, baking powder, salt, and cinnamon in a wide dish. Transfer the milk, eggs, lemon juice and 1 teaspoon of vanilla extract leftover; whisk until it is moistened. Fold the apples in.

3. Drop 1/4 cup 2-in dough into batches. Detached from the air-fryer bowl. Spritz with spray for frying. Cook for 5-6 minutes till it is lightly browned. Switch the fritters over; proceed to fried for 1-2 minutes till lightly browned.

4. Melt butter over medium-high heat in a shallow saucepan. Cook gently for 5 minutes, before the butter and foam begins to tan. Remove from heat; mildly cold. Add browned butter with confectioner's sugar, milk and 1/2 teaspoon vanilla extract: whisk until smooth. Drizzle before serving over the fritters.

14. Air Fryer French Toast Sticks

Ingredients

❖ Bread pieces 4

❖ Eggs 2

❖ Salt and cinnamon 1 pinch

❖ Nutmeg 1 pinch

❖ Icing sugar 1 teaspoon

❖ Butter 2 tablespoon

Steps

1. Heat the air fryer at 180 degrees centigrade.

2. Two eggs, a sprinkle of salt, a few hard-cinnamon shakes, and tiny pinches of both nutmeg and ground cloves are softly pounded together in a cup.

3. Butter all sides of the pieces of bread and break them into segments.

4. In the egg mixture, dredge-strip and place it in an air fryer.

5. After 2 minutes of frying, stop the Air Fryer, remove the oil, make sure you put the oil on a heat-safe surface and sprinkle the bread with cooking spray.

6. Flip and spray the second side till you have adequately sprayed the strips, as well.

7. Return the pan to the fryer and cook for another 4 minutes, testing after a few minutes to ensure that they are uniformly fried and not burnt.

8. Take from the Air Fryer till the egg is fried, and the bread is lightly browned and eat immediately.

9. Sprinkle with icing sugar for garnishing and serving, finish with ice cream, drizzle with maple syrup, or represent a little dipping cup of syrup.

15. Air Fryer Breakfast Toad-in-the-Hole Tarts

Ingredients

❖ Frozen puff pastry 1 sheet
❖ Sliced cooked ham 4 tablespoons
❖ Cheddar cheese 4 tablespoons
❖ Sliced fresh chives 1 tablespoon
❖ Large Eggs 4

Steps

1. Heat up to 400 degrees F for the air fryer.
2. On a flat surface, spread the pastry sheet and break it into 4 squares.
3. In the air-fryer bowl, put 2 pastry squares and cook for 6 to 8 minutes.
4. Remove the air fryer from the bowl. To form an oval shape, use a metal tablespoon to press every square gently. In each hole, put 1 tbsp of Cheddar cheese and 1 tbsp of ham and pour 1 egg on top.

5. Move the basket back to the air fryer. Cook until necessary, around 6 more minutes. Take the tart out of the basket and let it cool for 5 minutes. With the leftover squares of pastry, cheese, ham, and eggs, repeat.
6. Tarts with chives to garnish.

16. Air Fryer Churros

Ingredients

- ❖ Butter ¼ cup
- ❖ Salt 1 pinch
- ❖ Milk ½ cup
- ❖ Eggs 2 large
- ❖ Flour ½ cup
- ❖ Ground cinnamon ½ teaspoon
- ❖ White sugar ¼ cup

Steps

1. Melt butter on medium-high heat in a saucepan. Sprinkle with milk and apply salt. Lower the flame to low and carry it to a boil, stirring vigorously with a wooden spoon. Add flour easily all at a time. Keep stirring until it fits along with the pastry.
2. Turn off the heat and leave for 5 to 7 minutes to cool down. Mix the wooden spoon with the eggs before the pastry is blended. Spoon the dough into a pastry bag with a big star tip attached. Pipe the dough into strips directly into the basket of the air fryer.

3. Air fried the churros for 5 minutes at 340 degrees F.
4. Meanwhile, in a small bowl, combine the sugar and cinnamon and pour over a shallow plate.
5. Take the fried churros from the air fryer and roll them in the mixture of cinnamon-sugar.

17. Air Fryer Hard Boiled Eggs

Ingredients

❖ Eggs 4

Steps

1. To 250F / 120C, heat the air fryer.

2. In the air fryer bowl, put the wire rack and position the eggs on top.

3. For 16 minutes, cook.

4. To interrupt the frying method, extract the air fryer's eggs and quickly immerse them in ice water.

5. Peel and serve until cooled.

18. Air Fryer Omelette

Ingredients

❖ Salt 1 pinch

❖ Milk ¼ cup

❖ Eggs 2

❖ Shredded cheese ¼ cup

❖ Breakfast seasoning Garden herb 1 teaspoon

❖ Fresh meat and veggies

Steps

1. Mix the eggs and milk in a shallow bowl until well mixed.

2. Add the egg mixture with a sprinkle of salt.

3. Apply the egg mixture to vegetables.

4. Pour a well-greased 6"x3" pan into the egg mixture.

5. Place the pan in the air fryer's basket.

6. Cook for 8-10 minutes at 350 ° Fahrenheit.

7. Sprinkle the breakfast seasoning on the eggs and sprinkle the cheese over the surface midway during preparation.

8. Soften the omelet from the pan's sides with a thin spatula and pass it to a tray.

19. Air Fryer McDonald's Copycat Egg McMuffin

Ingredients

❖ Eggs 2

❖ Muffins 2

❖ Bacon 2 slices

❖ Cheese 2 slices

Steps

1. Heat the air fryer at 400 degrees.

2. Put foil on the rack.

3. Sprinkle the cooking oil spray.

4. Break one egg in every jar cover.

5. Put bacon on the rack.

6. Heat up to 5 mins and rotate the bacon.

7. Cook further for another 5 mins.

8. Take off the eggs.

9. Put sliced muffin in the air fryer and bake for 5 mins till light brown.

10. Place a piece of cheese on the muffin, bacon, and egg.

20. Air Fryer Breakfast Pizza

Ingredients

❖ Crescent Dough

❖ Eggs 3 scrambled

❖ Crumbled sausage

❖ Pepper 1/2 minced

❖ Cheddar cheese 1/2 cup

❖ Mozzarella cheese 1/2 cup

Steps

1. Sprinkle oil on the pan.

2. Spread out the dough in the lower layer of a pan.

3. Put the air fryer for 5 mins at 350 degrees till the upper layer is lightly browned.

4. Take off the air fryer.

5. Cover it with sausage, cheese, peppers, and eggs.

6. Put air fryer for extra 5-10 mins.

21. Air Fryer Cherry and Cream Cheese Danish

Ingredients

❖ Icing
❖ Pillsbury Crescent Rolls Dough
❖ Cream Cheese 8 oz
❖ Cherry Pie Filling 16 oz

Steps

1. Heat the air fryer at 350 degrees.

2. Wrapped out the crescent dough.

3. Wrap the very upper layer for one time. Packed the edges to make a circle and fill every roll with cream cheese.

4. Put an air fryer on a rack.

5. Heat up to 390 degrees for 10 mins.

6. The upper layer will become lightly browned.

7. Put foil on the top of the tray and heat again for extra 10 mins.

8. Take it off and drizzle with icing.

22. Air-Fryer Southern Bacon, Egg, and Cheese Breakfast Sandwich

Ingredients

- ❖ Bread slices 2
- ❖ Eggs 2
- ❖ Bacon 3 to 4 pieces
- ❖ Mayonnaise 1 tablespoon
- ❖ Butter ½-1 tablespoon

Steps

1. At high temperatures, put 3 to 4 slices of bacon in an air-fryer, around 375-390 degrees.

2. Cook the bacon for around 3 minutes or set aside for your preferred crispiness.

3. Set aside with a medium-hot skillet, butter, and a slightly toasted slice of bread.

4. Fry two eggs in a skillet and form the sandwich bread to order.

5. To cook on both sides, flip the egg halfway.

6. Put one slice of cheese on top before moving the fried egg to the toasted crust.

7. Next, on top of a scrambled egg with cheese, incorporate air-fried, crispy bacon.

8. To complete the sandwich, put the other slice of cheese on top of the bacon, then position the other slice of toasted bread.

9. Finally, for around one to two minutes, place the breakfast sandwich in the air-fryer to toast your sandwich and make it good, sweet, and crispy.

10. Take from the freezer.

23. Air-Fried Breakfast Bombs

Ingredients

- ❖ Bacon slices 3
- ❖ Eggs 3 large
- ❖ Fresh chives 1 tablespoon
- ❖ Cream cheese 1 ounce
- ❖ Cooking oil spray
- ❖ Wheat pizza dough 4 ounces

Steps

1. Cook the bacon in a small skillet for around 10 minutes, mild to crisp. Bring the bacon out of the pan, crumble. Add the eggs to the bacon drippings in the pan; cook, constantly stirring, around 1 minute, until almost firm but still loose. Put the eggs in a bowl; add the cream cheese, the chives, and the crumbled bacon.

2. Cut the dough into four identical pieces. Wrap each piece into a 5-inch circle on a lightly floured. Place a quarter of the egg mixture in the center of each circle of dough. Clean the dough's outer edge with water; tie the dough around the egg mixture to shape a purse and pinch the seams along with the dough.

3. Put dough purses in air fryer baskets in a single layer, cover with cooking spray. Cook for 5 to 6 minutes at 350 ° F until golden brown, checking after 5 minutes.

24. Air Fryer Breakfast Biscuit Bombs

Ingredients

- ❖ Vegetable oil 1 tablespoon
- ❖ Bulk breakfast sausage 1 / 4lb
- ❖ Eggs 2
- ❖ Salt 1 / 8 teaspoon
- ❖ Pepper 1 / 8 teaspoon

- ❖ Biscuits bomb
- ❖ Pillsbury 1 can
- ❖ Cheddar cheese 2 oz
- ❖ Egg wash and water 1 tablespoon

Steps

1. Break the cooking parchment paper into two 8-inch rounds. Set one round at the bottom of the basket of the air fryer.

2. Heat oil over medium to high heat in a 10-inch nonstick skillet. Cook the sausage in oil for 2 to 5 minutes, frequently stirring to crumble, till it is no longer pink; transfer to a medium bowl with a slotted spoon. Decrease the heat to medium. To skillet drippings, add pounded eggs, salt, and pepper; cook until eggs are thickened, but still moist, stirring regularly. Stir the eggs in the cup onto the sausage. Cool for five minutes.

3. Meanwhile, divide the dough into five biscuits; divide each biscuit into two layers. Push into a 4-inch round each. Spoon 1 into the middle of each circular heaping tablespoonful of the egg mixture. Cover it with one of the cheese bits. Fold the sides carefully up and over the filling, press to seal. Beat most of the egg and water in a shallow cup. Rub the biscuits with egg wash on both ends.

4. Put 5 of the biscuit bombs on the parchment in the air fryer bowl, seam side down. With cooking water, water all sides of the second round of parchment. Cover the second parchment round biscuit bombs in the bowl, then cover it with the leftover 5 biscuit bombs.

5. Set to 325 degrees F; cook for 8 minutes. Remove the circular parchment; use tongs to carefully transform the biscuits and position them in a single layer in the basket. Heat again 4 to 6 minutes longer or (at least 165 ° F) before cooked through.

25. Air Fryer Stuffed Breakfast Bombs with Eggs & Bacon

Ingredients

- ❖ Bacon ½ cup
- ❖ Eggs 1 cup
- ❖ Cheddar cheese ½ cup
- ❖ Salt and pepper
- ❖ Freeze biscuits 1 package

Steps

1. Merge the fried eggs, baked bacon, and melted Cheddar cheese in a little bowl.

2. Add a few teaspoons of combination to the biscuit and put it in the middle of it.

3. Just use and cover another biscuit or surround the biscuit on itself and cover the corners by pushing tightly. Put on the air fryer bowl.

4. Adjust the temperature to an air fryer level of 320 degrees F for 5 minutes.

5. Table, eat and enjoy.

26. Air Fryer Breakfast Burritos

Ingredients

- ❖ Ground sausage ½ lb.
- ❖ Bacon bits 1/3 cup
- ❖ Bell pepper ½
- ❖ Shredded cheese ½ cup
- ❖ Spraying oil
- ❖ Flour tortillas 6 medium
- ❖ Eggs 6

Steps

1. In a large bowl, mix the fried sausage, scrambled eggs, cheese, bell pepper, bacon bits. Stir to blend.

2. Spoon about half a cup of the combination into the flour tortilla core.

3. Fold the ends, and then move.

4. With the remaining ingredients, repeat.

5. Put filled burritos in the basket of the air fryer & liberally spray with oil.

6. Cook for 5 minutes at 330 degrees.

27. Air Fryer Breakfast Frittata

Ingredients

- ❖ Cheddar cheese ½ cup
- ❖ Breakfast sausage ¼ pound
- ❖ Eggs 4 large
- ❖ Red Bell pepper 2 tablespoon
- ❖ Green onion 1

- ❖ Cayenne pepper 1 pinch
- ❖ Cooking spray

Steps

1. Mix all the ingredients in a bowl.
2. Heat the air fryer at 360 degrees.
3. Put the mixture in already ready cake pan.
4. Cook till frittata is adjusted for 19-20 mins.

28. Air Fryer Crispy Bacon

Ingredients

- ❖ Thick one bacon ¾ lb.

Steps

1. Put bacon within the air fryer in the form of a thin layer.
2. Heat the air fryer to 400 degrees and cook for 8-10 mins till become crispy in taste.

29. Air Fryer Raspberry Muffins

Ingredients

- ❖ Baking powder 1 teaspoon
- ❖ Flour 1 cup
- ❖ Orange zest ½ teaspoon
- ❖ Sugar 1/3 cup
- ❖ Milk 1/3 cup
- ❖ Egg 1
- ❖ Vegetable oil 2.5 tablespoons
- ❖ Salt 1/8 teaspoon
- ❖ Vanilla essence ½ teaspoon
- ❖ Raw vanilla sugar ½ tablespoon
- ❖ Raspberries ½ cup

Steps

1. Put a muffin paper inside the muffin tray.
2. Blend baking powder, salt, and flour in a bowl.
3. In another bowl, blend sugar, egg, vanilla, and milk properly until mix.
4. Add the wet ingredients into dry ones and softly cover them in raspberries.
5. Split the muffin batter having surface covering of vanilla sugar into muffin cups.
6. Put them in an air fryer and bake them for 15 mins till muffins come out. Keep them aside to cool down properly.

30. Air Fryer Tofu

© Cindy Gordon VegetarianMamma

Ingredients

- ❖ Soy sauce 2 tablespoons
- ❖ Black firm tofu 453 g
- ❖ Olive oil 1 tablespoon
- ❖ Sesame oil 1 tablespoon
- ❖ Garlic 1 clove

Steps

1. Push the tofu for at least 14 mins, using either a hard pan or placing it on top, enabling the moisture to drain away. When done, bite-sized chunks of tofu are cut and moved to a dish.
2. In a tiny cup, combine all the leftover ingredients. Drizzle and throw over the tofu to coat. Let the tofu marinate for 15 more minutes.
3. Heat the air-fryer to 190-degree C. In a single layer, apply tofu blocks to the Air Fryer bowl. Cook for 15 minutes, frequently shaking the pan to facilitate frying. Before transferring a rack to them, let the muffins cool a bit in the baking pan to cool completely.

31. Air Fryer Brussel Sprouts

Ingredients

- ❖ Brussel sprouts 1 pound

- ❖ Olive oil 1 tablespoon
- ❖ Shallot 1 medium
- ❖ Salt ½ teaspoon
- ❖ Unsalted butter 2 tablespoons
- ❖ Red wine vinegar 1 teaspoon

Steps

1. Heat an air fryer at 375ºF. Meanwhile, cut 1 pound of sprouts from Brussels and halve any sprouts longer than an inch across. Apply 1 tablespoon of olive oil and 1/2 teaspoon of kosher salt to a medium bowl and blend.
2. To the air fryer, add the Brussels sprouts and shake them into one single plate. Air fry, stopping to move the bowl around midway through, for a total of 15 minutes. Begin preparing the shallot butter, meanwhile.
3. Chop 1 medium shallot finely. In a medium microwave-safe dish, put 2 tablespoons of unsalted butter and heat it in the microwave. Add the shallots and 1 tsp vinegar of red wine and mix to incorporate.
4. When the Brussels sprouts are set, move the shallot butter into the bowl or saucepan and toss to mix. Immediately serve.

Air Fryer Main Dishes

1. Parmesan Breaded Air Fryer Chicken Tenders

Ingredients

- ❖ Chicken tenders 8
- ❖ Egg 1
- ❖ Water 2 tablespoon
- ❖ Canola cooking spray

For Dredge coating

- ❖ Panko breadcrumbs 1 cup
- ❖ Salt ½ tsp
- ❖ Black pepper ¼ tsp
- ❖ Garlic powder 1 tsp
- ❖ Onion powder ½
- ❖ Parmesan ¼ cup

Steps

1. In a shallow bowl or baking pan wide enough to accommodate the chicken bits, mix the dredge-coating ingredients.
2. Put the egg and water in a second shallow bowl or baking pan and whisk to mix.
3. Dip the chicken tenders in the egg wash and then into the combination of the panko dredge.
4. In the fry basket, bring the breaded tenders in it.
5. Over the panko, spray a light coat of canola oil.
6. Fix the temperature and fry for 12 minutes at 400 degrees. Half through the cooking time, check the chicken and switch the chicken off to brown the other side.

2. Air Fryer Garlic Mushrooms Steaks

Ingredients

- ❖ Mushrooms, washed and dried, 8 oz.
- ❖ Olive oil 2 tablespoons

- ❖ Garlic powder ½ teaspoon
- ❖ Soy sauce 1 teaspoon
- ❖ Salt and pepper according to taste
- ❖ Sliced parsley 1 tablespoon

Steps

1. Slice out the mushrooms in half and add to a bowl and mix with garlic powder, oil, pepper, salt, and soy sauce.

2. Heat the air fryer at 380-degree F for 12 mins and move it midway thoroughly.

3. Sprinkle lemon and cover it with sliced parsley.

3. Air Fryer Falafels

Ingredients

- ❖ Chickpeas 2 cans
- ❖ Fresh parsley ¼ cup
- ❖ Cilantro ¼ cup
- ❖ Garlic 2 cloves
- ❖ Shallot 1 large
- ❖ Flour 3 tablespoons
- ❖ Ground cumin 2 teaspoons
- ❖ Paprika 1 teaspoon
- ❖ Lemon juice ½
- ❖ Salt 1 teaspoon
- ❖ Olive oil spray

Steps

1. Add the shallot, chickpeas, parsley, garlic, cilantro, sesame seeds, rice, paprika, salt, lemon, and cumin to a food processor bowl.

2. Form the falafel mixture, around 1-inch in diameter, into tablespoon-sized discs. Repeat this before enough of the falafel combination is used. Get 25 to 30 discs of falafel.

3. Spray the basket with non-adhesive olive oil for your air fryer. Add as many falafel discs to the basket as you can without hitting them and gently brush them with olive oil. Air fried the falafel for 8 minutes at 350 ° F. Flip and fried the second side for an extra 6 minutes.

4. Repeat before you have all the falafel fried.

5. Serve falafel in a warm pita. Serve with some toppings you want and tahini yogurt sauce.

4. Air Fryer Pita Bread Pizza

Ingredients

- ❖ Pita bread 1
- ❖ Olive oil 1 tsp
- ❖ Tomato sauce 1 ½ tsp
- ❖ Shredded mozzarella cheese ¼ cup

Steps

1. Sprinkle the air fryer bowl within from cooking oil spray.

2. Place the pita in the air fryer bowl.

3. Rub the pita with olive oil.

4. Spread out the tomato sauce on the pita.

5. Spray the pita with shredded cheese.

6. Heat the pita pizza in the air fryer at 400-degree F for 5 mins.

5. Air Fryer Chicken Quesadilla

Ingredients

- ❖ Soft taco shells
- ❖ Chicken fajita strips
- ❖ Green pepper sliced ½ cup
- ❖ Shredded Mexican cheese
- ❖ Sliced onion ½ cup

Steps

1. For around 3 minutes, heat the Air Fryer to 370 degrees.

2. Lightly coat the plate with vegetable oil, and in the bowl, position 1 soft taco shell.

3. Put on the shell with shredded cheese.

4. Layout the strips of fajita chicken until they are in a continuous layer.

5. On top of your chicken, place your onions and green peppers on top.

6. Apply more cheese that is shredded.

7. Put on the top of another soft taco shell and gently spray with vegetable oil.

8. Set a four-minute timer.

9. Flip the broad spatula over cautiously.

10. Lightly spray with vegetable oil and set the rack on top of the shell to support it in line.

11. Set a four-minute timer.

12. Leave in for a few more minutes if it's not crispy enough for you.

13. Remove and break into 4 or 6 slices, respectively.

14. If needed, serve with salsa and sour cream.

6. Crispy Golden Air Fryer Fish

Ingredients

- ❖ Salt and black pepper
- ❖ Flour ½ cup
- ❖ Catfish 4 strips around 1 lb.
- ❖ Egg 1 large
- ❖ Old Bay seasoning 1 tsp.
- ❖ Panko breadcrumbs 2 cup
- ❖ Lemon wedges and Tartar sauce

Steps

1. Heat an air fryer at 400-degree F.
2. Mix the first 5 ingredients and add them to a Ziploc bag.
3. Wash the catfish, pat it off, and add the Ziploc bag to the fillets.
4. Enclose the bag, and then shake until it is thoroughly coated with the fillets.

5. Insert the coated fillets into the basket of the air fryer.

6. Spray the low-calorie spray on the fish fillets, cover the air fryer and cook for 9-10 mins.

7. Switch over the fillets of air fryer fish and continue to cook 3-4 mins, or until finished.

8. Serve the fillets of air fryer fish with a small salad.

7. Air Fryer Chicken Fried Rice

Ingredients

❖ Cold cooked white rice 3 cups

❖ Frozen peas and carrots 1 cup

❖ Soy sauce 6 tablespoons

❖ Vegetable oil 1 tablespoon

❖ Packed cup chicken 1

❖ Onion ½ cup

Steps

1. Put in the mixing bowl with the cold cooked white rice.

2. Add the soy sauce and vegetable oil, then mix well.

3. Add the onion and the diced ham, the frozen peas & carrots and blend completely.

4. In the nonstick plate, dump the rice mixture into it.

5. Place the Air Fryer in the bowl.

6. With a cooking period of 20 minutes, set the Air Fryer to 360-degree F.

7. Take off the pan from the Air Fryer as soon as the timer goes off.

8. Serve with your meat of preference, or just take a bowl and enjoy it.

8. Air Fryer Steak Bites and Mushrooms

Ingredients

❖ Sirloin fillet 1 pound

❖ Olive oil 1 tablespoon

❖ Montreal seasoning 1 tablespoon

❖ Mushrooms 8 ounces

❖ Blue cheese sauce

Steps

1. Heat the empty air fryer at 390 ° F for 3 minutes with the crisper plate.

2. Toss the beef cubes with the olive oil and Montreal seasoning when the air fryer is heating up.

3. Chop halves or thirds of the mushrooms.

4. In the hot oven air fryer, pour the beef cubes and mushrooms and gently shake to combine.

5. Set the temperature of the air fryer to 390 ° F and set the timer for 7 minutes.

6. Pause and shake the basket after 3 minutes. Do this again at intervals of 2 minutes until the beef cubes achieve the desired doneness. Dependent on the thickness of the cubes, the period can differ by machine. Lift a large piece out and test it to see the progress with a meat thermometer. Once it is removed from the air fryer, note that the meat will continue to cook. The meat is medium and has a warm pink center at 145 ° F.

7. Allow the meat a few minutes before serving to rest and then enjoy it.

9. Juicy Air Fryer Pork Chops with Rub

Ingredients

- ❖ Boneless pork chops 2-4
- ❖ Pork rub 2 tablespoon
- ❖ Olive oil 1 tablespoon

Steps

1. Rub both sides of the pork chops with olive oil.

2. Spread seasoning on all sides of the pork chops with pork rub. To get the seasoning to adhere, it works best to push the rub softly into the pork chops.

3. To help make clean-up easier, spray the aluminum air fryer basket with cooking spray.

4. Insert 2-4 boneless pork chops into the basket of the air fryer.

5. Set the temperature setting to 400-degree F with a total cooking time of 12 minutes.

6. Cook the pork chops for 7 minutes on one side of the air fryer.

7. Flip them over and cook for another 5 minutes, or until the internal temperature hits 145-degree F.

8. If you are frying 4 pork chops in an air fryer, make sure to turn and ROTATE the pan to maintain an even cooking period. In other words, the pork chops that were in the front for the first 7 minutes, turn them and position them in the back of the pan for when they are finished frying.

9. Before serving, rest for 5 + minutes. It is important.

10. Air Fryer Steak with Garlic Mushrooms

Ingredients

- ❖ Avocado oil 1 tablespoon
- ❖ Ribeye steak 16 oz.
- ❖ Mushrooms 2 cup
- ❖ Salt ½ teaspoon
- ❖ Black pepper ½ teaspoon
- ❖ Unsalted butter 2 tablespoon
- ❖ Minced garlic 2 tablespoon
- ❖ Red pepper flakes ¼ teaspoon

Steps

1. For 4 minutes, heat the Air Fryer at 400 ° F.
2. Dry the steaks and split them into 1/2-inch pieces. Pass the pieces of steak to a wide bowl.
3. Cut out the fresh mushrooms in half and move them into the large bowl with the cubed steak.
4. Add the garlic, salt, melted butter, pepper and red pepper flakes, and toss to cover the steak bites and mushrooms equally to the wide bowl.
5. In an even, non-overlapping layer, pass the mixture to an air fryer basket.
6. Air fried for 7-15 minutes, tossing the steak and mushrooms twice during this period. Test the steak after 7 minutes to see whether it's according to taste. If it's too pink, proceed to cook as required.
7. Garnish with parsley and serve with the finest taste and feel right away.
8. Turn them over and continue to cook for 5 more minutes or until 145-degree F is hit in the inner temperature.
9. Make sure to turn and ROTATE the pan and maintain an equal cooking period while you're frying 4 pork chops in an air fryer.
10. Before serving, leave to rest for 5 + minutes. Quite necessary.

11. Low Carb Coconut Shrimp

Ingredients

- ❖ Large shrimp, peeled off, 1 lb.
- ❖ Coconut flour ¼ cup
- ❖ Eggs 2
- ❖ Unsweetened flaked coconut 1 cup

Steps

1. Add coconut flour in a tiny bowl. In a 2nd cup, put eggs and mix well. In a 3rd tub, incorporate flaked coconut.

2. In the coconut flour, dip the shrimp. Then dip the eggs, making sure the excess egg is removed. Finally, add the shrimp to the coconut bowl and push to coat the whole coconut shrimp.

3. Put covered shrimp in the air fryer bowl. Continue to add shrimp until the basket has a full layer of shrimp.

4. Cook in an air fryer for 6-8 minutes at 400 degrees. To flip the shrimp, stop cooking midway through. When the shrimp is yellow, and the coconut is golden brown, they are finished.

12. Tandoori Fish Tikka

Ingredients

For Tikka

- ❖ Fish (Salmon) 1 lb.
- ❖ Nell pepper 1
- ❖ Onion 1 medium

Tandoori Marinade

- ❖ Light olive oil 2 tablespoon
- ❖ Plain yogurt 4 tablespoons
- ❖ Ginger 2 teaspoon
- ❖ Garlic 2 teaspoon
- ❖ Lime juice 1 tablespoon
- ❖ Salt 1 teaspoon
- ❖ Turmeric ½ teaspoon
- ❖ Coriander 2 teaspoon

- ❖ Cumin powder 1 teaspoon
- ❖ Garam masala 1.5 teaspoon
- ❖ Kashmiri red chili powder 1 teaspoon
- ❖ Kasoori methi 2 teaspoon

Steps

1. Mix the yogurt, oil, ginger-garlic paste, and lemon juice all the spices together in a mixing bowl.

2. In the marinade, incorporate fish bits, capsicum and onion and toss well before it gets covered.

3. Use an air fryer for cooking Tikka

4. For quick clean-up, cover the drip pan with aluminum foil. Place the basket of fried food in the drip pan.

5. In a single layer, place the tuna, peppers, and onions in the basket. Otherwise, they will not crisp up while cooking.

6. Reinsert the basket. Use the 360°F temperature set-button. Depending on the thickness of the fish, set the timer for 8-10 mins.

13. Bharwa Bhindi (Stuffed Okra)

Ingredients

- ❖ Okra (bhindi) 10.5 oz.
- ❖ Oil for frying 2 tablespoons

- ❖ Lime ½

Spice stuffing

- ❖ Coriander powder 2 tablespoon
- ❖ Ground cumin 2 teaspoon
- ❖ Dry mango powder 1 teaspoon
- ❖ Kashmiri red chili powder 1 teaspoon
- ❖ Garam masala 1 teaspoon
- ❖ Ground turmeric ¼ teaspoon
- ❖ Salt 1 teaspoon
- ❖ Oil 2 teaspoon

Steps

1. Use water to wash the bhindi and let it air dry.
2. Trim the ends and slit each bhindi lengthwise.
3. Mix all the stuffed spices in a bowl.
4. Take one bhindi at a time and use the spice blend to stuff it. With all the slit bhindi, repeat. When filling the bhindi, be generous; it's all right with some masala falls out.
1. In the air-fryer basket, put the stuffed okra in a single sheet. Cook for 12 mins at 360-degree F. To flip the okra, cut the basket after about 8 minutes.
2. It can be served by Bharwa bhindi. With a generous squeeze of lime juice on top, we enjoy it. Represent with warm roti or paratha.

14. Greek-Style Chicken Wings

Ingredients

- ❖ Extra virgin olive oil ½ cup
- ❖ Fresh lemon juice ¼ cup
- ❖ Minced garlic 2 cloves
- ❖ Dried oregano 2 teaspoon
- ❖ Dried thyme 1 teaspoon
- ❖ Salt 1 teaspoon
- ❖ Ground pepper ½ teaspoon

- ❖ Red pepper flakes ½ teaspoon
- ❖ Crushed red pepper flakes ¼ teaspoon
- ❖ Chicken wings drumettes 2 lb.
- ❖ Tzatziki sauce

Steps

1. Mix all the ingredients, except the Tzatziki sauce and chicken. Put the marinade in a large bag that can be resealed and add the chicken.

2. Refrigerate overnight for 4 hours, turning over occasionally.

3. Heat the air fryer to 370 ° F.

4. Add half of the chicken and simmer for 20 minutes, flipping the chicken midway through.

5. After 20 minutes, offer the air fryer bowl a shake to throw the chicken a bit. Cook 1-2 minutes more or till juices run clear and meat is no longer pink.

6. Repeat for the chicken that remains. Represent with Tzatziki sauce.

15. Air Fryer Garlic Ranch Wings

Ingredients

- ❖ Ranch seasoning mix 3 tablespoons
- ❖ Butter melted ¼ cup
- ❖ Fresh garlic minced 6 cloves
- ❖ Chicken wings 2 pounds

Steps

1. Melt the butter and mix with Ranch dry seasoning mix as well as minced garlic.

2. Put wings into a bowl and marinade it.

3. Put the bag into the freezer for the whole night.

4. Put wings in the air fryer and heat up to 360 degrees for 15-20 mins, while shaking two times.

5. Increase the temperature to 390 degrees and heat more for 5 mins.

16. Air Fryer Crispy Buffalo Chicken Hot Wings

Ingredients

- ❖ Chicken wings drumettes 16
- ❖ Low sodium soy sauce 2 teaspoons
- ❖ Montreal Grill Mate chicken seasoning
- ❖ Garlic powder 1 teaspoon
- ❖ Pepper according to taste
- ❖ Cooking spray
- ❖ Frank's Red-hot buffalo wing sauce ¼ cup

Steps

1. Drizzle over the chicken with the soy sauce.
2. To eat, prepare the chicken with the garlic powder, chicken seasoning, and pepper.
3. Put the chicken in a fryer in the air. Stacking the chicken on top of each other is fine.
4. Over the top of the meat, spray cooking oil.
5. Simmer the chicken at 400 degrees for five minutes. To ensure all the parts are thoroughly prepared, cut the pan, and shake the meat.
6. Throw the chicken back into an air fryer. Give an extra five minutes for the chicken to cook.
7. Take the chicken out of an air fryer.
8. Glaze the buffalo wing sauce with each slice of meat.
9. Throw the chicken back into an air fryer. Cook for 7-12 minutes till the chicken reaches the crisp you want and is not pink on the inside anymore.

17. Air Fryer Marinated Steak

Ingredients

- ❖ Butcher Box New York Strip Steaks 2
- ❖ Soy sauce 1 tablespoon
- ❖ Liquid smoke 1 teaspoon
- ❖ McCormick's Grill Mates seasoning 1 tablespoon
- ❖ Unsweetened cocoa powder ½ tablespoon
- ❖ Salt and pepper to taste
- ❖ Melted butter as an option

Steps

1. Drizzle the liquid smoke and soy sauce with the Butcher Box Steak.

2. With the seasonings, season the steak.

3. Refrigerate, ideally overnight, for a minimum of a couple of hours.

4. In an air fryer, put the steak. Cook two steaks at a time. An accessory grill tray, sheet shelf, or the regular air fryer basket may be used.

5. Cook it at 370 degrees for 5 minutes. Open the air fryer after 5 minutes and check your steak. Based on the target thickness, cooking time can differ. Cook to 125 ° F for rare, 135 ° F for medium-rare, 145 ° F for medium, 155 ° F for medium-well, and 160 ° F for well cooked. Using a meat thermometer.

6. For an extra 2 minutes of medium-done beef, I grilled the beef.

7. Remove the steak and drizzle with the melted butter from the air-fryer.

18. Air Fryer Bacon and egg Bite Cups

Ingredients

❖ Eggs 6 large

❖ Milk 2 tablespoons

❖ Salt and pepper to taste

❖ Sliced green peppers ¼ cup

❖ Red peppers sliced ¼ cup

❖ Sliced onions ¼

❖ Fresh spinach sliced ¼ cup

❖ Shredded cheese ½ cup

❖ Mozzarella cheese ¼ cup

❖ Cooked and crumbled bacon 3 slices

Steps

1. Add eggs in a bowl along with salt, pepper, and cream. Whisk together.

2. Spray green and red peppers, onions, cheeses, spinach, and bacon. Whisk them.

3. Put silicone molds in the air fryer before this mixture preparation.

4. Add the egg mixture into every silicon molds. Sprinkle all the remaining veggies.

5. Heat the air fryer for 12-15 minutes at 300 degrees till the toothpick comes out clearly from the egg mixture.

19. Air Fryer Tender Juicy Smoked BBQ Ribs

Ingredients

- ❖ Ribs rack 1
- ❖ Liquid smoke 1 tablespoon
- ❖ Pork rub 2-3 tablespoons
- ❖ Salt and pepper according to taste
- ❖ BBQ sauce ½ cup

Steps

1. There is a thin film that can be difficult to strip. Remove the skin from the back of the ribs. It can peel straight off occasionally. You should split it, too, and then take it off. Break the ribs in half so that the ribs will fit into the air fryer.

2. Drizzle along all sides of the ribs with the liquid smoke, and with the pork paste, salt and pepper, season all ends.

3. Wrap the ribs and enable the ribs to rest for 30 minutes at room temperature.

4. Use an air fryer to add the ribs. Stacking the ribs is okay.

5. Simmer at 360 degrees for 15 minutes.

6. Open a fryer in the air. The ribs flip. For an extra 15 minutes, cook.

7. Remove from the air fryer from the ribs. Drizzle BBQ sauce on the ribs.

20. Air Fryer Bacon and Cream Cheese Stuffed Jalapeno Poppers

Ingredients

- ❖ Fresh jalapenos 10
- ❖ Cream cheese 6 oz.
- ❖ Shredded cheddar cheese ¼ cup
- ❖ Bacon 2 slices
- ❖ Cooking oil spray

Steps

1. To produce 2 halves per jalapeno, break the jalapenos in two, vertically.

2. Put it in a bowl with the cream cheese. 15 seconds in the oven to soften.

3. Remove the jalapeno and seeds from the inside.

4. In a cup, mix the crumbled bacon, cream cheese, and grilled cheese. Mix thoroughly.

5. With the cream cheese mixture, stuff each of the jalapenos.

6. Through the Air Fryer, fill the poppers. With cooking oil, brush the poppers.

7. Air Fryer Close Up. Cook the poppers for 5 minutes at 370 degrees.

8. Remove and cool from the Air Fryer before serving.

21. Air Fryer Italian Herb Pork loin

Ingredients

- ❖ Boneless pork loin (not tenderloin), 3-4 pound
- ❖ Italian Vinaigrette Marinade 1/4 cup
- ❖ Garlic 4 cloves, minced
- ❖ Rosemary (crushed) 1 teaspoon
- ❖ Thyme 1 teaspoon
- ❖ Italian Seasoning 1/2 teaspoon
- ❖ Salt and pepper to taste

Steps

1. Drizzle both sides of the pork loin with the Italian marinade. The leftover seasoning is sprinkled on both ends.

2. It is recommended, though optional, to marinate the pork loin for 2 hours. Marinate the covered pork loin in a bowl or the refrigerator in a sealable bag.

3. Place the pork loin on parchment paper in the air fryer basket.

4. Fry the pork loin at 360 degrees for 25 minutes.

5. Open and rotate the pork loin with the air fryer. Cook for a further 12-15 minutes or until the pork loin's internal temperature hits at least 145 degrees. Use a thermometer for meat.

6. Use the air fryer to cut the pork loin. Until slicing, enable the meat to rest for at least 9-10 minutes. If wanted, you may glaze them with extra vinaigrette.

22. Air Fryer Grilled Chicken Kebabs

Ingredients

* Skinless chicken breasts, cut into 1-inch cubes, 16 oz
* Soy sauce 2 tablespoons
* McCormick's Grill Mates Chicken Seasoning 1 tablespoon
* McCormick's Grill Mates BBQ Seasoning 1 teaspoon
* Salt and pepper to taste
* Green pepper sliced ½
* Red pepper sliced ½
* Yellow pepper sliced ½
* Zucchini sliced ½
* Red onion sliced ¼
* 4-5 grape tomatoes
* Cooking oil spray optional

Steps

1. Marinating the chicken is desired but not needed. Put the chicken in a sealable plastic bag or wide bowl with chicken seasoning, soy sauce, BBQ seasoning, salt, and pepper to taste if you intend to marinate the chicken.

Shake the bag to ensure that it is evenly covered and seasoned with the chicken.

2. Remove and thread the chicken onto a skewer.

3. Layer the zucchini, tomatoes, and onions with the chicken. Cover each skewer with a grape tomato.

4. With cooking oil, spray the chicken and vegetables.

5. Line up the air fryer with parchment paper liners for simple clean up.

6. Put the skewers on a grill rack in the air fryer bowl. Cook at 350 degrees for 10 minutes.

7. Open and rotate the skewers with the air fryer. Cook for a further 7-10 minutes before the chicken hits an internal temperature of 165 degrees. Evaluate the interior of one of the chicken parts by using a meat thermometer.

23. Air Fryer Shrimp and Vegetables

Ingredients

- ❖ Small shrimp
- ❖ Frozen mixed vegetables 1 bag
- ❖ Gluten-free Cajun seasoning 1 tablespoon
- ❖ Olive oil spray
- ❖ Cooked rice

Steps

1. Add vegetables and the shrimp to the air fryer.

2. Cover it with Cajun seasoning and sprinkle it with oil spray.

3. Heat it at 355 degrees for 10 mins.

4. Now open and mix the vegetables and shrimp.

5. Continue to cook for extra 10 mins. Serve on cooked rice.

24. Air Fryer Bratwurst and Vegetables

Ingredients

- ❖ Bratwurst 1 package
- ❖ Red bell pepper 1
- ❖ Green bell pepper 1
- ❖ Red onion ¼ cup
- ❖ Gluten-free Cajun seasoning ½ tablespoon

Steps

1. Line up the air fryer with foil and add vegetables.

2. Break down the bratwurst into ½ inch size and put on top of the vegetables.

3. Spray the Cajun seasoning smoothly on it.

4. Air fryer at 390 degrees for 5-10 mins. Now open and mix it well.

5. Remove an air fryer after another extra 10 mins and serve.

25. Air Fryer Turkey Legs

Ingredients

- ❖ Turkey drumsticks 1 package
- ❖ Olive oil cooking spray
- ❖ BBQ sauce

Steps

1. Put the turkey legs in the bowl of an air fryer and sprinkle it with olive oil cooking spray.

2. Heat it to 390 degrees for 5-10 mins. Turn on and cook for more than 10 mins till 165-degree temperature.

3. Add sauce and roll it in foil. Let it cool and serve.

26. Air Fryer Roasted Edamame

Ingredients

- ❖ Edamame 2 cups
- ❖ Olive oil spray
- ❖ Garlic salt

Steps

1. Put edamame in the air fryer bowl, and it can be fresh or frozen.
2. Cover it with olive spray and pinch of garlic salt.
3. Heat the air fryer at 390 degrees for 10 mins.
4. Mix midway through the cooking time and roasted it more for extra 5 mins. Serve it.

27. Air Fryer Bulgogi Burgers

Ingredients

For the Bulgogi Burgers

- ❖ Lean ground beef 1 pound
- ❖ Gochujang 2 tablespoon
- ❖ Dark soy sauce 1 tablespoon
- ❖ Minced garlic 2 teaspoon

- ❖ Minced ginger 2 teaspoon
- ❖ Sugar 2 teaspoon
- ❖ Sesame oil 1 tablespoon
- ❖ Chopped green Scallions ¼ cup
- ❖ Salt ½ teaspoon

For the Gochujang Mayonnaise

- ❖ Mayonnaise ¼ cup
- ❖ Gochujang 1 tablespoon
- ❖ Sesame oil 1 tablespoon
- ❖ Sesame seeds 1 tablespoon
- ❖ Chopped green Scallions ¼ cup
- ❖ Hamburger buns 4

Steps

1. Mix the ground beef, soy sauce, gochujang, garlic, sugar, ginger, sesame oil, minced onions and salt in a big bowl and let the mixture sit in the refrigerator for 30 minutes up to 24 hours.

2. With a small depression in the center, divide the beef into four portions and create circular patties to keep the burgers from puffing out during cooking into a dome-shape.

3. For 10 minutes, set the air fryer to 360-degree F and put the patties in the air fryer bowl in one single sheet.

4. Make the Gochujang Mayonnaise: Mix the gochujang, mayonnaise, sesame oil, scallions, and sesame seeds while the patties are cooking.

5. Ensure that the beef has achieved an internal temperature of 160F using a meat thermometer and remove it onto a serving tray.

6. Serve the patties and the gochujang mayonnaise with hamburger buns.

28. Air Fryer Carne Asada

Ingredients

- ❖ Limes juiced 2 mediums
- ❖ Orange peeled 1 medium
- ❖ Cilantro 1 cup

- ❖ Jalapeno pepper 1
- ❖ Vegetable oil 2 tablespoons
- ❖ White vinegar 2 tablespoons
- ❖ Ancho chile powder 2 teaspoons
- ❖ Sugar 2 teaspoon
- ❖ Salt 1 teaspoon
- ❖ Cumin seeds 1 teaspoon
- ❖ Skirt steak 1.5 pound
- ❖ Coriander powder 1 teaspoon

Steps

1. In a blender, put all the ingredients except the skirt steak and combine until a smooth sauce is obtained.

2. Split the skirt steak into four sections and put it in a plastic zip-top container.

3. Add the marinade on the steak and keep the beef marinated for 30 minutes.

4. Place the steaks in the air fryer basket and adjust the air fryer to 400-degree F.

5. Cook for 8 minutes, or until your steak's internal temperature has hit 145-degree F. It is necessary not to overcook skirt steak to toughen the beef.

6. For 10 minutes, let the steak rest. Don't hurry at this stage.

7. Slice (this aspect is important) the steak against the grain and serve.

29. Keto Steak Nuggets

Ingredients

- ❖ Beefsteak 1 pound
- ❖ Egg1 large
- ❖ Palm oil for frying
- ❖ Parmesan cheese ½ cup
- ❖ Pork panko ½ cup
- ❖ Homemade seasoned salt ½ teaspoon
- ❖ Mayonnaise ¼ cup
- ❖ Sour cream ¼ cup

- ❖ Chipotles paste 1 teaspoon
- ❖ Dip mix ½ teaspoon
- ❖ Lime juiced ¼ medium

Steps

1. For the Chipotle Ranch Dip: Add all the ingredients together and mix properly. A medium-spice version produces 1 teaspoon of chipotle paste. Before serving, refrigerate for at least 30 minutes and hold for up to 1 week.

2. Combine Panko pork, parmesan cheese and seasoned salt-use my homemade stuff again, not the store-bought.

3. Beat the egg 1. Place 1 bowl of beaten egg and another breading mix in another.

4. Dip the steak chunks into the egg, then bread it. Place it on a sheet pan or plate lined with wax paper.

5. FREEZE breaded bites of raw steak 30 minutes before frying.

6. Heat your lard to approximately 325 degrees F. Fry steak nuggets (from frozen or chilled) once browned, around 2-3 minutes, working in batches as needed.

7. Switch to a lined plate with paper towels, season with a salt spray, and serve with Chipotle Ranch.

30. Korean Short BBQ Ribs

Ingredients

- ❖ Short ribs
- ❖ Korean BBQ sauce
- ❖ Pineapple 2 tablespoon

Steps

1. Mix all the ingredients and leave for 24 hours.

2. Put the rack in the air fryer bowl. Heat the air fryer at 360-degree F for 12 minutes. Switch the other side. Serve it.

31. Air Fryer Korean Hot Dogs

Ingredients

- ❖ Hot dogs 6
- ❖ Mozzarella cheese and sausages
- ❖ Wooden chopsticks 3 pairs

- ❖ Panko breadcrumbs 1 cup
- ❖ Oil spray, sugar, and mustard sauce

Steps

1. Without cutting open, cut a slice down each hot dog; cut the slice with a half cheese handle.
2. Heat the air fryer at 350 °. Mix the butter, rice, vinegar, jalapenos, chili powder, and half a cup of broken tortilla chips in a wide bowl to form a smooth mixture. On a lightly floured board, position the dough; divide into sixths. Roll the dough into 15-inch large pieces; tie the cheese-stuffed hot dog along one strip. Repeat with the dough and the hot dogs that remain. Spray the cooking spray on the dogs and move softly onto the leftover smashed chips. Spray the air fryer container with cooking spray and, without contact, put the dogs in the bowl, leaving space for expansion.
3. Cook in batches for 8-10 minutes until the dough is finely browned, and the cheese begins to melt. Represent with extra chips, sour cream and guacamole if needed.

Chapter 3: Lunch

1. Air Fryer Sweet Chili Chicken Wings

Ingredients

- ❖ Chicken Wings 12
- ❖ Baking Powder ½ Tbsp
- ❖ Black Pepper 1 Tsp
- ❖ Sea Salt ½ Tsp
- ❖ Garlic Powder 1 Tsp
- ❖ Onion Powder ¼ Tsp
- ❖ Paprika ¼ Tsp

Steps

1. Dry the chicken wings with a paper towel. With baking powder and seasoning, add the chicken wings to a zip-lock container. Cover the bag (make sure all the air is out) and chuck it around until it covers the wings.

2. Spray with cooking spray on the metal rack and place the chicken wings into a single layer. Close the Ninja Foody lid and press AIR CRISP, then set the TEMP to 400 ° F, set the Period to 20 minutes, and then press START. The sweet chili sauce is made when frying the chicken wings.

3. Open the cover for 10 minutes and toss/flip the chicken wings with tongs to keep them from sticking. Cover the lid and allow the remaining 10 minutes to cook for them.

4. However, monitor the internal temperature to guarantee that they are cooked after the time has passed. Before tossing in the sweet chili sauce, encouraged to rest for 5 minutes.

Warm Sauce with Chili

1. In a shallow saucepan, mix all ingredients and cook over medium heat on the burner. Carry the sauce to a boil and then reduce heat until the sauce has decreased and thickened gradually to a simmer, stirring. Hold the sauce warm before you're done with the chicken wings.
2. In the gravy, toss or drop the fried chicken wings. I want to make sure that they are coated thoroughly.
3. Put a single layer of the sauced chicken wings on a greased baking sheet with a wire rack cover. Broil the chicken wings for 2-4 minutes at HIGH on the top rack. Stay

tight to the oven and periodically. Check the wings till they burn easily. Remove them from the oven till the sauce is crispy, and the wings have some flavor. Serve immediately.

2. Air Fryer Fish

Ingredients

- ❖ Fish fillets 8
- ❖ Olive oil 1 tablespoon
- ❖ Garlic powder ¼ tsp
- ❖ Dry breadcrumbs 1 cup
- ❖ Black pepper ¼ tsp
- ❖ Paprika ½ teaspoon
- ❖ Chili powder ¼ tsp
- ❖ Salt ½ teaspoon
- ❖ Onion powder ¼ teaspoon

Steps

1. Blend the breadcrumbs with chili powder, paprika, black pepper, onion powder, garlic powder, and salt in a shallow bath.
2. Coat-fillet of fish with breadcrumbs and move to the bowl of the air fryer.
3. Cook in an air fryer for 12-15 minutes at 390 ° f (200 ° c). Open the air fryer for the first 8-10 minutes and then turn the fish fillets on the opposite side and cook.

3. Air Fryer Wonton Mozzarella Sticks

Ingredients

- ❖ Mozzarella cheese sticks 6
- ❖ Egg roll 6
- ❖ Olive oil spray
- ❖ Salt

Steps

1. Put a slice of string cheese on the egg roll wrapper's bottom corner. Roll up halfway and fold the sides over the cheese carefully into the middle. Soak finger in water and examine the wrapper's edges. Roll over the mozzarella stick with the remaining wrapper. Repeat for the leftover cheese and wrappers.
2. In the air fryer, put 6 of the mozzarellas sticks and spray with an olive oil spray. Using kosher salt to sprinkle.
3. Fry for 3 minutes at 350 degrees, flip, sprinkle the other side with a spray of olive oil and sprinkle with salt, and proceed to fry for another 3 minutes. If needed, provide with a marinara sauce for soaking.

4. Air Fryer Steak

Ingredients

- ❖ Loin steaks 2 strip
- ❖ Salt 2 tsp
- ❖ Black pepper 2 tsp
- ❖ Butter 2 tsp

Steps

1. Spray with pepper and salt on the steaks, put on a plate and refrigerate, uncovered, for 2-3 days. Flip it with a paper towel every 11-12 hours or so, blotting the fluids.

2. For advanced tenderness and enriched taste, this stage is suggested, but one may miss it if pressed for time.

3. 45-60 minutes before serving, take the steaks from the fridge and allow them to stay at room temperature.

4. Rub the steaks on both sides with melted butter and put on the rack of the air fryer. For medium thickness, steam at 410F for 14 minutes, without raising the temperature.

5. If air-fried steaks are thicker or thinner than 1,25 "thick, the times may need to be modified.

6. This cooking time is an estimate, so use an instant reading thermometer in the Notes segment in conjunction with the bowl.

7. Remove the steaks from the air fryer, cover them in foil or wax paper, and let them sit for 10 minutes, then eat.

5. Air Fryer Caramelized Bananas

Ingredients

- ❖ Bananas 2
- ❖ Lemon 1/4
- ❖ Coconut sugar 1 tbsp

Steps

1. Wash bananas, then cut them straight down the center, lengthwise

2. Try squeezing the lemon juice over each banana's top.

3. When combined with coconut sugar using cinnamon, rub the bananas' surface until covered with coconut sugar.

4. At 400F, put in the parchment-lined air fryer for 7-9 minutes.

5. Eat as is or top up with favorite toppings until removed from the air fryer and enjoy.

6. Air Fryer Sesame Chicken

Ingredients

- ❖ Boneless Chicken Thighs 6
- ❖ Cornstarch 1/2 Cup
- ❖ Olive Oil Spray

Steps

1. Break the chicken into cubed pieces, then add the cornstarch into a dish.
2. Put it in the air fryer and cook it according to the chicken air fryer manual. So, when chicken is in the air fryer, put a good even layer of olive oil spray; it works well to mix things up midway through cooking time and add an extra coat of spray.
3. While the chicken is frying, start preparing the sauce in a tiny saucepan.
4. On a medium-high fire, add sugar, orange juice, ginger, hoisin sauce, garlic, and soy sauce to the saucepan. When well mixed, whisk this away.
5. Stir in the water and cornstarch till the sugar has fully melted, and a low boil is achieved.
6. Mix the sesame seeds in it and take the sauce from the heat. Put aside to thicken for 5 minutes.
7. Take from the air fryer and put in a bowl until the chicken is cooked, and then cover with the sauce.
8. Topped over rice and beans and eat.

7. Air Fryer Donuts

Ingredients

- ❖ Milk 1 cup
- ❖ Instant yeast 2 ½ tsp.
- ❖ Sugar ¼ cup
- ❖ Salt ½ tsp
- ❖ Egg 1
- ❖ Butter ¼ cup
- ❖ Flour 3 cups
- ❖ Oil spray

Steps

1. Gently whisk together milk, 1 tsp of sugar, and yeast in the bowl of a stand mixer equipped with a dough handle. Let it stay for 10 minutes until it is foamy

2. To the milk mixture, add the cinnamon, egg, and sugar, melted butter and 2 cups of flour. Mix until mixed at a low level, then add the remaining cup of flour slowly with the mixer going, until the dough no longer sticks to the pipe. Increase the pace to medium-low and knead until the dough is elastic and smooth for 5 minutes.

3. Place the dough and cover it with plastic wrap in a greased bowl. In a warm spot, let it grow before it doubles.

4. Place the dough on a floured board, punch it down and stretch it out softly to a thickness of around 1/2 inch. 1- To extract the middle, cut out 11-13 donuts.

5. Switch to thinly floured parchment paper donuts and donut holes and cover loosely with oiled plastic wrap. Let the donuts grow for about 30 minutes before the amount has doubled. Preheat the 350F Air Fryer.

6. Spray the Air Fryer bowl with oil spray and gently move the donuts in a single layer to the Air Fryer jar. Using oil spray to spray donuts and cook at 350F until golden brown, around 4 minutes. Repeat for donuts and gaps left.

7. Melt butter over medium heat in a shallow saucepan while the donuts are in the Air Fryer. Stir in the sugar and vanilla extract powder until smooth. Remove from the heat and mix one tablespoon at a time in hot water until the icing is a little thin, still not watery.

8. Using forks to dip hot donuts and donut holes into the glaze to submerge them. To encourage the excess glaze to drip off, position it on a wire rack placed over a rimmed baking sheet. Let it hang for about 10 minutes before the glaze hardens.

8. Bang Bang Chicken

Ingredients

- Mayonnaise 1/2 cup
- Honey 2 tablespoons
- Sriracha sauce 1/2 tablespoon
- Buttermilk 1 cup
- Flour ¾
- Cornstarch ½ cup
- Egg 1
- Oil

Steps

1. Add all ingredients in a mixing bowl to create bang bang chicken sauce. Whisk before it's all mixed.
2. In the air fryer, first create buttermilk batter by mixing flour, egg, corn starch, pepper, salt, sriracha sauce, and buttermilk to produce bang bang meat. And whisk until mixed.
3. Before inserting the poultry, grease your Air Fryer with some oil of your choosing. Next, work in plenty, drop bits of chicken in buttermilk batter and then apply breadcrumbs to the Air Fryer. Air Fried for 8-10 minutes at 375F or until chicken is boiling thru. When on the other hand, rotate the chicken bits.
4. Drizzle over the chicken with the sauce and serve with leafy greens or Eggs and Green Onion Fried Rice Recipe.

9. Crispy Air Fryer Eggplant Parmesan

Ingredients

- ❖ Eggplant 1 large
- ❖ Wheat breadcrumbs ½ cup
- ❖ Parmesan cheese 3 tbsp
- ❖ Salt
- ❖ Italian seasoning 1 tsp
- ❖ Flour 3 tbsp
- ❖ Water 1 tbsp
- ❖ Olive oil spray
- ❖ Marinara sauce 1 cup
- ❖ Mozzarella cheese ¼ cup

❖ Fresh parsley

Steps

1. Break the eggplant into slices of approximately 1/2. "Add some salt on both ends of the slices and hold for at least 10-15 minutes.
2. Meanwhile, combine the egg with water and flour in a small bowl to make the batter.
3. Put cheese, breadcrumbs, Italian seasoning, and salt in a medium shallow bowl. Mix thoroughly.
4. Now equally add the batter to every eggplant slice. To cover it equally to both sides, add the battered halves in the breadcrumb mix.
5. On a clean, dry flat plate, put breaded eggplant slices and spray oil on them.
6. Heat the Air Fryer to 360F. Then place the slices of eggplant on the wire mesh and fry for around 8 minutes.
7. With around 1 tsp of marinara sauce and fresh mozzarella cheese thinly scattered on it, cover the air fried slices with around 1 tablespoon. Fry the eggplant for another 2 min or till the cheese melts.
8. On the side of your favorite pasta, serve soft.

10. Air Fryer Shrimp Fajitas

Ingredients

❖ Medium Shrimp 1 Pound

❖ Red Bell Pepper 1

❖ Green Bell Pepper 1

❖ Sweet Onion 1/2 Cup

❖ Gluten-Free Fajita 2 Tbsp

❖ Olive Oil Spray

❖ White Corn Tortillas or Flour Tortillas

Steps

1. Spray with olive oil or cover with foil on the air fryer bowl.
2. To get the ice off, pass cold water over it if the shrimp is stuck with ice on it.
3. Add to the bowl the tomatoes, seafood, seasoning, and cabbage.
4. Attach a layer with a mist with olive oil.
5. Mix everything.
6. Cook for 12 minutes at 390 degrees using the Ninja Foody Air Fryer.
7. Place the cap open and sprinkle it again and blend it up.

8. Cook for 10 more minutes.
9. On soft tortillas, eat.

11. Honey Glazed Air Fryer Salmon

Ingredients

* ❖ Salmon Fillets 4
* ❖ Salt
* ❖ Black Pepper
* ❖ Soy Sauce 2 teaspoons
* ❖ Honey 1 tablespoon
* ❖ Sesame Seeds 1 teaspoon

Steps

1. Heat the air fryer (it takes 1-2 mins).
2. Additionally: Season with pepper and salt on each salmon fillet. Rub the fish with soy sauce.
3. Put the fillets in the air fryer's bowl and cook for 8 minutes or till ready at 375 ° F (190 ° C).
4. Glaze every fillet with honey around a minute or two until the time is up and spray with sesame seeds. Bring them back in to have the cooking finished.
5. With a side of your choosing, serve.

12. Crispy Air Fryer Roasted Brussels Sprouts With Balsamic

Ingredients

* ❖ Brussels sprouts 1 pound
* ❖ Olive oil 2 Tablespoons
* ❖ Balsamic vinegar 1 Tablespoon
* ❖ Salt and Black pepper

Steps

1. Place the cut sprouts in a bowl. Sprinkle the vinegar and oil generously over the sprouts in Brussels. Don't pour vinegar and oil in one place, or just brush one of the sprouts in Brussels.
2. Sprinkle generously with pepper and salt around the Brussels sprouts. Mix to combine all and long enough so that the marinade soaks up all the Brussels sprouts.

3. Add the Brussels to the bowl of the air fryer. For around 15-20 minutes, fry the air at 359 ° F. Shake and softly stir halfway through to cook for about 7-8 minutes. At the halfway point, make sure the shaking. Shake and flip a third time if necessary, to ensure sure it cooks equally.

4. For the rest of the period, aim to air-fried Brussels completely. To make sure nothing burns, you should search earlier if necessary.

5. If needed, add extra salt, and pepper to the Brussels sprouts and enjoy.

13. Air Fryer Chicken Nuggets

Ingredients

- ❖ Cooking spray
- ❖ Chicken breasts 2
- ❖ Olive oil 1/3 cup
- ❖ Panko 1.5 cup
- ❖ Parmesan ¼ cup
- ❖ Sweet paprika 2 tsp

Steps

1. Break the chicken breasts into cubes from 1 "to 1.5" and put them aside and with one dish holding olive oil, while the other carrying panko, parmesan, and paprika, set up the station.

2. Lightly spritz the interior of your air fryer with some grease.

3. Dip the cube of chicken in the olive oil, then placed it on the top of the suit. Make sure you have a well-covered nugget and put it in the air fryer. Repeat until it's complete on your air fryer.

4. Adjust air fryer to 400F and cook for 8 minutes with homemade chicken nuggets.

5. Serve with the side of your choosing.

14. Air Fryer Baked Apples

Ingredients

- ❖ Apples 2
- ❖ Butter 1 tsp
- ❖ Cinnamon ½ tsp

Steps

1. Break the chicken breasts into cubes from 1 "to 1.5" and put them aside.

2. With one dish holding olive oil, the other carrying parmesan, paprika blend, and panko, set up the station.

3. Lightly spritz the interior of your air fryer with some grease.

4. Dip the cube of chicken in the olive oil, then placed it on the top of the suit. Make sure you have a well-covered nugget and put it in the air fryer. Repeat until it's complete on your air fryer.

5. Adjust air fryer to 400F and cook for 8 minutes with homemade chicken nuggets.

6. Serve with the side of your choosing.

15. Air Fryer Fish Tacos

Ingredients

- ❖ Firm white fish fillets 24 oz
- ❖ Grill seasoning 1 tbsp
- ❖ Avocado 1 large
- ❖ Oranges 2 medium
- ❖ Red onion 1/4 cup
- ❖ Fresh cilantro 2 tbsp
- ❖ Salt 1 tsp
- ❖ Mayonnaise 1/4 cup
- ❖ Chipotle sauce 1/4 cup
- ❖ Lime juice 1 tbsp
- ❖ Corn tortillas

Steps

1. Mix the orange, avocado, cilantro, cabbage, and half a teaspoon of salt.

2. Stir the chipotle sauce, mayonnaise, lime juice and half a teaspoon of salt together.

3. Spray the fish generously, mostly with grill seasoning.

4. To stop sticking, quickly spray the air-fryer basket with vegetable oil.

5. Organize the fish in the bowl in a single sheet. Cook for 8-12 minutes at 400 degrees f, or until the fish's internal temperature exceeds 145 degrees f. Flipping the fish during frying is not required.

6. To make tacos, eat the fish with warmed avocado citrus salsa, corn tortillas, and chipotle mayonnaise.

16. Air Fryer Dumplings

Ingredients

❖ Chicken dumplings 8 ounces

❖ Soy sauce 1/4 cup

❖ Water 1/4 cup

❖ Maple syrup 1/8 cup

❖ Garlic powder 1/2 teaspoon

❖ Rice vinegar 1/2 teaspoon

❖ Small pinch of red pepper flakes

Steps

1. Preheat the air fryer for about 4 minutes to 370 degrees.
2. Put the frozen dumplings in one layer within the air fryer and spray them with gasoline.
3. Fry for 5 minutes, rotate the bowl and then apply a little more oil to the mist.
4. For another 4-6 minutes, cook the dumplings.
5. Meanwhile, make the dipping sauce by adding together the ingredients.
6. Take the fried dumplings from the bowl and let stay before enjoying for another 2 minutes.

17. Air Fryer Pork Chops

Ingredients

- ❖ Boneless 4 pork chops
- ❖ Grill seasoning 1 tbsp
- ❖ Maple syrup 1/4 cup
- ❖ Dijon mustard 2 tbsp
- ❖ Lemon juice 2 tsp
- ❖ Salt 1/2 tsp
- ❖ Vegetable oil

Steps

1. Rub air-fryer basket lightly with vegetable oil.
2. Clean pork chops with towels and generously brush with the barbecue seasoning on both sides.
3. Place the pork chops in one layer in the basket of the air fryer. You can need to bake the pork chops in two batches, depending on your air fryer's capacity.
4. Cook the pork chops for 12-15 minutes at 375 degrees F (more time is required if your pork chops are thick). Halfway into cooking time, turn over the pork chops.
5. Test the pork chops' internal temperature-when they are 145 degrees F, and they are finished frying.
6. In an air fryer, mix the vinegar, lemon juice, maple syrup, and salt while the pork chops are frying.
7. After extracting them from the air fryer, dump the sauce over the pork chops instantly.
8. Until eating, cause the pork chops to rest for 2 minutes.

18. Air Fryer Chicken Chimichangas

Ingredients

- ❖ Rotisserie chicken white meat 1
- ❖ Cooked rice 1 1/2 cups
- ❖ Salsa 1 cup
- ❖ Salt 1/2 tsp
- ❖ Soft taco size flour tortillas about 8 inches across
- ❖ Vegetable oil 2 tbsp

Steps

1. Rub the bottom of the basket with vegetable oil for the air fryer. The air fryer should be preheated to 360 degrees.
2. Mix the rice, chicken, salt, and salsa in a big bowl until well mixed.
3. In the middle of each tortilla, position about 1/2 cup of the chicken filling. With the ends bent in to lock in the lining, firmly wrap them back.
4. Place the chimichangas in the oiled bowl, two at a time and seam side down. With vegetable oil, gently clean the tops of the chimichangas.
5. Air-fry the chimichangas at 360 degrees for around 4 minutes. To flip the chimichangas, open an air fryer and use metal tongs. Once the chimichangas are crispy and browned, proceed to air fry for another 4 minutes.
6. The filling will be stored for up to two days in the refrigerator in an air-tight container so that the chimichangas can be prepared as desired.

7. Placed sour cream, white cheese sauce, onion, spinach, and guacamole on top of the chimichangas.

19. Simple Chicken Burrito Bowls

Ingredients

- ❖ Rotisserie chicken 1
- ❖ Black beans 1 15 oz
- ❖ Corn 1 15 oz
- ❖ Taco Skillet Sauce 1 8 oz packet
- ❖ Vegetable oil 1 tbsp
- ❖ White rice 1 cup
- ❖ Salt 1 tsp
- ❖ Water 1 3/4 cup
- ❖ Taco sauce 2 tbsp
- ❖ Iceberg lettuce 1 cup
- ❖ Avocado 1
- ❖ Lime wedges 4
- ❖ Medium cheddar cheese 6 oz
- ❖ Sour cream ½ cup
- ❖ Jalapenos 4 oz

Steps

1. Add the corn, chicken, taco skillet sauce, and black beans to a wide saucepan. Mix, cover, and heat until simmering, over medium-low heat.
2. Meanwhile, over medium-high pressure, heat the oil in a different saucepan. Add the rice and cook for a minute, sometimes stirring, before the rice begins to toast. Add the sauce to the water, salt and taco and bring it to a boil. Cover and boil the rice for 15-20 minutes or until the water is absorbed. Lower the pressure.
3. Add a large scoop of rice to the cups, then cover with the mixture of meat, beans, then maize. Add lime wedge, diced avocado, shredded lettuce, shredded cheese, sliced jalapeños, and sour cream to the option. Immediately serve.

20. Chicken Soft Tacos

Ingredients

- ❖ Unsalted butter 3 tbsp
- ❖ Garlic 4 cloves
- ❖ Chipotle chiles 2 tsp
- ❖ Orange 1/2 cup
- ❖ Worcestershire sauce 1/2 cup
- ❖ Cilantro 3/4 cup
- ❖ Boneless, skinless chicken breasts 4
- ❖ Yellow mustard 1 tsp
- ❖ Salt and pepper
- ❖ Flour tortillas 12 4-inch

Steps

1. In a broad skillet over the medium-high fire, melt the butter.
2. Add the garlic and chipotle and roast for around 1 minute before it is fragrant.
3. Stir in Worcestershire, orange juice, and 1/2 cup of cilantro and bring to a simmer.
4. Add the chicken and boil, covered, over medium-low heat for 10 to 15 minutes, until the meat is 160 degrees, flipping the chicken midway through cooking. Move to the foil-plate and tent.
5. Increase the heat to medium-high and simmer for around 5 minutes, until the liquid is reduced to 1/4 cup.
6. Whisk in the mustard, off the heat.
7. Shred the chicken into bite-sized bits using 2 forks, then return to the skillet.
8. In a pot, apply the remaining cilantro and mix until well mixed. With salt and pepper, season.
9. Serve with shredded cabbage, tortillas, sauce, cheese, sour cream, and wedges of lime.

21. Ground Pork Tacos - Al Pastor Style

Ingredients

- ❖ Pork 1 1/3 lbs.
- ❖ Orange 1/3 cup

- ❖ Canned chipotle sauce 3 tbsp
- ❖ Smoked paprika 1 tsp
- ❖ Cumin 1 tsp
- ❖ Salt 1 tsp
- ❖ Garlic powder 1/2 tsp
- ❖ Cayenne pepper 1/4 tsp
- ❖ Pineapple 1 1/2 cups
- ❖ Red onion finely diced 1/3 cup
- ❖ Cilantro 1/3 cup
- ❖ Juice of one-half lime
- ❖ Salt 1/2 tsp
- ❖ Pepper Jack cheese 6 oz
- ❖ Corn tortillas

Steps

1. Place the red onion, pineapple, lime juice, cilantro, and 1/2 tsp together in a bowl and set aside.
2. Add the chopped pork and cook till it is no longer pink in a non-stick skillet on medium heat, cutting ties the meat with a spatula.
3. Stir the chipotle sauce, orange juice, smoked paprika, garlic powder, cumin, and the remaining tsp and cayenne pepper into the fried pork. Stir well and allow for about 5 minutes to simmer.
4. Serve with tortillas, organic pineapple salsa and sliced Pepper Jack cheese on the pork taco meat.

22. Air-Fryer Southern-Style Chicken

Ingredients

- ❖ Crushed Ritz crackers 2 cups
- ❖ Fresh parsley 1 tablespoon
- ❖ Garlic salt 1 teaspoon
- ❖ Paprika 1 teaspoon
- ❖ Pepper 1/2 teaspoon
- ❖ Cumin 1/4 teaspoon
- ❖ Rubbed sage 1/4 teaspoon
- ❖ Egg 1 large
- ❖ 1 broiler/fryer chicken
- ❖ Cooking spray

Steps

1. Heat an air fryer at 375 °. Blend the first seven ingredients in a small dish. Put the egg in a different shallow bowl. Dip the chicken in the shell, then pat in the cracker combination to help adhere to the coating. Place the chicken in batches in a thin layer on the oiled tray in the air-fryer bowl and sprinkle with the cooking mist.
2. Cook for 10 minutes. With cooking oil, transform the spritz and chicken; cook until the chicken is lightly browned, and the juices are transparent, 15-20 mins longer.

23. Air-Fryer Fish and Fries

Ingredients

- ❖ Potatoes 1 pound
- ❖ Olive oil 2 tablespoons
- ❖ Pepper 1/4 teaspoon
- ❖ Salt 1/4 teaspoon

FISH:

- ❖ Flour 1/3 cup
- ❖ Pepper 1/4 teaspoon
- ❖ Egg 1 large
- ❖ Water 2 tablespoons
- ❖ Cornflakes 2/3 cup
- ❖ Parmesan cheese 1 tablespoon
- ❖ Cayenne pepper 1/8 teaspoon
- ❖ Salt 1/4 teaspoon
- ❖ Haddock 1 pound

Steps

1. Heat air fryer at 400 °. Lengthwise, peel and cut the potatoes into 1/2-in.-thick slices; cut the slices into 1/2-in.-thick sticks.
2. Toss the potatoes with oil, pepper, and salt in a wide bowl. Place potatoes in batches in a single layer on the air-fryer basket tray; cook until only soft, 5-10 minutes to redistribute tossed potatoes; cook until slightly golden brown and crisp, 5-10 minutes longer.
3. Meanwhile, combine the flour and pepper in a small dish. Mix the egg with water in another small dish. Toss the cornflakes with the cheese and cayenne in a third bowl. Sprinkle salt on the fish; dip in the flour mixture to cover all sides; shake off the residue. Dip in the mixture of shells, then pat in the cornflake mixture to bind to the coating.
4. Take the fries out of the bowl and stay warm. In an air-fryer bowl, put the fish in a single layer on the plate. Cook until fish is gently browned and, 9 minutes, turning midway through cooking, only begins to flake easily with a fork. Do not overcook

it anymore. To heat up, return the fries to the basket. Immediately serve. Serve with tartar sauce if needed.

24. Air-Fryer Ground Beef Wellington

Ingredients

- ❖ Butter 1 tablespoon
- ❖ Mushrooms 1/2 cup
- ❖ Flour 2 teaspoons
- ❖ Pepper 1/4 teaspoon
- ❖ Half-and-half cream 1/2 cup
- ❖ Egg yolk 1 large
- ❖ Onion 2 tablespoons
- ❖ Salt 1/4 teaspoon
- ❖ Beef 1/2 pound
- ❖ Freeze Crescent rolls 1 tube (4 ounces)
- ❖ Egg 1 large
- ❖ Parsley flakes 1 teaspoon

Steps

1. Heat the air fryer at 300 °. Heat the butter over medium-high heat in a saucepan. Insert mushrooms; boil and mix for 5-6 minutes, until soft. Add flour and 1/8 of a teaspoon of pepper when combined. Add cream steadily. Cook and whisk until thickened, about 2 minutes.
2. Combine the egg yolk, carrot, 2 teaspoons of salt, mushroom sauce, and 1/8 teaspoon of pepper in a cup. Crumble over the mixture of beef and blend properly. Unroll and divide the crescent dough into 2 rectangles; force the perforations to close. Place each rectangle with the meatloaf. Bring together the sides and press to cover. Clean the broken egg if needed.
3. Put Wellingtons in a thin layer in an air-fryer basket on a greased plate. Cook until a thermometer placed into the meatloaf measures 160 °, 18-22 minutes, until golden brown.
4. Meanwhile, over low heat, steam the remaining sauce; mix in the parsley. With Wellingtons, serve the sauce.

25. Air-Fryer Ravioli

Ingredients

- ❖ Breadcrumbs 1 cup
- ❖ Parmesan cheese 1/4 cup
- ❖ Dried basil 2 teaspoons
- ❖ Flour 1/2 cup
- ❖ Eggs 2 large
- ❖ 1 package frozen beef ravioli
- ❖ Cooking spray
- ❖ 1 cup marinara sauce, warmed

Steps

1. Heat the air fryer at 350 °. Mix the breadcrumbs, the cheese, and the basil in a small dish. In different shallow cups, position the flour and eggs. To cover all ends, dip the ravioli in flour; shake off the waste. Dip in the shells, then pat in the crumb mixture to help bind to the coating.
2. Arrange the ravioli in batches on a greased tray in the air-fryer basket in a single layer; spritz with olive oil. Cook for 3-4 minutes before it's golden brown. Flip; spritz with spray for cooking. Fry till lightly browned, for 3-4 more minutes. Sprinkle instantly with basil and extra Parmesan cheese if needed. With marinara sauce, eat warm.

26. Popcorn Shrimp Tacos with Cabbage Slaw

Ingredients

- ❖ Coleslaw 2 cups
- ❖ Cilantro 1/4 cup
- ❖ Lime juice 2 tablespoons
- ❖ Honey 2 tablespoons
- ❖ Salt 1/4 teaspoon
- ❖ Eggs 2 large
- ❖ 2% Milk 2 tablespoon
- ❖ Flour 1/2 cup
- ❖ Panko breadcrumbs 1-1/2 cups
- ❖ ground cumin 1 tablespoon
- ❖ Garlic powder 1 tablespoon
- ❖ Non cooked shrimp 1 pound
- ❖ Cooking spray
- ❖ Corn tortillas 8
- ❖ Avocado 1 medium

Steps

1. Combine the cilantro, coleslaw blend, sugar, lime juice, salt, and jalapeno, if needed, in a small bowl; toss to cover.
2. Heat an air fryer at 375 °. Whisk the eggs and milk together in a small dish. Place flour in a different shallow bowl. Cumin, Panko, and garlic powder are combined in a final small cup. To cover all ends, dip the shrimp in flour; shake off the waste. Dip in the egg mixture, then pat onto the panko mixture to help bind to the coating.
3. Organize shrimp in a thin layer in an oiled air-fryer bowl in batches, dust with cooking spray. For 2-3 minutes, cook till lightly browned. Turn; spritz with spray for cooking. Cook until the shrimp turns pink and lightly browned, 3 minutes longer.
4. Serve shrimp in coleslaw blend and avocado in tortillas.

27. Bacon-Wrapped Avocado Wedges

Ingredients

- ❖ Avocados 2 medium
- ❖ Bacon strips 12
- ❖ Mayonnaise 1/2 cup
- ❖ Sriracha chili sauce 2 to 3 tablespoons
- ❖ Lime juice 1 to 2 tablespoons

Steps

1. Heat the air fryer at 400 degrees. Break each avocado in half; peel and extract the pit. Break the halves into thirds each. Wrap over each avocado wedge with 1 bacon slice. If required, operate in batches, put slices in a thin layer in the fryer basket and cook 10-15 minutes until the bacon is fried through.
2. Meanwhile, whisk together the sriracha sauce, mayonnaise, lime juice and zest in a shallow dish. Serve with sauce on the wedges.

28. Air-Fryer Steak Fajitas

Ingredients

- ❖ Tomatoes 2 large
- ❖ Red onion 1/2 cup
- ❖ Lime juice 1/4 cup
- ❖ Pepper 1 jalapeno
- ❖ Cilantro 3 tablespoons

- ❖ Cumin 2 teaspoons
- ❖ Salt 3/4 teaspoon
- ❖ 1 beef flank steak
- ❖ Onion 1 large
- ❖ 6 whole-wheat tortillas (8 inches), warmed

Steps

1. Place five ingredients in a little bowl for salsa first; mix in 1 tsp cumin and 1/4 tsp salt. Let it stand until you serve.
2. Heat an air fryer at 400 °. Sprinkle the residual cumin and salt with the steak. Place the air-fryer basket on a greased plate. Cook until the meat hits the appropriate thickness (a thermometer can read 135 ° for medium-rare; medium, 140 °; moderate-well, 145 °), 6-8 minutes on each hand. Remove from the basket and quit for 5 minutes to stand.
3. Meanwhile, put the onion in the air-fryer basket on the counter. Cook till crisp-tender, stirring once, 2-3 minutes. Thinly slice the steak around the grain; eat with salsa and onion in tortillas. Serve with lime and avocado slices if needed.

29. Air-Fryer Sweet and Sour Pork

Ingredients

- ❖ Pineapple 1/2 cup
- ❖ Cider vinegar 1/2 cup
- ❖ Sugar 1/4 cup
- ❖ Dark brown sugar 1/4 cup
- ❖ Ketchup 1/4 cup
- ❖ Reduced-sodium soy sauce 1 tablespoon
- ❖ Dijon mustard 1-1/2 teaspoons
- ❖ Garlic powder 1/2 teaspoon
- ❖ 1 pork tenderloin
- ❖ Salt 1/8 teaspoon
- ❖ Pepper 1/8 teaspoon
- ❖ Cooking spray

Steps

1. Integrate the first eight ingredients in a shallow saucepan. Get it to a boil; lower the flame. Simmer, exposed, for 6-8 minutes till thickened, stirring periodically.
2. Heat the air fryer at 350 °. Sprinkle salt and pepper on the bacon. Place the pork in the air-fryer bowl on a greased tray; spritz with the cooking mist. Cook for 7-8 minutes before the pork starts to brown around the edges. Place 2 teaspoons of sauce over the pork. Heat till at least 145 ° is read by a thermometer placed into the bacon, 11-13 minutes longer. Let the pork stand before slicing for 5 minutes. Serve with the sauce that exists. Cover with chopped green onions if needed.

30. Air-Fryer Taco Twists

Ingredients

- ❖ Beef 1/3 pound
- ❖ Onion 1 large
- ❖ Cheddar cheese 2/3 cup
- ❖ Salsa 1/3 cup
- ❖ Canned chopped green chiles 3 tablespoons
- ❖ Garlic powder 1/4 teaspoon
- ❖ Hot pepper sauce 1/4 teaspoon
- ❖ Salt 1/8 teaspoon
- ❖ Cumin 1/8 teaspoon

❖ Freeze Crescent rolls 1 tube

Steps

1. Heat the air fryer at 300 °. Cook the beef and onion on medium heat in a large skillet until the meat is no longer pink, rinse. Integrate salsa, garlic powder, cheese, salt, and cumin with sweet pepper sauce.

2. Unroll and divide the crescent roll dough into 4 rectangles; push the sealing perforations. Put in the middle of each rectangle with 1/2 cup of meat mixture. Twist and put 4 corners to the center: pinch to cover. Place in a thin layer on the greased tray in the air-fryer bowl in batches. Cook for 18-22 minutes before it is golden brown. Serve with condiments of your choosing, if needed.

31. Air-Fryer Potato Chips

Ingredients

❖ Potatoes 2 large
❖ Olive oil spray
❖ Sea salt ½ teaspoon

Steps

1. Preheat the air fryer at 360 °. Cut the potatoes into thinly sliced using a mandolin or vegetable peeler. Switch to a wide bowl; to fill, add sufficiently ice water. Take a 15-minute soak, rinse. Soak for 15 more minutes.

2. Drain potatoes, put, and pat dry on towels. Sprinkle with cooking spray on the potatoes; sprinkle with salt. Put potato slices in batches in a thin layer on the oiled air-fryer basket plate. Cook for 15-17 minutes until it is crisp and lightly browned, stirring and rotating every 6 minutes. Sprinkle with parsley if needed.

32. Air-Fryer Greek Breadsticks

Ingredients

❖ Marinated quartered artichoke hearts 1/4 cup

❖ Pitted Greek olives 2 tablespoons

❖ Frozen puff pastry 1 package

❖ Spreadable spinach and artichoke cream cheese 1 carton

❖ Parmesan cheese 2 tablespoons

❖ Egg 1 large

* Water 1 tablespoon
* Sesame seeds 2 teaspoons

Steps

1. Heat an air fryer at 325 °. In a food processor, put the artichokes and olives; cover and pulse till finely chopped. On a lightly floured board, unfold 1 pastry sheet; scatter half the cream cheese on half of the pastry. Comb with a variation of half the artichoke. Sprinkle the Parmesan cheese with half of it. Fold the simple half over the filling; pressure to close softly.
2. Repeat with the remaining cookie, cream cheese, Parmesan cheese and artichoke mixture. Whisk the water and egg; clean the tips. Sprinkle the seeds with sesame. Split into 16 3/4-in.-wide strips for each rectangle.
3. Adjust bread pieces in a single sheet in batches on a greased tray in the air-fryer basket. Cook for 12-15 minutes until it is golden brown.

33. Air-Fryer Crumb-Topped Sole

Ingredients

* Mayonnaise 3 tablespoons
* Parmesan cheese 3 tablespoons
* Mustard seed 2 teaspoons
* Pepper 1/4 teaspoon
* Sole fillets 4
* Soft breadcrumbs 1 cup
* Onion 1
* Mustard 1/2 teaspoon
* Butter 2 teaspoons
* Cooking spray

Steps

1. Heat an air fryer at 375 °. Combine mayonnaise, bacon, mustard seed, pepper, 2 tablespoons: place over the fillets' tops.
2. In the air-fryer bowl, put the fish in a single layer on the greased plate. Cook for 3-5 minutes before the fish quickly flakes with a fork.

3. Meanwhile, mix breadcrumbs, carrot, ground mustard and 1 remaining tablespoon of cheese in a small bowl: whisk in butter. Cook until golden brown, for 2-3 more minutes. Sprinkle with additional green onions if needed.

34. Air-Fried Radishes

Ingredients

- ❖ Radishes 2-1/4 pounds
- ❖ Olive oil 3 tablespoons
- ❖ Oregano 1 tablespoon
- ❖ Salt 1/4 teaspoon
- ❖ Pepper 1/8 teaspoon

Steps

1. Heat the air fryer at 375 degrees. Mix all the ingredients.
2. Place radishes on an oiled tray in the air fryer bowl. Fry till crispy, 15 minutes, blend frequently.

35. Air-Fryer Ham and Egg Pockets

Ingredients

- ❖ Egg 1 large

- ❖ 2% Milk 2 teaspoons
- ❖ Butter 2 teaspoons
- ❖ Sliced deli ham 1 ounce
- ❖ Cheddar cheese 2 tablespoons
- ❖ Freeze Crescent rolls 1 tube

Steps

1. Heat the air fryer at 300 °. Combine the egg and milk in a shallow dish. Heat the butter in a small skillet until sweet. Add the egg combination; cook and stir until the eggs are formed, over medium heat. Distance yourself from the steam. Fold in the cheese and ham.
2. Divide the crescent dough into two rectangles. Fold the dough over the filling, close with a squeeze. In the air-fryer basket, put it in a single layer on a greased plate. Cook for 8-10 minutes until it is lightly browned.

36. Air-Fryer Eggplant Fries

Ingredients

- ❖ Eggs 2 large
- ❖ Parmesan cheese 1/2 cup
- ❖ Toasted wheat germ 1/2 cup
- ❖ Italian seasoning 1 teaspoon
- ❖ Garlic salt 3/4 teaspoon
- ❖ Eggplant 1 medium
- ❖ Cooking spray
- ❖ Meatless pasta sauce 1 cup

Steps

1. Heat an air fryer at 375 °. Whisk the eggs together in a small dish. Mix the cheese, seasonings, and wheat germ in another small dish.
2. Trim the eggplant ends; split the eggplant into 1/2-in.-thick pieces lengthwise. Split elongated into 1/2-in pieces. Dip the eggplant in the eggs, then cover with the mixture of cheese.
3. Adjust eggplant in batches on a greased tray in the air-fryer bowl in a single layer; spritz with olive oil. Cook for 4-5 minutes until it is golden brown. Turn; spritz with

spray for cooking. Cook for 4-5 minutes until it is golden brown. Serve with pasta sauce directly.

37. Air-Fryer Turkey Croquettes

Ingredients

- ❖ Mashed potatoes 2 cups
- ❖ Parmesan cheese 1/2 cup
- ❖ Swiss cheese 1/2 cup
- ❖ Shallot 1
- ❖ Rosemary 2 teaspoons
- ❖ Sage 1 teaspoon
- ❖ Salt 1/2 teaspoon
- ❖ Pepper 1/4 teaspoon
- ❖ Cooked turkey 3 cups
- ❖ Egg 1 large
- ❖ Water 2 tablespoons
- ❖ Panko breadcrumbs 1-1/4 cups
- ❖ Butter-flavored cooking spray

Steps

1. Heat the air fryer at 350 °. Mix the cheese, sage, pepper, salt, mashed potatoes, shallot, and rosemary in a big bowl, whisk in the turkey.
2. Whisk the egg and water in a small dish. In another shallow cup, position the breadcrumbs. Dip the croquettes in the egg mixture, then pat them onto the breadcrumbs to make the coating hold.
3. Place croquettes in batches on a greased tray in the air-fryer bowl in a single layer; spritz with olive oil. Cook for 4-5 minutes until it is golden brown. Turn; spritz with spray for cooking. Cook for 4-5 minutes, until golden brown. Serve with sour cream if needed.

38. Garlic-Herb Fried Patty Pan Squash

Ingredients

- ❖ Small pattypan squash 5 cups

- ❖ Olive oil 1 tablespoon
- ❖ Garlic cloves 2
- ❖ Salt 1/2 teaspoon
- ❖ Oregano 1/4 teaspoon
- ❖ Dried thyme 1/4 teaspoon
- ❖ Pepper 1/4 teaspoon
- ❖ Parsley 1 tablespoon

Steps Heat the air fryer at 375 degrees and put the squash in a bowl. Blend salt, oil, garlic, pepper, oregano, and thyme. Toss to coat.

1. Put the squash on an oiled tray in the air fryer bowl. Fry till tender, 15 mins, stirring frequently. Spray with parsley.

Conclusion

A reason is why the air fryer diet is so popular: it works, and weight reduction is merely only the beginning. Research has been conducted on-air fryer diet that is gluten-free and low carbs containing diet. Studies have shown that this diet enhances energy levels, stabilizes mood, controls sugar in the blood, boosts cholesterol, lowers blood pressure, and more. Despite its long history, though, much remains uncertain about the diet, including its modes of operation, the right therapy, and the broad reach of its applicability. However, the inappropriate implementation of the diet may have significant health consequences and may not be the safest solution for maintaining good well-being. It takes at least two weeks for the body to react to the drastic carbohydrate loss, and occasionally four times as much.

The air fryer low carbs and gluten-free diet usually have unique effects on the body and cells that have benefits beyond what nearly every diet can offer. Carbohydrate restriction and ketone output mixtures reduce insulin rates, activate autophagy (cell clean-up), improve mitochondrial chemicals' development and productivity, reduce inflammation, and burn fat.

Vegan Air Fryer Cookbook

Cook and Taste 50+ High-Protein Recipes. Kickstart Muscles and Body Transformation, Kill Hunger and Feel More Energetic

By

Chef Ludovico L'Italiano

Table of Contents

Introduction..**269**

What is Cooking Vegan?...271

What advantages would veganism have?................................272

Air Fryer 273

Air fryer's Working Process:...275

Tips for using an Air Fryer...277

Outcome..278

CHAPTER 1: Breakfast Recipes...**279**

1. Toasted French toast 279

2. Vegan Casserole 280

3. Vegan Omelet 282

4. Waffles with Vegan chicken..284

5. Tempeh Bacon 287

6. Delicious Potato Pancakes 289

CHAPTER 2: Air Fryer Main Dishes..................................**291**

1. **Mushroom 'n Bell Pepper Pizza** 292

2. Veggies Stuffed Eggplants..294

3. Air-fried Falafel 296

4. Almond Flour Battered Wings.......................................297

5. Spicy Tofu..298

6. Sautéed Bacon with Spinach 299

7. Garden Fresh Veggie Medley...300

8. Colorful Vegetable Croquettes.......................................301

9. Cheesy Mushrooms 302

10. Greek-style Roasted Vegetables 303

11. Vegetable Kabobs with Simple Peanut Sauce 304

12. Hungarian Mushroom Pilaf..305

13. Chinese cabbage Bake 306

14.   Brussels sprouts With Balsamic Oil...308

15.   Aromatic Baked Potatoes with Chives..309

16.   Easy Vegan "chicken" 309

17.   Paprika Vegetable Kebab's..311

18.   Spiced Soy Curls 312

19.   Cauliflower & Egg Rice Casserole..313

20.   Hollandaise Topped Grilled Asparagus...314

21.   Crispy Asparagus Dipped In Paprika-garlic Spice 315

22.   Eggplant Gratin with Mozzarella Crust...316

23.   Asian-style Cauliflower..317

24.   Two-cheese Vegetable Frittata 318

25.   Rice & Beans Stuffed Bell Peppers..319

26.   Parsley-loaded Mushrooms 320

27.   Cheesy Vegetable Quesadilla..321

28.   Creamy 'n Cheese Broccoli Bake..322

29.   Sweet & Spicy Parsnips...323

30.   Zucchini with Mediterranean Dill Sauce 324

31.   Zesty Broccoli...325

32.   Chewy Glazed Parsnips...326

33.   Hoisin-glazed Bok Choy 327

34.   Green Beans with Okra 328

35.   Celeriac with some Greek Yogurt Dip 329

36.   Wine & Garlic Flavored Vegetables 330

37.   Spicy Braised Vegetables...331

CHAPTER 3: Air Fryer Snack Side Dishes and Appetizer Recipes **333**

1.   Crispy 'n Tasty Spring Rolls 333

2.   Spinach & Feta Crescent Triangles 334

3.   Healthy Avocado Fries 335

4.   Twice-fried Cauliflower Tater Tots...336

5. Cheesy Mushroom & Cauliflower Balls..337

6. Italian Seasoned Easy Pasta Chips...339

7. Thai Sweet Potato Balls...339

8. Barbecue Roasted Almonds 340

9. Croissant Rolls..341

10. Curry' n Coriander Spiced Bread Rolls..342

11. Scrumptiously Healthy Chips 343

12. Kid-friendly Vegetable Fritters...344

13. Avocado Fries 345

14. Crispy Wings with Lemony Old Bay Spice.......................................347

15. Cold Salad with Veggies and Pasta...348

16. Zucchini and Minty Eggplant Bites..349

17. Stuffed Potatoes 351

18. Paneer Cutlet..352

19. Spicy Roasted Cashew Nuts 352

CHAPTER 4: Deserts...**354**

1. Almond-apple Treat...354

2. Pepper-pineapple With Butter-sugar Glaze.....................................354

3. True Churros with Yummy Hot Chocolate 355

Conclusion...**357**

Introduction

To have a good, satisfying life, a balanced diet is important. Tiredness and susceptibility to illnesses, many severe, arise from a lifestyle so full of junk food. Our community, sadly, does not neglect unsafe choices. People turn to immoral practices in order to satisfy desire, leading to animal torture. Two of the key explanations that people adhere to vegetarianism, a vegan-based diet that often excludes animal foods such as cheese, beef, jelly, and honey, are fitness and animal welfare.

It's essential for vegetarians to get the most nutrients out of any food, and that's where frying using an air fryer shines. The air fryer cooking will maintain as many nutrients as possible from beans and veggies, and the gadget makes it incredibly simple to cook nutritious food.

Although there are prepared vegan alternatives, the healthier choice, and far less pricey, is still to prepare your own recipes. This book provides the very first moves to being a vegan and offers 50 quick breakfast recipes, sides, snacks, and much more, so you have a solid base on which to develop.

This book will teach you all you need to thrive, whether you are either a vegan and only need more meal choices or have just begun contemplating transforming your diet.

What is Cooking Vegan?

In recent decades, vegetarianism has become quite common, as individuals understand just how toxic the eating patterns of civilization have become. We are a society that enjoys meat, and, unfortunately, we go to dishonest measures to get the food we like. More citizens are choosing to give up beef and, unlike vegans, other livestock items due to various health issues, ethical issues, or both. Their diet moves to one focused on plants, whole grains, beans, fruit, seeds, nuts, and vegan varieties of the common dish.

What advantages would veganism have?

There are a lot of advantages to a diet away from all animal items. Only a few includes:

- Healthier hair, skin, and nails

- High energy

- Fewer chances of flu and cold

- Fewer migraines

- Increased tolerance to cancer

- Strengthened fitness of the heart

Although research has proven that veganism will contribute to reducing BMI, it must not be followed for the mere sake of weight reduction. "Vegan" does not indicate "lower-calorie," and if you wish to reduce weight, other healthier activities, including exercising and consuming water, can complement the diet.

Air Fryer

A common kitchen gadget used to create fried foods such as beef, baked goods and potato chips is an air fryer. It provides a crunchy, crisp coating by blowing hot air across the food. This also leads to a chemical reaction commonly known as the Maillard effect, which happens in the presence of heat in between reducing sugar and amino acid. This adds to shifts in food color and taste. Due to the reduced amount of calories and fat, air-fried items are marketed as a healthier substitute to deep-fried foods.

Rather than fully soaking the food in fat, air-frying utilizes just a teaspoon to create a flavor and feel equivalent to deep-fried foods.

The flavor and appearance of the fried food in the air are similar to the deep fryer outcomes: On the surface, crispy; from the inside, soft. You do need to use a limited amount of oil, though, or any at all (based on what you're baking). But indeed, contrary to deep frying, if you agree to use only 1-2 teaspoons of plant-based oil with spices and you stuck to air-frying vegetables rather than anything else, air frying is certainly a better option.

The secret to weight loss, decreased likelihood of cardiovascular illness and better long-term wellbeing as we mature is any gadget that assists you and your friends in your vegetarian game.

Air fryer's Working Process:

The air fryer is a worktop kitchen gadget that operates in the same manner as a traditional oven. To become acquainted with the operating theory of the traditional oven, you will need a little study. The air fryer uses rotating hot air to fry and crisp your meal, close to the convection oven. In a traditional convection oven, the airflow relies on revolving fans, which blast hot air around to produce an even or equalized temperature dispersal throughout the oven.

This is compared to the upward airflow of standard ovens, where the warm place is typically the oven's tip. And although the air fryer is not quite like the convection oven, it is a great approximation of it in the field of airflow for most components. The gadget has an air inlet at the top that lets air in and a hot air outlet at the side. All of these features are used to monitor the temperature within the air fryer. Temperatures will rise to 230 ° C, based on the sort of air fryer you're buying.

In conjunction with any grease, this hot air is used for cooking the food in the bowl within the device, if you like. Yes, if you want a taste of the oil, you should apply more oil. To jazz up the taste of the meal, simply add a little more to the blend. But the key concept behind the air fryer is to reduce the consumption of calories and fat without reducing the amount of taste.

Using air frying rather than deep frying saves between 70-80 calories, according to researchers. The growing success of recipes for air fryers is simply attributed to its impressive performance. It is simple to use and less time-consuming than conventional ovens.

This is more or less a lottery win for people searching for healthy alternative to deep-frying, as demonstrated by its widespread popularity in many homes today. In contrast to conventional ovens or deep frying, the air fryer creates crispy, crunchy, wonderful, and far fewer fatty foods in less duration. For certain individuals like us; this is what distinguishes air fryer recipes.

Tips for using an Air Fryer

1. The food is cooked easily. Air fried, unlike conventional cooking techniques, cut the cooking time a great deal. Therefore, to stop burning the food or getting a not-so-great flavor, it is best to hold a close eye on the gadget. Notice, remember that the smaller the food on the basket, the shorter the cooking period, which implies that the food cooks quicker.

2. You may need to reduce the temperature at first. Bear in mind that air fryers depend on the flow of hot air, which heats up rapidly. This ensures that it's better, to begin with, a low temperature so that the food cooks equally. It is likely that when the inside is already cooking, the exterior of the food is all cooked and begins to become dark or too dry.

3. When air fryers are in operation, they create some noise. If you are new to recipes for air fryers, you may have to realize that air fryers create noise while working. When it's in service, a whirring tone emanates from the device. However, the slight annoyance pales in contrast to the various advantages of having an air fryer.

4. Hold the grate within the container at all hours. As previously mentioned, the air fryer has a container inside it, where the food is put and permitted to cook. This helps hot air to flow freely around the food, allowing for even cooking.

5. Don't stuff the air fryer with so much food at once. If you plan to make a meal for one guy, with only one batch, you would most definitely be able to get your cooking right. If you're cooking for two or more individuals, you can need to plan the food in groups. With a 4 - 5 quart air fryer, you can always need to cook in groups, depending on the size and sort of air fryer you have. This not only means that your device works longer but also keeps

your food from cooking unevenly. You shouldn't have to turn the air fryer off as you pull out the basket since it simply turns off on its own until the basket is out. Often, make sure the drawer is completely retracted; otherwise, the fryer would not turn back on.

6. Take the basket out of the mix and mix the ingredients. You might need to move the food around or switch it over once every few minutes, based on the dish you're preparing and the time it takes to prepare your dinner.

The explanation for this is that even cooking can be done. Certain recipes involve the foods in the basket to shake and shuffle throughout the cooking phase. And an easy-to-understand checklist is given for each recipe to direct you thru the cycle.

7. The air fryer does not need cooking mist. It isn't needed. In order to prevent the urge to use non-stick frying spray in the container, you must deliberately take care of this. The basket is now coated with a non-stick covering, so what you need to do is fill your meal inside the container and push it back in.

Outcome

You can create nutritious meals very simply and fast, right in the comfort of your house. There are many excellent recipes for producing healthier meals and nutritious foods, which you can notice in the air fryer recipes illustrated in this book. However, you'll need to pay careful attention to the ingredients and know-how to easily use the air fryer to do this. To get straightforward guidance on installation and usage, you can need to refer to the company's manual.

CHAPTER 1: Breakfast Recipes

1. Toasted French toast

Preparation time: 2 minutes

Cooking time: 5 minutes

Servings: 1 people

Ingredients:

- ½ Cup of Unsweetened Shredded Coconut

- 1 Tsp. Baking Powder

- ½ Cup Lite Culinary Coconut Milk

- 2 Slices of Gluten-Free Bread (use your favorite)

Directions:

1. Stir together the baking powder and coconut milk in a large rimmed pot.

2. On a tray, layout your ground coconut.

3. Pick each loaf of your bread and dip it in your coconut milk for the very first time, and then pass it to the ground coconut, let it sit for a few minutes, then cover the slice entirely with the coconut.

4. Place the covered bread loaves in your air fryer, cover it, adjust the temperature to about 350 ° F and set the clock for around 4 minutes.

5. Take out from your air fryer until done, and finish with some maple syrup of your choice. French toast is done. Enjoy!

2. Vegan Casserole

Preparation time: 10-12 minutes

Cooking time: 15-20 minutes

Servings: 2-3 people

Ingredients:

- 1/2 cup of cooked quinoa

- 1 tbsp. of lemon juice

- 2 tbsp. of water

- 2 tbsp. of plain soy yogurt

- 2 tbsp. of nutritional yeast

- 7 ounces of extra-firm tofu about half a block, drained but not pressed

- 1/2 tsp. of ground cumin

- 1/2 tsp. of red pepper flakes

- 1/2 tsp. of freeze-dried dill

- 1/2 tsp. of black pepper

- 1/2 tsp. of salt

- 1 tsp. of dried oregano

- 1/2 cup of diced shiitake mushrooms

- 1/2 cup of diced bell pepper I used a combination of red and green

- 2 small celery stalks chopped

- 1 large carrot chopped

- 1 tsp. of minced garlic

- 1 small onion diced

- 1 tsp. of olive oil

Directions:

1. Warm the olive oil over medium-low heat in a big skillet. Add your onion and garlic and simmer till the onion is transparent (for about 3 to 6 minutes). Add your bell

pepper, carrot, and celery and simmer for another 3 minutes. Mix the oregano, mushrooms, pepper, salt, cumin, dill, and red pepper powder. Mix completely and lower the heat to low. If the vegetables tend to cling, stir regularly and add in about a teaspoon of water.

2. Pulse the nutritional yeast, tofu, water, yogurt, and some lemon juice in a food mixer until fluffy. To your skillet, add your tofu mixture. Add in half a cup of cooked quinoa. Mix thoroughly.

3. Move to a microwave-proof plate or tray that works for your air fryer basket.

4. Cook for around 15 minutes at about 350°F (or 18 to 20 minutes at about 330°F, till it turns golden brown).

5. Please take out your plate or tray from your air fryer and let it rest for at least five minutes before eating.

3. Vegan Omelet

Preparation time: 15 minutes

Cooking time: 16 minutes

Servings: 3 people

Ingredients:

- ½ cup of grated vegan cheese

- 1 tbsp. of water

- 1 tbsp. of brags

- 3 tbsp. of nutritional yeast

- ¼ tsp. of basil

- ¼ tsp. of garlic powder

- ¼ tsp. of onion powder

- ¼ tsp. of pepper

- ½ tsp. of cumin

- ½ tsp. of turmeric

- ¼ tsp. of salt

- ¼ cup of chickpea flour (or you may use any bean flour)

- ½ cup of finely diced veggies (like chard, kale, dried mushrooms, spinach, watermelon radish etc.)

- half a piece of tofu (organic high in protein kind)

Directions:

4. Blend all your ingredients in a food blender or mixer, excluding the vegetables and cheese.

5. Move the batter from the blender to a container and combine the vegetables and cheese in it. Since it's faster, you could use both hands to combine it.

6. Brush the base of your air fryer bucket with some oil.

7. Put a couple of parchment papers on your counter. On the top of your parchment paper, place a cookie cutter of your desire.

8. In your cookie cutter, push 1/6 of the paste. Then raise and put the cookie cutter on a different section of your parchment paper.

9. Redo the process till you have about 6 pieces using the remainder of the paste.

10. Put 2 or 3 of your omelets at the base of your air fryer container. Using some oil, brush the topsides of the omelets.

11. Cook for around 5 minutes at about 370 °, turn and bake for another 4 minutes or more if needed. And redo with the omelets that remain.

12. Offer with sriracha mayo or whatever kind of dipping sauce you prefer. Or use them for a sandwich at breakfast.

4. Waffles with Vegan chicken

Preparation time: 10 minutes

Cooking time: 15 minutes

Servings: 2 people

Ingredients:

Fried Vegan Chicken:

- ¼ to ½ teaspoon of Black Pepper

- ½ teaspoon of Paprika

- ½ teaspoon of Onion Powder

- ½ teaspoon of Garlic Powder

- 2 teaspoon of Dried Parsley

- 2 Cups of Gluten-Free Panko

- ¼ Cup of Cornstarch

- 1 Cup of Unsweetened Non-Dairy Milk

- 1 Small Head of Cauliflower

Yummy Cornmeal Waffles:

- ½ teaspoon of Pure Vanilla Extract

- ¼ Cup of Unsweetened Applesauce

- ½ Cup of Unsweetened Non-Dairy Milk

- 1 to 2 TB Erythritol (or preferred sweetener)

- 1 teaspoon Baking Powder

- ¼ Cup of Stoneground Cornmeal

- ⅔ Cup of Gluten-Free All-Purpose Flour

Toppings:

- Vegan Butter

- Hot Sauce

- Pure Maple Syrup

Directions:

For making your Vegan Fried Chicken:

1. Dice the cauliflower (you wouldn't have to be careful in this) into big florets and put it aside.

2. Mix the cornstarch and milk in a tiny pot.

3. Throw the herbs, panko, and spices together in a big bowl or dish.

4. In the thick milk mixture, soak your cauliflower florets, then cover the soaked bits in the prepared panko mix before putting the wrapped floret into your air fryer bucket.

5. For the remaining of your cauliflower, redo the same process.

6. Set your air fryer clock for around 15 minutes to about 400 ° F and let the cauliflower air fry.

For making you're Waffles:

1. Oil a regular waffle iron and warm it up.

2. Mix all your dry ingredients in a pot, and then blend in your wet ingredients until you have a thick mixture.

3. To create a big waffle, utilize ½ of the mixture and redo the process to create another waffle for a maximum of two persons.

To Organize:

1. Put on dishes your waffles, place each with ½ of the cooked cauliflower, now drizzle with the hot sauce, syrup, and any extra toppings that you want. Serve warm!

5. Tempeh Bacon

Preparation time: 15 minutes plus 2 hour marinating time

Cooking time: 10 minutes

Servings: 4 people

Ingredients:

- ½ teaspoon of freshly grated black pepper

- ½ teaspoon of onion powder

- ½ teaspoon of garlic powder

- 1 ½ teaspoon of smoked paprika

- 1 teaspoon of apple cider vinegar

- 1 tablespoon of olive oil (plus some more for oiling your air fryer)

- 3 tablespoon of pure maple syrup

- ¼ cup of gluten-free, reduced-sodium tamari

- 8 oz. of gluten-free tempeh

Directions:

1. Break your Tempeh cube into two parts and boil for about 10 minutes, some more if required. To the rice cooker bowl, add a cup of warm water. Then, put the pieces of tempeh into the steamer basket of the unit. Close the cover, push the button for heat or steam cooking (based on your rice cooker's type or brand), and adjust the steaming timer for around 10 minutes.

2. Let the tempeh cool completely before taking it out of the rice cooker or your steamer basket for around 5 minutes.

3. Now make the sauce while cooking the tempeh. In a 9" x 13" baking tray, incorporate all the rest of your ingredients and mix them using a fork. Then set it aside and ready the tempeh.

4. Put the tempeh steamed before and cooled on a chopping board, and slice into strips around 1/4' wide. Put each slice gently in the sauce. Then roll over each slice gently. Seal and put in the fridge for two to three hours or even overnight, rotating once or twice during the time.

5. Turn the bits gently one more time until you are about to create the tempeh bacon. And if you would like, you may spoon over any leftover sauce.

6. Put your crisper plate/tray into the air fryer if yours came with one instead of a built-in one. Oil the base of your crisper tray or your air fryer basket slightly with some olive oil or using an olive oil spray that is anti-aerosol.

7. Put the tempeh slices in a thin layer gently in your air fryer bucket. If you have a tiny air fryer, you will have to air fry it in two or multiple rounds. Air fry for around 10-15 minutes at about 325 ° F before the slices are lightly golden but not burnt. You

may detach your air fryer container to inspect it and make sure it's not burnt. It normally takes about 10 minutes.

6. Delicious Potato Pancakes

Preparation time: 5 minutes

Cooking time: 15 minutes

Servings: 4 people

Ingredients:

- black pepper according to taste

- 3 tablespoon of flour

- ¼ teaspoon of pepper

- ¼ teaspoon of salt

- ½ teaspoon of garlic powder

- 2 tablespoon of unsalted butter

- ¼ cup of milk

- 1 beaten egg

- 1 medium onion, chopped

Directions:

1. Preheat the fryer to about 390° F and combine the potatoes, garlic powder, eggs, milk, onion, pepper, butter, and salt in a small bowl; add in the flour and make a batter.

2. Shape around 1⁄4 cup of your batter into a cake.

3. In the fryer's cooking basket, put the cakes and cook for a couple of minutes.

4. Serve and enjoy your treat!

CHAPTER 2: Air Fryer Main Dishes

1. Mushroom 'n Bell Pepper Pizza

Preparation time: 5 minutes

Cooking time: 10 minutes

Servings: 10 people

Ingredients:

- salt and pepper according to taste

- 2 tbsp. of parsley

- 1 vegan pizza dough

- 1 shallot, chopped

- 1 cup of oyster mushrooms, chopped

- ¼ red bell pepper, chopped

Directions:

1. Preheat your air fryer to about 400°F.

2. Cut the pie dough into small squares. Just set them aside.

3. Put your bell pepper, shallot, oyster mushroom, and parsley all together into a mixing dish.

4. According to taste, sprinkle with some pepper and salt.

5. On top of your pizza cubes, put your topping.

6. Put your pizza cubes into your air fryer and cook for about 10 minutes.

2. Veggies Stuffed Eggplants

Preparation time: 5 minutes

Cooking time: 14 minutes

Servings: 5 people

Ingredients:

- 2 tbsp. of tomato paste

- Salt and ground black pepper, as required

- ½ tsp. of garlic, chopped

- 1 tbsp. of vegetable oil

- 1 tbsp. of fresh lime juice

- ½ green bell pepper, seeded and chopped

- ¼ cup of cottage cheese, chopped

- 1 tomato, chopped

- 1 onion, chopped

- 10 small eggplants, halved lengthwise

Directions:

1. Preheat your air fryer to about 320°F and oil the container of your air fryer.

2. Cut a strip longitudinally from all sides of your eggplant and scrape out the pulp in a medium-sized bowl.

3. Add lime juice on top of your eggplants and place them in the container of your Air Fryer.

4. Cook for around a couple of minutes and extract from your Air Fryer.

5. Heat the vegetable oil on medium-high heat in a pan and add the onion and garlic.

6. Sauté for around 2 minutes and mix in the tomato, salt, eggplant flesh, and black pepper.

7. Sauté and add bell pepper, tomato paste, cheese, and cilantro for roughly 3 minutes.

8. Cook for around a minute and put this paste into your eggplants.

9. Shut each eggplant with its lids and adjust the Air Fryer to 360°F.

10. Organize and bake for around 5 minutes in your Air Fryer Basket.

11. Dish out on a serving tray and eat hot.

3. Air-fried Falafel

Preparation time: 10 minutes

Cooking time: 25 minutes

Servings: 6 people

Ingredients:

- Salt and black pepper according to taste

- 1 teaspoon of chili powder

- 2 teaspoon of ground coriander

- 2 teaspoon of ground cumin

- 1 onion, chopped

- 4 garlic cloves, chopped

- Juice of 1 lemon

- 1 cup of fresh parsley, chopped

- ½ cup of chickpea flour

Directions:

1. Add flour, coriander, chickpeas, lemon juice, parsley, onion, garlic, chili, cumin, salt, turmeric, and pepper to a processor and mix until mixed, not too battery; several chunks should be present.

2. Morph the paste into spheres and hand-press them to ensure that they are still around.

3. Spray using some spray oil and place them in a paper-lined air fryer bucket; if necessary, perform in groups.

4. Cook for about 14 minutes at around 360°F, rotating once mid-way through the cooking process.

5. They must be light brown and crispy.

4. Almond Flour Battered Wings

Preparation time: 10 minutes

Cooking time: 25 minutes

Servings: 4 people

Ingredients:

- Salt and pepper according to taste

- 4 tbsp. of minced garlic

- 2 tbsp. of stevia powder

- 16 pieces of vegan chicken wings

- ¾ cup of almond flour

- ¼ cup of butter, melted

Directions:

1. Preheat your air fryer for about 5 minutes.

2. Mix the stevia powder, almond flour, vegan chicken wings, and garlic in a mixing dish. According to taste, sprinkle with some black pepper and salt.

3. Please put it in the bucket of your air fryer and cook at about 400°F for around 25 minutes.

4. Ensure you give your fryer container a shake midway through the cooking process.

5. Put in a serving dish after cooking and add some melted butter on top. Toss it to coat it completely.

5. Spicy Tofu

Preparation time: 5 minutes

Cooking time: 13 minutes

Servings: 3 people

Ingredients:

- Salt and black pepper, according to taste

- 1 tsp. of garlic powder

- 1 tsp. of onion powder

- 1½ tsp. of paprika

- 1½ tbsp. of avocado oil

- 3 tsp. of cornstarch

- 1 (14-ounces) block extra-firm tofu, pressed and cut into ¾-inch cubes

Directions:

1. Preheat your air fryer to about 390°F and oil the container of your air fryer with some spray oil.

2. In a medium-sized bowl, blend the cornstarch, oil, tofu, and spices and mix to cover properly.

3. In the Air Fryer basket, place the tofu bits and cook for around a minute, flipping twice between the cooking times.

4. On a serving dish, spread out the tofu and enjoy it warm.

6. Sautéed Bacon with Spinach

Preparation time: 5 minutes

Cooking time: 9 minutes

Servings: 2 people

Ingredients:

- 1 garlic clove, minced

- 2 tbsp. of olive oil

- 4-ounce of fresh spinach

- 1 onion, chopped

- 3 meatless bacon slices, chopped

Directions:

1. Preheat your air fryer at about 340° F and oil the air fryer's tray with some olive oil or cooking oil spray.

2. In the Air Fryer basket, put garlic and olive oil.

3. Cook and add in the onions and bacon for around 2 minutes.

4. Cook and mix in the spinach for approximately 3 minutes.

5. Cook for 4 more minutes and plate out in a bowl to eat.

7. Garden Fresh Veggie Medley

Preparation time: 5 minutes

Cooking time: 15 minutes

Servings: 4 people

Ingredients:

- 1 tbsp. of balsamic vinegar

- 1 tbsp. of olive oil

- 2 tbsp. of herbs de Provence

- 2 garlic cloves, minced

- 2 small onions, chopped

- 3 tomatoes, chopped

- 1 zucchini, chopped

- 1 eggplant, chopped

- 2 yellow bell peppers seeded and chopped

- Salt and black pepper, according to taste.

Directions:

1. Preheat your air fryer at about 355° F and oil up the air fryer basket.

2. In a medium-sized bowl, add all the ingredients and toss to cover completely.

3. Move to the basket of your Air Fryer and cook for around 15 minutes.

4. After completing the cooking time, let it sit in the air fryer for around 5 minutes and plate out to serve warm.

8. Colorful Vegetable Croquettes

Preparation time: 5 minutes

Cooking time: 10 minutes

Servings: 4 people

Ingredients:

- 1/2 cup of parmesan cheese, grated

- 2 eggs

- 1/4 cup of coconut flour

- 1/2 cup of almond flour

- 2 tbsp. of olive oil

- 3 tbsp. of scallions, minced

- 1 clove garlic, minced

- 1 bell pepper, chopped

- 1/2 cup of mushrooms, chopped

- 1/2 tsp. of cayenne pepper

- Salt and black pepper, according to taste.

- 2 tbsp. of butter

- 4 tbsp. of milk

- 1/2 pound of broccoli

Directions:

1. Boil your broccoli in a medium-sized saucepan for up to around 20 minutes. With butter, milk, black pepper, salt, and cayenne pepper, rinse the broccoli and mash it.

2. Add in the bell pepper, mushrooms, garlic, scallions, and olive oil and blend properly. Form into patties with the blend.

3. Put the flour in a deep bowl; beat your eggs in a second bowl; then put the parmesan cheese in another bowl.

4. Dip each patty into your flour, accompanied by the eggs and lastly the parmesan cheese, push to hold the shape.

5. Cook for around 16 minutes, turning midway through the cooking period, in the preheated Air Fryer at about 370° F. Bon appétit!

9. Cheesy Mushrooms

Preparation time: 3 minutes

Cooking time: 8 minutes

Servings: 4 people

Ingredients:

- 1 tsp. of dried dill

- 2 tbsp. of Italian dried mixed herbs

- 2 tbsp. of olive oil

- 2 tbsp. of cheddar cheese, grated

- 2 tbsp. of mozzarella cheese, grated

- Salt and freshly ground black pepper, according to taste

- 6-ounce of button mushrooms stemmed

Directions:

Preheat the air fryer at around 355° F and oil your air fryer basket.

In a mixing bowl, combine the Italian dried mixed herbs, mushrooms, salt, oil, and black pepper and mix well to cover.

In the Air Fryer bucket, place the mushrooms and cover them with some cheddar cheese and mozzarella cheese.

To eat, cook for around 8 minutes and scatter with dried dill.

10. Greek-style Roasted Vegetables

Preparation time: 10 minutes

Cooking time: 25 minutes

Servings: 3 people

Ingredients:

- 1/2 cup of Kalamata olives, pitted

- 1 (28-ounce) canned diced tomatoes with juice

- 1/2 tsp. of dried basil

- Sea salt and freshly cracked black pepper, according to taste

- 1 tsp. of dried rosemary

- 1 cup of dry white wine

- 2 tbsp. of extra-virgin olive oil

- 2 bell peppers, cut into 1-inch chunks

- 1 red onion, sliced

- 1/2 pound of zucchini, cut into 1-inch chunks

- 1/2 pound of cauliflower, cut into 1-inch florets

- 1/2 pound of butternut squash, peeled and cut into 1-inch chunks

Directions:

1. Add some rosemary, wine, olive oil, black pepper, salt, and basil along with your vegetables toss until well-seasoned.

2. Onto a lightly oiled baking dish, add 1/2 of the canned chopped tomatoes; scatter to fill the base of your baking dish.

3. Add in the vegetables and add the leftover chopped tomatoes to the top. On top of tomatoes, spread the Kalamata olives.

4. Bake for around 20 minutes at about 390° F in the preheated Air Fryer, turning the dish midway through your cooking cycle. Serve it hot and enjoy it!

11. Vegetable Kabobs with Simple Peanut Sauce

Preparation time: 10 minutes

Cooking time: 30 minutes

Servings: 4 people

Ingredients:

- 1/3 tsp. of granulated garlic

- 1 tsp. of dried rosemary, crushed

- 1 tsp. of red pepper flakes, crushed

- Sea salt and ground black pepper, according to your taste.

- 2 tbsp. of extra-virgin olive oil

- 8 small button mushrooms, cleaned

- 8 pearl onions, halved

- 2 bell peppers, diced into 1-inch pieces

- 8 whole baby potatoes, diced into 1-inch pieces

Peanut Sauce:

- 1/2 tsp. of garlic salt

- 1 tbsp. of soy sauce

- 1 tbsp. of balsamic vinegar

- 2 tbsp. of peanut butter

Directions:

1. For a few minutes, dunk the wooden chopsticks in water.

2. String the vegetables onto your chopsticks; drip some olive oil all over your chopsticks with the vegetables on it; dust with seasoning.

3. Cook for about 1 minute at 400°F in the preheated Air Fryer.

Peanut Sauce:

1. In the meantime, mix the balsamic vinegar with some peanut butter, garlic salt and some soy sauce in a tiny dish. Offer the kabobs with a side of peanut sauce. Eat warm!

12. Hungarian Mushroom Pilaf

Preparation time: 10 minutes

Cooking time: 50 minutes

Servings: 4 people

Ingredients:

- 1 tsp. of sweet Hungarian paprika

- 1/2 tsp. of dried tarragon

- 1 tsp. of dried thyme

- 1/4 cup of dry vermouth

- 1 onion, chopped

- 2 garlic cloves

- 2 tbsp. of olive oil

- 1 pound of fresh porcini mushrooms, sliced

- 2 tbsp. of olive oil

- 3 cups of vegetable broth

- 1 ½ cups of white rice

Directions:

1. In a wide saucepan, put the broth and rice, add some water, and bring it to a boil.

2. Cover with a lid and turn the flame down to a low temperature and proceed to cook for the next 18 minutes or so. After cooking, let it rest for 5 to 10 minutes, and then set aside.

3. Finally, in a lightly oiled baking dish, mix the heated, fully cooked rice with the rest of your ingredients.

4. Cook at about 200° degrees for around 20 minutes in the preheated Air Fryer, regularly monitoring to even cook.

5. In small bowls, serve. Bon appétit!

13. Chinese cabbage Bake

Preparation time: 15 minutes

Cooking time: 35 minutes

Servings: 4 people

Ingredients:

- 1 cup of Monterey Jack cheese, shredded

- 1/2 tsp. of cayenne pepper

- 1 cup of cream cheese

- 1/2 cup of milk

- 4 tbsp. of flaxseed meal

- 1/2 stick butter

- 2 garlic cloves, sliced

- 1 onion, thickly sliced

- 1 jalapeno pepper, seeded and sliced

- Sea salt and freshly ground black pepper, according to taste.

- 2 bell peppers, seeded and sliced

- 1/2 pound of Chinese cabbage, roughly chopped

Directions:

1. Heat the salted water in a pan and carry it to a boil. For around 2 to 3 minutes, steam the Chinese cabbage. To end the cooking process, switch the Chinese cabbage to cold water immediately.

2. Put your Chinese cabbage in a lightly oiled casserole dish. Add in the garlic, onion, and peppers.

3. Next, over low fire, melt some butter in a skillet. Add in your flaxseed meal steadily and cook for around 2 minutes to create a paste.

4. Add in the milk gently, constantly whisking until it creates a dense mixture. Add in your cream cheese. Sprinkle some cayenne pepper, salt, and black pepper. To the casserole tray, transfer your mixture.

5. Cover with some Monterey Jack cheese and cook for about 2 minutes at around 390° F in your preheated Air Fryer. Serve it warm.

14. Brussels sprouts With Balsamic Oil

Preparation time: 5 minutes

Cooking time: 15 minutes

Servings: 4 people

Ingredients:

- 2 tbsp. of olive oil

- 2 cups of Brussels sprouts, halved

- 1 tbsp. of balsamic vinegar

- ¼ tsp. of salt

Directions:

1. For 5 minutes, preheat your air fryer.

2. In a mixing bowl, blend all of your ingredients to ensure the zucchini fries are very well coated. Put the fries in the basket of an air fryer.

3. Close it and cook it at about 350°F for around 15 minutes.

15. Aromatic Baked Potatoes with Chives

Preparation time: 15 minutes

Cooking time: 45 minutes

Servings: 2 people

Ingredients:

- 2 tbsp. of chives, chopped

- 2 garlic cloves, minced

- 1 tbsp. of sea salt

- 1/4 tsp. of smoked paprika

- 1/4 tsp. of red pepper flakes

- 2 tbsp. of olive oil

- 4 medium baking potatoes, peeled

Directions:

1. Toss the potatoes with your seasoning, olive oil, and garlic.

2. Please put them in the basket of your Air Fryer. Cook at about 400° F for around 40 minutes just until the potatoes are fork soft in your preheated Air Fryer.

3. Add in some fresh minced chives to garnish. Bon appétit!

16. Easy Vegan "chicken"

Preparation time: 10 minutes

Cooking time: 20 minutes

Servings: 4 people

Ingredients:

- 1 tsp. of celery seeds

- 1/2 tsp. of mustard powder

- 1 tsp. of cayenne pepper

- 1/4 cup of all-purpose flour

- 1/2 cup of cornmeal

- 8 ounces of soy chunks

- Sea salt and ground black pepper, according to taste.

Directions:

1. In a skillet over medium-high flame, cook the soya chunks in plenty of water. Turn off the flame and allow soaking for several minutes. Drain the remaining water, wash, and strain it out.

2. In a mixing bowl, combine the rest of the components. Roll your soy chunks over the breading paste, pressing lightly to stick.

3. In the slightly oiled Air Fryer basket, place your soy chunks.

4. Cook at about 390° for around 10 minutes in your preheated Air Fryer, rotating them over midway through the cooking process; operate in batches if required. Bon appétit!

17.Paprika Vegetable Kebab's

Preparation time: 10 minutes

Cooking time: 20 minutes

Servings: 4 people

Ingredients:

- 1/2 tsp. of ground black pepper

- 1 tsp. of sea salt flakes

- 1 tsp. of smoked paprika

- 1/4 cup of sesame oil

- 2 tbsp. of dry white wine

- 1 red onion, cut into wedges

- 2 cloves garlic, pressed

- 1 tsp. of whole grain mustard

- 1 fennel bulb, diced

- 1 parsnip, cut into thick slices

- 1 celery, cut into thick slices

Directions:

1. Toss all of the above ingredients together in a mixing bowl to uniformly coat. Thread the vegetables alternately onto the wooden skewers.

2. Cook for around 15 minutes at about 380° F on your Air Fryer grill plate.

3. Turn them over midway during the cooking process.

4. Taste, change the seasonings if needed and serve steaming hot.

18. Spiced Soy Curls

Preparation time: 5 minutes

Cooking time: 10 minutes

Servings: 2 people

Ingredients:

- 1 tsp. of poultry seasoning

- 2 tsp. of Cajun seasoning

- ¼ cup of fine ground cornmeal

- ¼ cup of nutritional yeast

- 4 ounces of soy curls

- 3 cups of boiling water

- Salt and ground white pepper, as needed

Directions:

1. Dip the soy curls for around a minute or so in hot water in a heat-resistant tub.

2. Drain your soy coils using a strainer and force the excess moisture out using a broad spoon.

3. Mix the cornmeal, nutritional yeast, salt, seasonings, and white pepper well in a mixing bowl.

4. Transfer your soy curls to the bowl and coat well with the blend. Let the air-fryer temperature to about 380° F. Oil the basket of your air fryers.

5. Adjust soy curls in a uniform layer in the lined air fryer basket. Cook for about 10 minutes in the air fryer, turning midway through the cycle.

6. Take out the soy curls from your air fryer and put them on a serving dish. Serve it steaming hot.

19. Cauliflower & Egg Rice Casserole

Preparation time: 5 minutes

Cooking time: 15 minutes

Servings: 4 people

Ingredients:

- 2 eggs, beaten

- 1 tablespoon of soy sauce

- Salt and black pepper according to taste.

- ½ cup of chopped onion

- 1 cup of okra, chopped

- 1 yellow bell pepper, chopped

- 2 teaspoon of olive oil

Directions:

1. Preheat your air fryer to about 380° F. Oil a baking tray with spray oil. Pulse the cauliflower till it becomes like thin rice-like capsules in your food blender.

2. Now add your cauliflower rice to a baking tray mix in the okra, bell pepper, salt, soy sauce, onion, and pepper and combine well.

3. Drizzle a little olive oil on top along with the beaten eggs. Put the tray in your air fryer and cook for about a minute. Serve it hot.

20. Hollandaise Topped Grilled Asparagus

Preparation time: 2 minutes

Cooking time: 15 minutes

Servings: 6 people

Ingredients:

- A punch of ground white pepper

- A pinch of mustard powder

- 3 pounds of asparagus spears, trimmed

- 3 egg yolks

- 2 tbsp. of olive oil

- 1 tsp. of chopped tarragon leaves

- ½ tsp. of salt

- ½ lemon juice

- ½ cup of butter, melted

- ¼ tsp. of black pepper

Directions:

1. Preheat your air fryer to about 330° F. In your air fryer, put the grill pan attachment.

2. Mix the olive oil, salt, asparagus, and pepper into a Ziploc bag. To mix all, give everything a quick shake. Load onto the grill plate and cook for about 15 minutes.

3. In the meantime, beat the lemon juice, egg yolks, and salt in a double boiler over a moderate flame until velvety.

4. Add in the melted butter, mustard powder, and some white pepper. Continue whisking till the mixture is creamy and thick. Serve with tarragon leaves as a garnish.

5. Pour the sauce over the asparagus spears and toss to blend.

21. Crispy Asparagus Dipped In Paprika-garlic Spice

Preparation time: 2 minutes

Cooking time: 15 minutes

Servings: 5 people

Ingredients:

- ¼ cup of almond flour

- ½ tsp. of garlic powder

- ½ tsp. of smoked paprika

- 10 medium asparagus, trimmed

- 2 large eggs, beaten

- 2 tbsp. of parsley, chopped

- Salt and pepper according to your taste

Directions:

1. For about 5 minutes, preheat your air fryer.

2. Mix the almond flour, garlic powder, parsley, and smoked paprika in a mixing dish. To taste, season with some salt and black pepper.

3. Soak your asparagus in the beaten eggs, and then dredge it in a combination of almond flour.

4. Put in the bowl of your air fryer. Close the lid. At about 350°F, cook for around a minute.

22. Eggplant Gratin with Mozzarella Crust

Preparation time: 10 minutes

Cooking time: 30 minutes

Servings: 2 people

Ingredients:

- 1 tablespoon of breadcrumbs

- ¼ cup of grated mozzarella cheese

- Cooking spray

- Salt and pepper according to your taste

- ¼ teaspoon of dried marjoram

- ¼ teaspoon of dried basil

- 1 teaspoon of capers

- 1 tablespoon of sliced pimiento-stuffed olives

- 1 clove garlic, minced

- ⅓ cup of chopped tomatoes

- ¼ cup of chopped onion

- ¼ cup of chopped green pepper

- ¼ cup of chopped red pepper

Directions:

1. Put the green pepper, eggplant, onion, red pepper, olives, tomatoes, basil marjoram, garlic, salt, capers, and pepper in a container and preheat your air fryer to about 300° F.

2. Lightly oil a baking tray with a spray of cooking olive oil.

3. Fill your baking with the eggplant combination and line it with the vessel.

4. Place some mozzarella cheese on top of it and top with some breadcrumbs. Put the dish in the frying pan and cook for a few minutes.

23. Asian-style Cauliflower

Preparation time: 10 minutes

Cooking time: 25 minutes

Servings: 4 people

Ingredients:

- 2 tbsp. of sesame seeds

- 1/4 cup of lime juice

- 1 tbsp. of fresh parsley, finely chopped

- 1 tbsp. of ginger, freshly grated

- 2 cloves of garlic, peeled and pressed

- 1 tbsp. of sake

- 1 tbsp. of tamari sauce

- 1 tbsp. of sesame oil

- 1 onion, peeled and finely chopped

- 2 cups of cauliflower, grated

Directions:

1. In a mixing bowl, mix your onion, cauliflower, tamari sauce, sesame oil, garlic, sake, and ginger; whisk until all is well integrated.

2. Air-fry it for around a minute at about 400° F.

3. Pause your Air Fryer. Add in some parsley and lemon juice.

4. Cook for an extra 10 minutes at about 300° degrees F in the air fryer.

5. In the meantime, in a non-stick pan, toast your sesame seeds; swirl them continuously over medium-low heat. Serve hot on top of the cauliflower with a pinch of salt and pepper.

24. Two-cheese Vegetable Frittata

Preparation time: 15 minutes

Cooking time: 35 minutes

Servings: 2 people

Ingredients:

- ⅓ cup of crumbled Feta cheese

- ⅓ cup of grated Cheddar cheese

- Salt and pepper according to taste

- ⅓ cup of milk

- 4 eggs, cracked into a bowl

- 2 teaspoon of olive oil

- ¼ lb. of asparagus, trimmed and sliced thinly

- ¼ cup of chopped chives

- 1 small red onion, sliced

- 1 large zucchini, sliced with a 1-inch thickness

- ⅓ cup of sliced mushrooms

Directions:

1. Preheat your air fryer to about 380° F. Set aside your baking dish lined with some parchment paper. Put salt, milk, and pepper into the egg bowl; whisk evenly.

2. Put a skillet on the stovetop over a moderate flame, and heat your olive oil. Add in the zucchini, asparagus, baby spinach, onion, and mushrooms; stir-fry for around 5 minutes. Transfer the vegetables into your baking tray, and finish with the beaten egg.

3. Put the tray into your air fryer and finish with cheddar and feta cheese.

4. For about 15 minutes, cook. Take out your baking tray and add in some fresh chives to garnish.

25. Rice & Beans Stuffed Bell Peppers

Preparation time: 10 minutes

Cooking time: 15 minutes

Servings: 5 people

Ingredients:

- 1 tbsp. of Parmesan cheese, grated

- ½ cup of mozzarella cheese, shredded

- 5 large bell peppers, tops removed and seeded

- 1½ tsp. of Italian seasoning

- 1 cup of cooked rice

- 1 (15-ounces) can of red kidney beans, rinsed and drained

- 1 (15-ounces) can of diced tomatoes with juice

- ½ small bell pepper, seeded and chopped

Directions:

1. Combine the tomatoes with juice, bell pepper, rice, beans, and Italian seasoning in a mixing dish. Using the rice mixture, fill each bell pepper uniformly.

2. Preheat the air fryer to 300° F. Oil the basket of your air fryer with some spray oil. Put the bell peppers in a uniform layer in your air fryer basket.

3. Cook for around 12 minutes in the air fryer. In the meantime, combine the Parmesan and mozzarella cheese in a mixing dish.

4. Remove the peppers from the air fryer basket and top each with some cheese mix. Cook for another 3 -4 minutes in the air fryer

5. Take the bell peppers from the air fryer and put them on a serving dish. Enable to cool slowly before serving. Serve it hot.

26. Parsley-loaded Mushrooms

Preparation time: 5 minutes

Cooking time: 15 minutes

Servings: 2 people

Ingredients:

- 2 tablespoon of parsley, finely chopped

- 2 teaspoon of olive oil

- 1 garlic clove, crushed

- 2 slices white bread

- salt and black pepper according to your taste

Directions:

1. Preheat the air fryer to about 360° F. Crush your bread into crumbs in a food blender. Add the parsley, garlic, and pepper; blend with the olive oil and mix.

2. Remove the stalks from the mushrooms and stuff the caps with breadcrumbs. In your air fryer basket, position the mushroom heads. Cook for a few minutes, just until golden brown and crispy.

27.Cheesy Vegetable Quesadilla

Preparation time: 2 minutes

Cooking time: 15 minutes

Servings: 1 people

Ingredients:

- 1 teaspoon of olive oil

- 1 tablespoon of cilantro, chopped

- ½ green onion, sliced

- ¼ zucchini, sliced

- ¼ yellow bell pepper, sliced

- ¼ cup of shredded gouda cheese

Directions:

1. Preheat your air fryer to about 390° F. Oil a basket of air fryers with some cooking oil.

2. Put a flour tortilla in your air fryer basket and cover it with some bell pepper, Gouda cheese, cilantro, zucchini, and green onion. Take the other tortilla to cover and spray with some olive oil.

3. Cook until slightly golden brown, for around 10 minutes. Cut into 4 slices for serving when ready. Enjoy!

28. Creamy 'n Cheese Broccoli Bake

Preparation time: 10 minutes

Cooking time: 30 minutes

Servings: 2 people

Ingredients:

- 1/4 cup of water

- 1-1/2 teaspoons of butter, or to taste

- 1/2 cup of cubed sharp Cheddar cheese

- 1/2 (14 ounces) can evaporate milk, divided

- 1/2 large onion, coarsely diced

- 1 tbsp. of dry bread crumbs, or to taste

- salt according to taste

- 2 tbsp. of all-purpose flour

- 1-pound of fresh broccoli, coarsely diced

Directions:

1. Lightly oil the air-fryer baking pan with cooking oil. Add half of the milk and flour into a pan and simmer at about 360° F for around 5 minutes.

2. Mix well midway through the cooking period. Remove the broccoli and the extra milk. Cook for the next 5 minutes after fully blending.

3. Mix in the cheese until it is fully melted. Mix the butter and bread crumbs well in a shallow tub. Sprinkle the broccoli on top.

4. At about 360° F, cook for around 20 minutes until the tops are finely golden brown. Enjoy and serve warm.

29. Sweet & Spicy Parsnips

Preparation time: 12 minutes

Cooking time: 44 minutes

Servings: 6 people

Ingredients:

- ¼ tsp. of red pepper flakes, crushed

- 1 tbsp. of dried parsley flakes, crushed

- 2 tbsp. of honey

- 1 tbsp. of n butter, melted

- 2 pounds of a parsnip, peeled and cut into 1-inch chunks

- Salt and ground black pepper, according to your taste.

Directions:

1. Let the air-fryer temperature to about 355° F. Oil the basket of your air fryers. Combine the butter and parsnips in a big dish.

2. Transfer the parsnip pieces into the lined air fryer basket arranges them in a uniform layer. Cook for a few minutes in the fryer.

3. In the meantime, combine the leftover ingredients in a large mixing bowl.

4. Move the parsnips into the honey mixture bowl after around 40 minutes and toss them to coat properly.

5. Again, in a uniform layer, organize the parsnip chunks into your air fryer basket.

6. Air-fry for another 3-4 minutes. Take the parsnip pieces from the air fryer and pass them onto the serving dish. Serve it warm.

30. Zucchini with Mediterranean Dill Sauce

Preparation time: 20 minutes

Cooking time: 60 minutes

Servings: 4 people

Ingredients:

- 1/2 tsp. of freshly cracked black peppercorns

- 2 sprigs thyme, leaves only, crushed

- 1 sprig rosemary, leaves only, crushed

- 1 tsp. of sea salt flakes

- 2 tbsp. of melted butter

- 1 pound of zucchini, peeled and cubed

For your Mediterranean Dipping:

- 1 tbsp. of olive oil

- 1 tbsp. of fresh dill, chopped

- 1/3 cup of yogurt

- 1/2 cup of mascarpone cheese

Directions:

1. To start, preheat your Air Fryer to 350° F. Now, add ice cold water to the container with your potato cubes and let them sit in the bath for about 35 minutes.

2. Dry your potato cubes with a hand towel after that. Whisk together the sea salt flakes, melted butter, thyme, rosemary, and freshly crushed peppercorns in a mixing container. This butter/spice mixture can be rubbed onto the potato cubes.

3. In the cooking basket of your air fryer, air-fry your potato cubes for around 18 to 20 minutes or until cooked completely; ensure you shake the potatoes at least once during cooking to cook them uniformly.

4. In the meantime, by mixing the rest of the ingredients, create the Mediterranean dipping sauce. To dip and eat, serve warm potatoes with Mediterranean sauce!

31. Zesty Broccoli

Preparation time: 10 minutes

Cooking time: 15 minutes

Servings: 4 people

Ingredients:

- 1 tbsp. of butter

- 1 large crown broccoli, chopped into bite-sized pieces

- 1 tbsp. of white sesame seeds

- 2 tbsp. of vegetable stock

- ½ tsp. of red pepper flakes, crushed

- 3 garlic cloves, minced

- ½ tsp. of fresh lemon zest, grated finely

- 1 tbsp. of pure lemon juice

Directions:

1. Preheat the Air fryer to about 355° F and oil an Air fryer pan with cooking spray. In the Air fryer plate, combine the vegetable stock, butter, and lemon juice.

2. Move the mixture and cook for about 2 minutes into your Air Fryer. Cook for a minute after incorporating the broccoli and garlic.

3. Cook for a minute with lemon zest, sesame seeds, and red pepper flakes. Remove the dish from the oven and eat immediately.

32. Chewy Glazed Parsnips

Preparation time: 15 minutes

Cooking time: 44 minutes

Servings: 6 people

Ingredients:

- ¼ tsp. of red pepper flakes, crushed

- 1 tbsp. of dried parsley flakes, crushed

- 2 tbsp. of maple syrup

- 1 tbsp. of butter, melted

- 2 pounds of parsnips, skinned and chopped into 1-inch chunks

Directions:

1. Preheat the Air fryer to about 355° F and oil your air fryer basket. In a wide mixing bowl, combine the butter and parsnips and toss well to cover. Cook for around 40 minutes with the parsnips in the Air fryer basket.

2. In the meantime, combine in a wide bowl the rest of your ingredients. Move this mix to your basket of the air fryer and cook for another 4 minutes or so. Remove the dish from the oven and eat promptly.

33. Hoisin-glazed Bok Choy

Preparation time: 5 minutes

Cooking time: 10 minutes

Servings: 4 people

Ingredients:

- 1 tbsp. of all-purpose flour

- 2 tbsp. of sesame oil

- 2 tbsp. of hoisin sauce

- 1/2 tsp. of sage

- 1 tsp. of onion powder

- 2 garlic cloves, minced

- 1 pound of baby Bok choy, roots removed, leaves separated

Directions:

1. In a lightly oiled Air Fryer basket, put the onion powder, garlic, Bok Choy, and sage. Cook for around 3 minutes at about 350° F in a preheated Air Fryer.

2. Whisk together the sesame oil, hoisin sauce, and flour in a deep mixing dish. Drizzle over the Bok choy with the gravy. Cook for an extra minute. Bon appétit!

34. Green Beans with Okra

Preparation time: 10 minutes

Cooking time: 20 minutes

Servings: 2 people

Ingredients:

- 3 tbsp. of balsamic vinegar

- ¼ cup of nutritional yeast

- ½ (10-ounces) of bag chilled cut green beans

- ½ (10-ounces) of bag chilled cut okra

- Salt and black pepper, according to your taste.

Directions:

1. Preheat your Air fryer to about 400° F and oil the air fryer basket.

2. In a wide mixing bowl, toss together the salt, green beans, okra, vinegar, nutritional yeast, and black pepper.

3. Cook for around 20 minutes with the okra mixture in your Air fryer basket. Dish out into a serving plate and eat warm.

35. Celeriac with some Greek Yogurt Dip

Preparation time: 12 minutes

Cooking time: 25 minutes

Servings: 2 people

Ingredients:

- 1/2 tsp. of sea salt

- 1/2 tsp. of ground black pepper, to taste

- 1 tbsp. of sesame oil

- 1 red onion, chopped into 1 1/2-inch piece

- 1/2 pound of celeriac, chopped into 1 1/2-inch piece

Spiced Yogurt:

- 1/2 tsp. of chili powder

- 1/2 tsp. of mustard seeds

- 2 tbsp. of mayonnaise

- 1/4 cup of Greek yogurt

Directions:

1. In the slightly oiled cooking basket, put the veggies in one uniform layer. Pour sesame oil over the veggies.

2. Season with a pinch of black pepper and a pinch of salt. Cook for around 20 minutes at about 300° F, tossing the basket midway through your cooking cycle.

3. In the meantime, whisk all the leftover ingredients into the sauce. Spoon the sauce over the veggies that have been cooked. Bon appétit!

36. Wine & Garlic Flavored Vegetables

Preparation time: 7-10 minutes

Cooking time: 15 minutes

Servings: 4 people

Ingredients:

- 4 cloves of garlic, minced

- 3 tbsp. of red wine vinegar

- 1/3 cup of olive oil

- 1 red onion, diced

- 1 package frozen diced vegetables

- 1 cup of baby Portobello mushrooms, diced

- 1 tsp. of Dijon mustard

- 1 ½ tbsp. of honey

- Salt and pepper according to your taste

- ¼ cup of chopped fresh basil

Directions:

1. Preheat the air fryer to about 330° F. In the air fryer, put the grill pan attachment.

2. Combine the veggies and season with pepper, salt, and garlic in a Ziploc container. To mix all, give everything a strong shake. Dump and cook for around 15 minutes on the grill pan.

3. Additionally, add the remainder of the ingredients into a mixing bowl and season with some more salt and pepper. Drizzle the sauce over your grilled vegetables.

37. Spicy Braised Vegetables

Preparation time: 10 minutes

Cooking time: 25 minutes

Servings: 4 people

Ingredients:

- 1/2 cup of tomato puree

- 1/4 tsp. of ground black pepper

- 1/2 tsp. of fine sea salt

- 1 tbsp. of garlic powder

- 1/2 tsp. of fennel seeds

- 1/4 tsp. of mustard powder

- 1/2 tsp. of porcini powder

- 1/4 cup of olive oil

- 1 celery stalk, chopped into matchsticks

- 2 bell peppers, deveined and thinly diced

- 1 Serrano pepper, deveined and thinly diced

- 1 large-sized zucchini, diced

Directions:

1. In your Air Fryer cooking basket, put your peppers, zucchini, sweet potatoes, and carrot.

2. Drizzle with some olive oil and toss to cover completely; cook for around 15 minutes in a preheated Air Fryer at about 350°F.

3. Make the sauce as the vegetables are frying by quickly whisking the remaining ingredients (except the tomato ketchup). Slightly oil up a baking dish that fits your fryer.

4. Add the cooked vegetables to the baking dish, along with the sauce, and toss well to cover.

5. Turn the Air Fryer to about 390° F and cook for 2-4 more minutes with the vegetables. Bon appétit!

CHAPTER 3: Air Fryer Snack Side Dishes and Appetizer Recipes

1. Crispy 'n Tasty Spring Rolls

Preparation time: 5 minutes

Cooking time: 15 minutes

Servings: 4 people

Ingredients:

- 8 spring roll wrappers

- 1 tsp. of nutritional yeast

- 1 tsp. of corn starch + 2 tablespoon water

- 1 tsp. of coconut sugar

- 1 tbsp. of soy sauce

- 1 medium carrot, shredded

- 1 cup of shiitake mushroom, sliced thinly

- 1 celery stalk, chopped

- ½ tsp. of ginger, finely chopped

Directions:

1. Mix your carrots, celery stalk, soy sauce, coconut sugar, ginger, and nutritional yeast with each other in a mixing dish.

2. Have a tbsp. of your vegetable mix and put it in the middle of your spring roll wrappers.

3. Roll up and secure the sides of your wraps with some cornstarch.

4. Cook for about 15 minutes or till your spring roll wraps is crisp in a preheated air fryer at 200F.

2. Spinach & Feta Crescent Triangles

Preparation time: 10 minutes

Cooking time: 20 minutes

Servings: 4 people

Ingredients:

- ¼ teaspoon of salt

- 1 teaspoon of chopped oregano

- ¼ teaspoon of garlic powder

- 1 cup of crumbled feta cheese

- 1 cup of steamed spinach

Directions:

1. Preheat your air fryer to about 350 F, and then roll up the dough over a level surface that is gently floured.

2. In a medium-sized bowl, mix the spinach, feta, salt, oregano, and ground garlic cloves. Split your dough into four equal chunks.

3. Split the mix of feta/spinach among the four chunks of dough. Fold and seal your dough using a fork.

4. Please put it on a baking tray covered with parchment paper, and then put it in your air fryer.

5. Cook until nicely golden, for around 1 minute.

3. Healthy Avocado Fries

Preparation time: 5 minutes

Cooking time: 20 minutes

Servings: 2 people

Ingredients:

- ¼ cup of aquafaba

- 1 avocado, cubed

- Salt as required

Directions:

1. Mix the aquafaba, crumbs, and salt in a mixing bowl.

2. Preheat your air fryer to about 390°F and cover the avocado pieces uniformly in the crumbs blend.

3. Put the ready pieces in the cooking bucket of your air fryer and cook for several minutes.

4. Twice-fried Cauliflower Tater Tots

Preparation time: 5 minutes

Cooking time: 16 minutes

Servings: 12 people

Ingredients:

- 3 tbsp. Of oats flaxseed meal + 3 tbsp. of water)

- 1-pound of cauliflower, steamed and chopped

- 1 tsp. of parsley, chopped

- 1 tsp. of oregano, chopped

- 1 tsp. of garlic, minced

- 1 tsp. of chives, chopped

- 1 onion, chopped

- 1 flax egg (1 tablespoon 3 tablespoon desiccated coconuts)

- ½ cup of nutritional yeast

- salt and pepper according to taste

- ½ cup of bread crumbs

Directions:

1. Preheat your air fryer to about 390 degrees F.

2. To extract extra moisture, place the steamed cauliflower onto a ring and a paper towel.

3. Put and mix the remainder of your ingredients, excluding your bread crumbs, in a small mixing container.

4. Use your palms, blend it until well mixed and shapes into a small ball.

5. Roll your tater tots over your bread crumbs and put them in the bucket of your air fryer.

6. For a minute, bake. Raise the cooking level to about 400 F and cook for the next 10 minutes.

5. Cheesy Mushroom & Cauliflower Balls

Preparation time: 10 minutes

Cooking time: 50 minutes

Servings: 4 people

Ingredients:

- Salt and pepper according to taste

- 2 sprigs chopped fresh thyme

- ¼ cup of coconut oil

- 1 cup of Grana Padano cheese

- 1 cup of breadcrumbs

- 2 tablespoon of vegetable stock

- 3 cups of cauliflower, chopped

- 3 cloves garlic, minced

- 1 small red onion, chopped

- 3 tablespoon of olive oil

Directions:

1. Over moderate flame, put a pan. Add some balsamic vinegar. When the oil is heated, stir-fry your onion and garlic till they become transparent.

2. Add in the mushrooms and cauliflower and stir-fry for about 5 minutes. Add in your stock, add thyme and cook till your cauliflower has consumed the stock. Add pepper, Grana Padano cheese, and salt.

3. Let the mix cool down and form bite-size spheres of your paste. To harden, put it in the fridge for about 30 minutes.

4. Preheat your air fryer to about 350°F.

5. Add your coconut oil and breadcrumbs into a small bowl and blend properly.

6. Take out your mushroom balls from the fridge, swirl the breadcrumb paste once more, and drop the balls into your breadcrumb paste.

7. Avoid overcrowding, put your balls into your air fryer's container and cook for about 15 minutes, flipping after every 5 minutes to ensure even cooking.

8. Serve with some tomato sauce and brown sugar.

6. Italian Seasoned Easy Pasta Chips

Preparation time: 5 minutes

Cooking time: 10 minutes

Servings: 2 people

Ingredients:

- 2 cups of whole wheat bowtie pasta

- 1 tbsp. of olive oil

- 1 tbsp. of nutritional yeast

- 1 ½ tsp. of Italian seasoning blend

- ½ tsp. of salt

Directions:

1. Put the accessory for the baking tray into your air fryer.

2. Mix all the ingredients in a medium-sized bowl, offer it a gentle stir.

3. Add the mixture to your air fryer basket.

4. Close your air fryer and cook at around 400°degrees F for about 10 minutes.

7. Thai Sweet Potato Balls

Preparation time: 10 minutes

Cooking time: 50 minutes

Servings: 4 people

Ingredients:

- 1 cup of coconut flakes

- 1 tsp. of baking powder

- 1/2 cup of almond meal

- 1/4 tsp. of ground cloves

- 1/2 tsp. of ground cinnamon

- 2 tsp. of orange zest

- 1 tbsp. of orange juice

- 1 cup of brown sugar

- 1 pound of sweet potatoes

Directions:

1. Bake your sweet potatoes for around 25 to 30 minutes at about 380° F till they become soft; peel and mash them in a medium-sized bowl.

2. Add orange zest, orange juice, brown sugar, ground cinnamon, almond meal, cloves, and baking powder. Now blend completely.

3. Roll the balls around in some coconut flakes.

4. Bake for around 15 minutes or until fully fried and crunchy in the preheated Air Fryer at about 360° F.

5. For the rest of the ingredients, redo the same procedure. Bon appétit!

8. Barbecue Roasted Almonds

Preparation time: 5 minutes

Cooking time: 20 minutes

Servings: 6 people

Ingredients:

- 1 tbsp. of olive oil

- 1/4 tsp. of smoked paprika

- 1/2 tsp. of cumin powder

- 1/4 tsp. of mustard powder

- 1/4 tsp. of garlic powder

- Sea salt and ground black pepper, according to taste

- 1 ½ cups of raw almonds

Directions:

1. In a mixing pot, mix all your ingredients.

2. Line the container of your Air Fryer with some baking parchment paper. Arrange the covered almonds out in the basket of your air fryer in a uniform layer.

3. Roast for around 8 to 9 minutes at about 340°F, tossing the bucket once or twice. If required, work in groups.

4. Enjoy!

9. Croissant Rolls

Preparation time: 2 minutes

Cooking time: 6 minutes

Servings: 8 people

Ingredients:

- 4 tbsp. of butter, melted

- 1 (8-ounces) can croissant rolls

Directions:

1. Adjust the air-fryer temperature to about 320°F. Oil the basket of your air fryers.

2. Into your air fryer basket, place your prepared croissant rolls.

3. Airs fry them for around 4 minutes or so.

4. Flip to the opposite side and cook for another 2-3 minutes.

5. Take out from your air fryer and move to a tray.

6. Glaze with some melted butter and eat warm.

10. Curry' n Coriander Spiced Bread Rolls

Preparation time: 5 minutes

Cooking time: 15 minutes

Servings: 5 people

Ingredients:

- salt and pepper according to taste

- 5 large potatoes, boiled

- 2 sprigs, curry leaves

- 2 small onions, chopped

- 2 green chilies, seeded and chopped

- 1 tbsp. of olive oil

- 1 bunch of coriander, chopped

- ½ tsp. of turmeric

- 8 slices of vegan wheat bread, brown sides discarded

- ½ tsp. of mustard seeds

Directions:

1. Mash your potatoes in a bowl and sprinkle some black pepper and salt according to taste. Now set aside.

2. In a pan, warm up the olive oil over medium-low heat and add some mustard seeds. Mix until the seeds start to sputter.

3. Now add in the onions and cook till they become transparent. Mix in the curry leaves and turmeric powder.

4. Keep on cooking till it becomes fragrant for a couple of minutes. Take it off the flame and add the mixture to the potatoes.

5. Mix in the green chilies and some coriander. This is meant to be the filling.

6. Wet your bread and drain excess moisture. In the center of the loaf, put a tbsp. of the potato filling and gently roll the bread so that the potato filling is fully enclosed within the bread.

7. Brush with some oil and put them inside your air fryer basket.

8. Cook for around 15 minutes in a preheated air fryer at about 400°F.

9. Ensure that the air fryer basket is shaken softly midway through the cooking period for an even cooking cycle.

11. Scrumptiously Healthy Chips

Preparation time: 5 minutes

Cooking time: 10 minutes

Servings: 2 people

Ingredients:

- 2 tbsp. of olive oil

- 2 tbsp. of almond flour

- 1 tsp. of garlic powder

- 1 bunch kale

- Salt and pepper according to taste

Directions:

1. For around 5 minutes, preheat your air fryer.

2. In a mixing bowl, add all your ingredients, add the kale leaves at the end and toss to completely cover them.

3. Put in the basket of your fryer and cook until crispy for around 10 minutes.

12. Kid-friendly Vegetable Fritters

Preparation time: 5 minutes

Cooking time: 20 minutes

Servings: 4 people

Ingredients:

- 2 tbsp. of olive oil

- 1/2 cup of cornmeal

- 1/2 cup of all-purpose flour

- 1/2 tsp. of ground cumin

- 1 tsp. of turmeric powder

- 2 garlic cloves, pressed

- 1 carrot, grated

- 1 sweet pepper, seeded and chopped

- 1 yellow onion, finely chopped

- 1 tbsp. of ground flaxseeds

- Salt and ground black pepper, according to taste

- 1 pound of broccoli florets

Directions:

1. In salted boiling water, blanch your broccoli until al dente, for around 3 to 5 minutes. Drain the excess water and move to a mixing bowl; add in the rest of your ingredients to mash the broccoli florets.

2. Shape the paste into patties and position them in the slightly oiled Air Fryer basket.

3. Cook for around 6 minutes at about 400° F, flipping them over midway through the cooking process; if needed, operate in batches.

4. Serve hot with some Vegenaise of your choice. Enjoy it!

13. Avocado Fries

Preparation time: 10 minutes

Cooking time: 50 minutes

Servings: 4 people

Ingredients:

- 2 avocados, cut into wedges

- 1/2 cup of parmesan cheese, grated

- 2 eggs

- Sea salt and ground black pepper, according to taste.

- 1/2 cup of almond meal

- 1/2 head garlic (6-7 cloves)

Sauce:

- 1 tsp. of mustard

- 1 tsp. of lemon juice

- 1/2 cup of mayonnaise

Directions:

1. On a piece of aluminum foil, put your garlic cloves and spray some cooking spray on it. Wrap your garlic cloves in the foil.

2. Cook for around 1-2 minutes at about 400°F in your preheated Air Fryer. Inspect the garlic, open the foil's top end, and keep cooking for an additional 10-12 minutes.

3. Once done, let them cool for around 10 to 15 minutes; take out the cloves by pressing them out of their skin; mash your garlic and put them aside.

4. Mix the salt, almond meal, and black pepper in a small dish.

5. Beat the eggs until foamy in a separate bowl.

6. Put some parmesan cheese in the final shallow dish.

7. In your almond meal blend, dip the avocado wedges, dusting off any excess.

8. In the beaten egg, dunk your wedges; eventually, dip in some parmesan cheese.

9. Spray your avocado wedges on both sides with some cooking oil spray.

10. Cook for around 8 minutes in the preheated Air Fryer at about 395° F, flipping them over midway thru the cooking process.

11. In the meantime, mix the ingredients of your sauce with your cooked crushed garlic.

12. Split the avocado wedges between plates and cover with the sauce before serving. Enjoy!

14. Crispy Wings with Lemony Old Bay Spice

Preparation time: 10 minutes

Cooking time: 25 minutes

Servings: 4 people

Ingredients:

- Salt and pepper according to taste

- 3 pounds of vegan chicken wings

- 1 tsp. of lemon juice, freshly squeezed

- 1 tbsp. of old bay spices

- ¾ cup of almond flour

- ½ cup of butter

Directions:

1. For about 5 minutes, preheat your air fryer. Mix all your ingredients in a mixing dish, excluding the butter. Put in the bowl of an air fryer.

2. Preheat the oven to about 350°F and bake for around 25 minutes. Rock the fryer container midway thru the cooking process, also for cooking.

3. Drizzle with some melted butter when it's done frying. Enjoy!

15. Cold Salad with Veggies and Pasta

Preparation time: 30 minutes

Cooking time: 1 hour 35 minutes

Servings: 12 people

Ingredients:

- ½ cup of fat-free Italian dressing

- 2 tablespoons of olive oil, divided

- ½ cup of Parmesan cheese, grated

- 8 cups of cooked pasta

- 4 medium tomatoes, cut in eighths

- 3 small eggplants, sliced into ½-inch thick rounds

- 3 medium zucchinis, sliced into ½-inch thick rounds

- Salt, according to your taste.

Directions:

1. Preheat your Air fryer to about 355° F and oil the inside of your air fryer basket. In a dish, mix 1 tablespoon of olive oil and zucchini and swirl to cover properly.

2. Cook for around 25 minutes your zucchini pieces in your Air fryer basket. In another dish, mix your eggplants with a tablespoon of olive oil and toss to coat properly.

3. Cook for around 40 minutes your eggplant slices in your Air fryer basket. Re-set the Air Fryer temperature to about 320° F and put the tomatoes next in the ready basket.

4. Cook and mix all your air-fried vegetables for around 30 minutes. To serve, mix in the rest of the ingredients and chill for at least 2 hours, covered.

16. Zucchini and Minty Eggplant Bites

Preparation time: 15 minutes

Cooking time: 35 minutes

Servings: 8 people

Ingredients:

- 3 tbsp. of olive oil

- 1 pound of zucchini, peeled and cubed

- 1 pound of eggplant, peeled and cubed

- 2 tbsp. of melted butter

- 1 ½ tsp. of red pepper chili flakes

- 2 tsp. of fresh mint leaves, minced

Directions:

1. In a large mixing container, add all of the ingredients mentioned above.

2. Roast the zucchini bites and eggplant in your Air Fryer for around 30 minutes at about 300° F, flipping once or twice during the cooking cycle. Serve with some dipping sauce that's homemade.

17. Stuffed Potatoes

Preparation time: 15 minutes

Cooking time: 31 minutes

Servings: 4 people

Ingredients:

- 3 tbsp. of canola oil

- ½ cup of Parmesan cheese, grated

- 2 tbsp. of chives, chopped

- ½ of brown onion, chopped

- 1 tbsp. of butter

- 4 potatoes, peeled

Directions:

1. Preheat the Air fryer to about 390° F and oil the air fryer basket. Coat the canola oil on the potatoes and place them in your Air Fryer Basket.

2. Cook for around 20 minutes before serving on a platter. Halve each potato and scrape out the middle from each half of it.

3. In a frying pan, melt some butter over medium heat and add the onions. Sauté in a bowl for around 5 minutes and dish out.

4. Combine the onions with the middle of the potato, chives and half of the cheese. Stir well and uniformly cram the onion potato mixture into the potato halves.

5. Top and layer the potato halves in your Air Fryer basket with the leftover cheese. Cook for around 6 minutes before serving hot.

18. Paneer Cutlet

Preparation time: 5 minutes

Cooking time: 15 minutes

Servings: 1 people

Ingredients:

- ½ teaspoon of salt

- ½ teaspoon of oregano

- 1 small onion, finely chopped

- ½ teaspoon of garlic powder

- 1 teaspoon of butter

- ½ teaspoon of chai masala

- 1 cup of grated cheese

Directions:

1. Preheat the air fryer to about 350° F and lightly oil a baking dish. In a mixing bowl, add all ingredients and stir well. Split the mixture into cutlets and put them in an oiled baking dish.

2. Put the baking dish in your air fryer and cook your cutlets until crispy, around a minute or so.

19. Spicy Roasted Cashew Nuts

Preparation time: 10 Minutes

Cooking time: 20 Minutes

Servings: 4

Ingredients:

- 1/2 tsp. of ancho chili powder

- 1/2 tsp. of smoked paprika

- Salt and ground black pepper, according to taste

- 1 tsp. of olive oil

- 1 cup of whole cashews

Directions:

1. In a mixing big bowl, toss all your ingredients.

2. Line parchment paper to cover the Air Fryer container. Space out the spiced cashews in your basket in a uniform layer.

3. Roast for about 6 to 8 minutes at 300 degrees F, tossing the basket once or twice during the cooking process. Work in batches if needed. Enjoy!

CHAPTER 4: Deserts

1. Almond-apple Treat

Preparation time: 5 minutes

Cooking time: 15 minutes

Servings: 4 people

Ingredients:

- 2 tablespoon of sugar

- ¾ oz. of raisins

- 1 ½ oz. of almonds

Directions:

1. Preheat your air fryer to around 360° F.

2. Mix the almonds, sugar, and raisins in a dish. Blend using a hand mixer.

3. Load the apples with a combination of the almond mixture. Please put them in the air fryer basket and cook for a few minutes. Enjoy!

2. Pepper-pineapple With Butter-sugar Glaze

Preparation time: 5 minutes

Cooking time: 10 minutes

Servings: 2 people

Ingredients:

- Salt according to taste.

- 2 tsp. of melted butter

- 1 tsp. of brown sugar

- 1 red bell pepper, seeded and julienned

- 1 medium-sized pineapple, peeled and sliced

Directions:

1. To about 390°F, preheat your air fryer. In your air fryer, put the grill pan attachment.

2. In a Ziploc bag, combine all ingredients and shake well.

3. Dump and cook on the grill pan for around 10 minutes to ensure you turn the pineapples over every 5 minutes during cooking.

3. True Churros with Yummy Hot Chocolate

Preparation time: 10 minutes

Cooking time: 25 minutes

Servings: 3 people

Ingredients:

- 1 tsp. of ground cinnamon

- 1/3 cup of sugar

- 1 tbsp. of cornstarch

- 1 cup of milk

- 2 ounces of dark chocolate

- 1 cup of all-purpose flour

- 1 tbsp. of canola oil

- 1 tsp. of lemon zest

- 1/4 tsp. of sea salt

- 2 tbsp. of granulated sugar

- 1/2 cup of water

Directions:

1. To create the churro dough, boil the water in a pan over a medium-high flame; then, add the salt, sugar, and lemon zest and fry, stirring continuously, until fully dissolved.

2. Take the pan off the heat and add in some canola oil. Stir the flour in steadily, constantly stirring until the solution turns to a ball.

3. With a broad star tip, pipe the paste into a piping bag. In the oiled Air Fryer basket, squeeze 4-inch slices of dough. Cook for around 6 minutes at a temperature of 300° F.

4. Make the hot cocoa for dipping in the meantime. In a shallow saucepan, melt some chocolate and 1/2 cup of milk over low flame.

5. In the leftover 1/2 cup of milk, mix the cornstarch and blend it into the hot chocolate mixture. Cook for around 5 minutes on low flame.

6. Mix the sugar and cinnamon; roll your churros in this combination. Serve with a side of hot cocoa. Enjoy!

Conclusion

These times, air frying is one of the most common cooking techniques and air fryers have become one of the chef's most impressive devices. In no time, air fryers can help you prepare nutritious and tasty meals! To prepare unique dishes for you and your family members, you do not need to be a master in the kitchen.

Everything you have to do is buy an air fryer and this wonderful cookbook for air fryers! Soon, you can make the greatest dishes ever and inspire those around you.

Cooked meals at home with you! Believe us! Get your hands on an air fryer and this handy set of recipes for air fryers and begin your new cooking experience. Have fun!